INTELLECTUAL PROPERTY AND DESKTOP 3D PRINTING

This innovative book explores the world of 3D printing from the perspective of intellectual property law, tackling theory and practice.

As 3D printing digitises tangibles and equips individual users with access to design and manufacturing tools, it also raises several pressing legal and policy issues. Does the IP framework – largely designed in the analogue age – adequately regulate the operation of the technology? How should the law respond to piracy in a digital environment where copying is the norm, not the exception? What are the community's experiences and views regarding IP? Is the law actually a concern?

To fully address these questions, the book begins with a contextual overview of 3D printing's history and broader socio-economic impact. It explains why the 'desktop' side of the technology is likely to be especially problematic when it comes to IP law and highlights key areas of concern. Drawing on its rich empirical data featuring world-leading experts, engineers, lawyers and users, it offers illuminating insights into the experiences and perspectives of stakeholders before finally considering potential regulatory responses.

Original and forward-looking, this book is essential reading for academics, practitioners, 3D printing users and any reader interested in the rapidly evolving field of law and technology.

Intellectual Property and Desktop 3D Printing

Law and Digital Innovation

Plamen Dinev

•HART•

OXFORD • LONDON • NEW YORK • NEW DELHI • SYDNEY

HART PUBLISHING

Bloomsbury Publishing Plc

Kemp House, Chawley Park, Cumnor Hill, Oxford, OX2 9PH, UK

1385 Broadway, New York, NY 10018, USA

Bloomsbury Publishing Ireland Limited, 29 Earlsfort Terrace, Dublin 2, D02 AY28, Ireland

HART PUBLISHING, the Hart/Stag logo, BLOOMSBURY and the Diana logo are trademarks of Bloomsbury Publishing Plc

First published in Great Britain 2025

A catalogue record for this book is available from the British Library.

A catalogue record for this book is available from the Library of Congress.

Library of Congress Control Number: 2025947202

ISBN: HB: 978-1-50997-473-3
ePDF: 978-1-50997-476-4
ePub: 978-1-50997-475-7

Typeset by Compuscript Ltd, Shannon

For product safety related questions contact productsafety@bloomsbury.com

To find out more about our authors and books visit www.hartpublishing.co.uk. Here you will find extracts, author information, details of forthcoming events and the option to sign up for our newsletters.

ACKNOWLEDGEMENTS

I am grateful to the Modern Law Review and the City Law School for their generous financial support. Completing the empirical component of this work would not have been possible without the Modern Law Review Scholarship for 2018.

I would like to thank all anonymous interviewees and survey participants in New York and elsewhere who gave up their valuable time to participate in the empirical study.

I am grateful to several people at the University of Manchester and other institutions who supported me during this process and offered valuable guidance and advice. In particular, I would like to thank Luke McDonagh, Enrico Bonadio, Andrew Choo and Javier Garcia Oliva.

I am thankful to the anonymous peer reviewers for their helpful feedback and recommendations. I would like to thank Roberta Bassi, Verity Stuart and Linda Goss at Hart Publishing for their exceptional professionalism and support as well as Chris Harrison for his excellent copy-editing.

Finally, I am grateful to all other friends and family members who have supported me during this period, with special thanks to Diana, Julie and Ivan.

CONTENTS

LIST OF ABBREVIATIONS

3D printing	Three-dimensional printing
AC	Law Reports, Appeal Cases
All ER	All England Law Reports
ALM	Additive layer manufacturing
AM	Additive manufacturing
AMF	Additive Manufacturing Format
Bus LR	Business Law Reports
CA	Court of Appeal
CAD	Computer-aided design
CC	Creative Commons
CDPA	Copyright, Designs and Patents Act
CERN	European Organization for Nuclear Research
Ch D	Law Reports, Chancery Division
Civ	Civil Division
CJEU	Court of Justice of the European Union
CNC	Computer numerical control
DMCA	Digital Millennium Copyright Act
DRM	Digital Rights Management
DSM Directive	Directive on Copyright in the Digital Single Market
e-Commerce Directive	Electronic Commerce Directive 2000
EEA	European Economic Area
EPC	European Patent Convention
EPO	European Patent Office

ER	English Reports
EU	European Union
EWCA	England and Wales Court of Appeal
EWHC	England and Wales High Court
FDM	Fused Deposition Modelling
FFF	Fused filament fabrication
FOSS	Free and open-source software
G-code	Geometric code
GDPR	General Data Protection Regulation
GNU	GNU's Not Unix
GPL	General Public License
InfoSoc	Information Society Directive
IP	Intellectual property
IPO	Intellectual Property Office
IPR	Intellectual Property Reports
MCQ	Multiple-choice question
NGO	Non-governmental Organisation
OSHW	Open-source hardware
OSHWA	Open-Source Hardware Association
PA	Patents Act
QB	Law Reports, Queen's Bench Division
RPC	Reports of Patent, Design and Trade Mark Cases
STL	Stereolithography
TMA	Trade Marks Act
TRIPS	Agreement on Trade-Related Aspects of Intellectual Property Rights
UK	United Kingdom
UKHL	United Kingdom House of Lords
UKIPO	The Intellectual Property Office of the United Kingdom

UKSC	United Kingdom Supreme Court
US	United States of America
USPTO	United States Patent and Trademark Office
WAC	Work of artistic craftsmanship
WIPO	World Intellectual Property Organisation

TABLE OF CASES

UK

EU

US

TABLE OF LEGISLATION

UK

EU

US

Ireland

International

1

Introduction

In March 2016, *The New York Times* reported that artists Nora al-Badri and Jan Nikolai Nelles smuggled 3D scanning equipment (concealed under a cashmere scarf) into Berlin's Neues Museum and made a digital replica of the Bust of Nefertiti, one of the most treasured – and copied – artworks of the ancient world.[1] This was carried out as part of an art project that aims to '[confront] … cultural theft and persisting colonialist notions of national ownership by making the object widely available'.[2] The resulting digital data, the story goes, were then given to 'hackers' who released a 3D printable version of the artwork to the public.

However, it quickly became apparent to experts that this was a high-quality scan that was likely to have been made by someone who had prolonged access to the work.[3] In other words, it was suspected that it may have been officially authorised by the Museum – and then leaked. When experts within the community asked the institution to release an official 3D printable model of the artwork to the public, the Museum – after a long battle and several freedom of information requests – shared a file that had a Creative Commons licence attached to it, digitally carved into the bottom of the 3D model itself. By doing so, the institution effectively attempted to claim ownership rights in a millennia-old public domain work, created during an era when the concept of intellectual property did not even exist:

> [The] Museum etched a copyright license into the bottom of the bust itself, claiming the authority to restrict how people might use the file. The museum was trying to pretend that it owned a copyright in the scan of a 3,000-year-old sculpture created 3,000 miles away.[4]

[1] C Wilder, 'Swiping a Priceless Antiquity … With a Scanner and a 3-D Printer' (*New York Times*, 1 March 2016) at nytimes.com/2016/03/02/arts/design/other-nefertiti-3d-printer.html.

[2] ibid.

[3] M Weinberg, 'The Nefertiti Bust Meets the 21st Century: When a German Museum Lost Its Fight Over 3D-Printing Files of the 3,000-Year-Old Artwork, It Made a Strange Decision' (*Slate*, 15 November 2019) at www.slate.com/technology/2019/11/nefertiti-bust-neues-museum-3d-printing.html; see also C Wilder, 'Nefertiti 3-D Scanning Project in Germany Raises Doubts' (*New York Times*, 10 March 2016) at www.nytimes.com/2016/03/11/arts/design/nefertiti-3-d-scanning-project-in-germany-raises-doubts.html.

[4] Weinberg (n 3).

This is but one fascinating example of the myriad of complex legal and policy issues raised by 3D printing technologies, which this book will explore from the perspective of IP law.

The Rationale for this Book

3D printing enables users to transform digital models into tangible three-dimensional products.[5] While the core technology behind this process has been quietly around for a while, the more accessible and affordable 'desktop' side of 3D printing is certainly new and fascinating.[6] It has captured the attention of engineers, economists, lawyers and the general public. Part of the reason for this is that desktop 3D printing has the potential to decentralise and 'democratise' manufacturing.[7] By equipping individual end users with access to design and precision manufacturing tools, it enables anyone with access to a 3D printer and modelling software to make various creative decisions and to have an active – as opposed to merely passive – role in production.

However, it is also precisely this aspect of the technology that is especially controversial from the perspective of IP law. Indeed, some of the key issues in this area stem from the question of not how things are done, but *who* does things.[8] As 3D printing introduces manufacturing capabilities at home and enables end users to model and print anything they can imagine, it also allows them to potentially interfere with virtually all major IP rights.[9] 3D printable models commonly shared online range from lucrative artistic works and action figures from popular culture (protectable by copyright) to functional items such as coffee grinder components and interlocking toy bricks (patentable or formerly patented) and

[5] 3D printing is based on an additive manufacturing process whereby raw material is deposited layer by layer. The technology will be discussed in detail in ch 2.

[6] 'Desktop' 3D printing generally refers to compact 3D printers that can be used at home or in an office environment (for more details, see ch 2).

[7] See, eg, B van Wiele, 'Decentralised, Democratised and Disruptive: How 3D Printing Challenges the Consumer Protection Rationale of Trade Marks' (2019) 41 *European Intellectual Property Review* 313, 314 ('The disruptive character of 3D printing lies in facilitating decentralised manufacturing supplemented with effortless sharing and customisation of the underlying digital designs. In doing so, 3D printing democratises not only manufacturing, but also creative design and distribution').

[8] P Troxler and C van Woensel, 'How Will Society Adopt 3D Printing?' in B van den Berg, S van der Hof and E Kosta (eds), *3D Printing: Legal, Philosophical and Economic Dimensions* (The Hague, Asser Press, 2016) 188; see also C Anderson, *Makers: The New Industrial Revolution* (London, Crown Business, 2006).

[9] While there are other methods of manufacturing things at home (and other technologies that operate in a similar manner), the ability to do so has traditionally remained outside the reach of most individuals owing to technological and economic reasons. For a more detailed discussion, see R Ballardini and N Lee, 'The Case of 3D Printing Technologies' in R Ballardini, M Norrgård and J Partanen (eds), *3D Printing, Intellectual Property and Innovation: Insights from Law and Technology* (Alphen aan den Rijn, Kluwer Law International, 2017) 173–4 (discussing this in the context of patent law).

various 'branded' items that may be subject to trade mark protection. While IP's early digital days were primarily concerned with copyright and content now largely consumed in digital form (such as music and film), 3D printing therefore goes one step further. As put by Deven Desai and Gerard Magliocca:

> 3D printing … will do for physical objects what MP3 files did for music … While 3D printers will unleash the creativity of producers and reduce costs for consumers, they will also make it far easier to infringe patents, copyrights, and trade dress.[10]

These concerns are not merely an academic exercise. Early skirmishes abound – for example, there have been several controversial takedown requests targeting fan-made 3D printable versions of Lego's interlocking toy bricks or other models based on items from popular culture.[11] What is more, the challenges posed by 3D printing have been explicitly acknowledged by several high-profile institutions and policymaking organisations around the world.[12] Yet, there is no case law on point and no scholarly consensus on how existing IP principles apply (or *should* apply) in this context, let alone on whether the existing framework is fit for purpose.

Amid the lack of legal certainty in this area, this monograph explores the extent to which 3D printing presents a challenge to IP theory and practice and aims to determine how the law should respond to these risks. Based on original empirical research, it also offers novel insights into the views and experiences of experts and 3D printing users – an important issue that has not been fully explored in the literature yet. In the next few sections, I will explain why this is necessary and how exactly I intend to address these issues.

The Need for an Interdisciplinary Approach

There have already been several alarming claims about the impact of 3D printing on IP law. Commentators have argued that 'business as usual will be disrupted as regular people gain access to power tools of design and production. Intellectual

[10] D Desai and G Magliocca, 'Patents, Meet Napster: 3D Printing and the Digitization of Things' (2014) 102 *Georgetown Law Journal* 1691, 1719.

[11] M Rimmer, 'The Maker Movement: Copyright Law, Remix Culture and 3D Printing' (2017) 41 *The University of Western Australia Law Review* 51; see also M Weinberg, 'Lego's IP Grab Bag' (2019) at michaelweinberg.org/blog/2019/10/10/lego-ip-grab-bag; N Hurst, 'HBO Blocks 3-D Printed Game of Thrones iPhone Dock' (Wired, 13 February 2013) at www.wired.com/2013/02/got-hbo-cease-and-desist.

[12] See, eg, I Hargreaves, 'Digital Opportunity: A Review of Intellectual Property and Growth' (2011) 5 ('With the emergence of fabrication through 3D printing, new technological challenges also arise, indicating the need for a thorough reassessment of IP') at www.gov.uk/government/publications/digital-opportunity-review-of-intellectual-property-and-growth; see also European Parliament resolution of 3 July 2018 on three-dimensional printing, a challenge in the fields of intellectual property rights and civil liability (2017/2007(INI)) [2020] OJ C118/10; World Intellectual Property Organization, 'World Intellectual Property Report: Breakthrough Innovation and Economic Growth' (2015) 106–7 at www.wipo.int/edocs/pubdocs/en/wipo_pub_944_2015.pdf.

property law will be brought to its knees'.[13] Others have hypothesised that 3D printing 'may relegate some IP rights to the scrap heap'.[14] However, are these scenarios actually likely to materialise? When considering possible regulatory responses, it is imperative that policymakers and rightsholders have a clear, nuanced, and up-to-date understanding of the risks *actually* posed by the technology. It is also important that they understand the existing community's values, experiences and views on these issues.

This is precisely why this monograph goes beyond purely library-based doctrinal research.[15] It examines these issues within their wider social context, relying on a combination of legal and empirical methods (needless to say, the law does not exist in a vacuum). While there have already been some empirical studies on 3D printing and IP law in recent years – and this book fits within that general analytical framework – qualitative data on the issue remain scarce, especially when it comes to *desktop* 3D printing in particular (which, coupled with the lack of case law on point, makes the need for such research even more compelling).[16]

In line with its interdisciplinary ethos, the monograph draws not only on classic IP theory and practice (engaging with the work of scholars, such as Mark Lemley, Lisa Ouellette and Lawrence Lessig, who have extensively discussed the intricate relationship between IP, creativity and innovation in the modern digital world), but also on contemporary debates from various other academic fields, including economics, philosophy and business.

[13] H Lipson and M Kurman, *Fabricated: The New World of 3D Printing* (Indianapolis, Wiley, 2013) 7.

[14] J Hornick, '3D Printing and IP Rights: The Elephant in the Room' (2015) 55 *Santa Clara Law Review* 801, 802 ('The potential result may be two-way disruption: IP may disrupt the growth and progress of 3D printing, but more importantly, 3D printing may relegate some IP rights to the scrap heap'); see also V Elam, 'The Transfer of Computer-Aided Design Files in the Era of 3D Printing: Trademark Infringement Under the Current European Framework' in *Building a European Digital Space: 12th International Conference on Internet, Law & Politics* (7–8 July 2016) 79 (argues that the availability of 3D printing to consumer masses could be a serious cause for concern for IP rightsholders).

[15] For an overview of the distinction between 'doctrinal' and 'socio-legal' research and legal methodologies more generally, see D Schiff, 'Socio-Legal Theory: Social Structure and Law' (1976) 39 *The Modern Law Review* 287; see also P Chynoweth, 'Legal Research' in L Ruddock and A Knight (eds), *Advanced Research Methods in the Built Environment* (Chichester, Wiley, 2003); T Hutchinson, 'The Doctrinal Method: Incorporating Interdisciplinary Methods in Reforming the Law' (2015) 8 *Erasmus Law Review* 130, 131–2.

[16] For some empirical studies in the area, see D Mendis, D Secchi and P Reeves, 'A Legal and Empirical Study into the Intellectual Property Implications of 3D Printing' (UK Intellectual Property Office Report 2015/41) at assets.publishing.service.gov.uk/government/uploads/system/uploads/attachment_data/file/549044/Legal-Empirical-_Executive-Summary.pdf (focusing on the industrial sector); see also S Santoso and S Wicker, 'The future of three-dimensional printing: Intellectual property or intellectual confinement?' (2016) 18 *New Media and Society* 138; J Nielsen and J Liddicoat, 'The Multiple Dimensions of Intellectual Property Infringement in the 3D Printing Era' (2017) 27 *Australian Intellectual Property Journal* (2017) 184; H Chan, H Choo, O Osuji and J Griffin, *Intellectual Property Rights and Emerging Technology: 3D Printing in China* (Abingdon, Routledge, 2020).

Empirical Design

Having obtained ethical approval from my institution, I relied on two streams of data collection in order to widen participation and to create a diverse and representative sample of participants involved in the 3D printing community.[17] This qualitative study features surveys and interviews with leading 3D printing experts, legal practitioners, engineers, designers and 'hobbyists' based in the UK, Europe and the United States.[18]

In line with the overarching aims of the book, the study aimed to shed light on the extent to which 3D printing presents a challenge to the IP framework and to gain a better understanding of the existing community and its relationship with the law, including individuals' experiences, concerns and views on a range of pertinent IP issues (for a full list of questions and further details about the study, see the Annex to this book). Both streams of data collection followed the same general structure and primarily relied on open-ended questions, given that the aim here was to invite participants to engage with the detail and, insofar as possible, to obtain data-rich insights into their diverse perspectives.[19]

First, a total of 10 semi-structured *interviews* were carried out between May and June 2019. With regards to creating the sample, I sought to include a wide range of professionals and users involved in the 3D printing community and took into account several relevant factors, including the level of experience of participants and, where applicable, the nature of their jobs and the type and size of their organisation.[20] When it came to approaching prospective interviewees, four individuals were contacted directly via email.[21] One was approached by using the 'snowball' method (where another interviewee was willing to provide me with their contact details). The remaining interviewees volunteered to participate after a call for participants was posted on several online discussion boards dedicated to 3D printing.[22]

The final sample composition included one 3D printing engineer; one 3D scanning expert; one lawyer; the chairperson of a global 3D printing retailer; the PR

[17] All participants were provided with a consent form and an information sheet containing a detailed overview of the study. This also included information about data protection and relevant contact details.

[18] In this study, the term 'hobbyist' was given its plain ordinary meaning, so as to include any user who uses the technology at home or as part of their hobby, as opposed to professionally.

[19] The study is primarily qualitative in nature, as its aim was to explore the views and experiences of users involved in the 3D printing community. Regarding qualitative approaches to empirical research more generally, see L Webley, 'Qualitative Approaches to Empirical Legal Research' in P Cane and H Kritzer (eds), *Oxford Handbook of Empirical Legal Research* (Oxford, OUP, 2010); see also J Kirk and M Miller, *Reliability and Validity in Qualitative Research* (Beverly Hills, Sage, 1986).

[20] On sampling in qualitative studies, see M Patton, *Qualitative Research and Evaluation Methods* (Thousand Oaks, Sage, 2002).

[21] Several prospective participants who were approached did not reply at all, or declined to participate due to existing commitments or scheduling conflicts.

[22] The call for participants was posted online in June 2019 and remained open for approximately six weeks.

director of an intermediary service (that prints on behalf of customers); the owner of a small 3D design and printing business; and four individual users who primarily print at home.[23]

The first round of interviews took place in New York, where four professionals were interviewed face-to-face. These initial interviews also served as pilots, which helped to confirm the suitability of the questions. The remaining interviews were conducted through video calls or instant messaging, depending on the availability and preferences of interviewees. The interviews were 'loose' and semi-structured so as to allow for follow-up questions and greater flexibility. For example, in light of interviewees' individual expertise and experiences, some participants were able to provide more detailed information regarding a certain point than others.

Second, the online *survey* was completed by 161 participants between June and July 2019.[24] In terms of the sample, the main selection criterion was that participants were part of the 3D printing community and either used the technology at home or as part of their profession. Approximately two-thirds of the survey respondents identified as hobbyists (only), less than a tenth as professionals (only), and approximately a quarter identified as *both* hobbyists and professionals, which clearly indicates that most professionals also use the technology at home.[25] There were both relative newcomers and highly experienced users. Nearly three-quarters were based in the US at the time of the survey, while the remaining participants were based in the UK or continental Europe.[26]

The findings of the study will be contextually analysed and discussed in chapter nine.[27]

Scope and Limitations

This monograph has several limitations. While 3D printing technologies raise a wide range of different legal issues (encompassing areas such as product liability,

[23] One of these four individual users (or 'hobbyists') explained that while they initially started using 3D printing as a hobby, they have recently also started using it professionally (indeed, it was not uncommon for participants to use the technology both at home and as part of their profession).

[24] Survey participants were approached through the same call for participants outlined above. The survey itself was completed online through Google Forms and it was available for approximately 6 weeks.

[25] Participants were able to select both options at the same time.

[26] In terms of age, the majority of survey participants fell within the 18–30 age bracket. Approximately a third were aged 31–45, and the remaining participants (less than a tenth) were older than 45.

[27] Data were primarily analysed through qualitative content analysis. The aim was to identify commonly recurring patterns and themes and to better understand participants' views, experiences and concerns regarding IP law (as opposed to providing a quantified measure of phenomena or producing statistically significant results). Where relevant, I use broad descriptive terms such as 'the majority', 'many', 'a few' to roughly indicate the prevalence of certain patterns and to guide interpretation. Regarding qualitative content analysis more generally (and its overlap with thematic analysis), see, eg, M Vaismoradi and others, 'Content Analysis and Thematic Analysis: Implications for Conducting a Qualitative Descriptive Study' (2013) 15 *Nursing and Health Sciences* 398.

gun control, data protection and intellectual property),[28] this book is exclusively confined to IP law and focuses on desktop 3D printing in particular.[29] Rather than attempting to cover each and every single aspect of the IP framework that may be relevant to the operation of 3D printing, it adopts a targeted approach that focuses on the issues that are especially problematic or novel from a legal or policy perspective.[30] In other words, there will be little or no legal analysis of more 'generic' issues where the same general rules and principles are likely to apply. In light of this approach and existing literature on the topic, the discussion is further primarily confined to copyright, patents and trade mark law, allowing for a more in-depth analysis of these critical areas of IP law (however, other relevant areas will be taken into account where applicable).[31]

In terms of its jurisdictional scope, the doctrinal analysis in this monograph primarily focuses on the legal framework in the UK, although it draws heavily on EU law and other relevant intergovernmental laws and treaties. Indeed, Brexit notwithstanding, several pertinent EU legal principles continue to play a key role

[28] For a monograph with a broader focus that explores the implications of 3D printing and scanning from the perspective of several different legal areas, including IP, data protection, and other legal fields, see A Daly, *Socio-Legal Aspects of the 3D Printing Revolution* (London, Palgrave Macmillan, 2016).

[29] For studies focusing on *industrial* 3D printing, see D Mendis and others, 'The Intellectual Property Implications of the Development of Industrial 3D Printing' (European Commission Final Report, 12 February 2020) at op.europa.eu/en/publication-detail/-/publication/e193a586-7f8c-11ea-aea8-01aa75ed71a1; see also Mendis, Secchi and Reeves (n 16).

[30] For an excellent book that similarly focuses on the novel issues raised by 3D printing and addresses the issue from the perspective of US law (and also several other major jurisdictions such as Japan, Australia, Canada and the EU), see L Osborn, *3D Printing and Intellectual Property* (Cambridge, CUP, 2019).

[31] There are already several comprehensive studies exploring design law. See P Malaquias, 'Consumer 3D Printing: Is the UK Copyright and Design Law Framework Fit for Purpose' (2016) 6 *Queen Mary Journal of Intellectual Property* 321 (argues that UK design law does not 'excessively constrain' 3D printing); V Elam, 'CAD Files and European Design Law' (2016) 7 *Journal of Intellectual Property Information Technology and E-Commerce Law* 146 (argues that EU design law 'should adapt to the reality of digitized goods and accommodate greater protection for right owners'); T Margoni, 'Design rights and 3D printing in the UK: Balancing innovation and creativity in a (dis)harmonised and fragmented legal framework' in D Mendis and others (eds), *3D Printing and Beyond: The Intellectual Property and Legal Implications Surrounding 3D Printing and Emerging Technologies* (Cheltenham, Edward Elgar, 2019) 77 (argues that the design framework is poorly coordinated, which could constitute a barrier to innovation when applied to 3D printing); D Mendis, 'Fit for Purpose? 3D Printing and the Implications for Design Law: Opportunities and Challenges' in T Aplin (ed), *Research Handbook on Intellectual Property and Digital Technologies* (Cheltenham, Edward Elgar, 2019) 445 (argues that the infringement exceptions should be reconsidered to strike a better balance between competing interests); D Hong, 'An Analysis of UK Copyright and Design Laws on 3D Printing and Product Design' (Doctoral thesis, Bournemouth 2020) at www.eprints.bournemouth.ac.uk/35915; V Elam, 'The challenge of three-dimensional printing: questioning established concepts in intellectual property law' (Doctoral thesis, EUI 2019) at www.cadmus.eui.eu/handle/1814/60404. For recent developments concerning 3D printing and design law at the EU level, see Regulation (EU) 2024/2822 of the European Parliament and of the Council of 23 October 2024 amending Council Regulation (EC) 6/2002 on Community designs and repealing Commission Regulation (EC) 2246/2002 [2024] OJ L 2822/18.11.2024 (in particular, see Art 19 and Recital 27). On trade secrets, see M Rimmer, 'Metal 3D Printing: Patent Law, Trade Secrets, and Additive Manufacturing' (2022) 7 *Frontiers in Research Metrics and Analytics*; see also B Vogel, 'Intellectual Property and Additive Manufacturing / 3D Printing: Strategies and Challenges of Applying Traditional IP Laws to a Transformative Technology' (2016) 17 *Minnesota Journal of Law, Science & Technology* 881.

in the UK today.[32] The book will also occasionally engage with relevant US literature on the topic (for example, to highlight key differences in legal approaches). This is especially important given the novelty of the issue and the fact that the US is not only a world leader in 3D printing technology, but also has rich legal scholarship on point.[33]

The empirical component has its own limitations. It is geographically confined to participants based in the UK, continental Europe and the US, and it was carried out over a relatively brief period of time.[34] As the sample primarily consists of users who are actively involved in the 3D printing community, the study also does not claim to reflect the views of all relevant stakeholders. Moreover, given the diversity of views expressed by participants and the fact that this is a primarily qualitative study, it does not claim to provide a definitive statement on the subject or to provide answers to all relevant IP issues raised by 3D printing.

Despite these limitations, this book is the first legal and empirical monograph of its kind to provide rich qualitative data on the IP issues raised by desktop 3D printing and the norms, experiences and views of users within the community. By adopting an innovative interdisciplinary approach, it works alongside recent successful books in the area that have examined the topic through a variety of different methods and perspectives, including the excellent work of scholars such as Lucas Osborn, Dinusha Mendis, Angela Daly, Rosa Ballardini, Matthew Rimmer, James Griffin and others.[35]

[32] While it remains to be seen whether UK courts will depart from EU intellectual property law in future, retained EU provisions remain applicable within the UK for the time being. On Brexit, see L Bently and others, *Intellectual Property Law* (Oxford, OUP, 2022) 17; L McDonagh, 'UK Patent Law and Copyright Law after Brexit: Potential Consequences' (Centre for International Governance Innovation Paper No 3, 2017) at www.cigionline.org/sites/default/files/documents/Brexit%20Series%20Paper%20no3.pdf.

[33] See, eg, M Lemley, 'IP in a World Without Scarcity' (2015) 90 *New York University Law Review* 460; L Osborn and T Holbrook, 'Digital Patent Infringement in an Era of 3D Printing' (2015) 48 *UC Davis Law Review* 1319; L Osborn, 'Doctrinal Quandaries with 3D Printing and Intellectual Property' (2016) 27 *Intellectual Property Litigation* 18; M Weinberg, 'It Will Be Awesome If They Don't Screw It Up: 3D Printing, Intellectual Property, and the Fight over the Next Great Disruptive Technology' (Public Knowledge 2010) at www.publicknowledge.org/files/docs/3DPrintingPaperPublicKnowledge.pdf; L Osborn, 'Regulating Three-Dimensional Printing: The Converging Worlds of Bits and Atoms' (2014) 51 *San Diego Law Review* 553.

[34] Besides data protection considerations, one of the key rationales for focusing on these jurisdictions is that these countries are world leaders when it comes to 3D printing technology.

[35] For a non-exhaustive list of some notable books in this area, see Osborn (n 30); see also D Mendis, M Lemley and M Rimmer, *3D Printing and Beyond: Intellectual Property and Regulation* (Cheltenham, Edward Elgar, 2019) (a comprehensive edited collection that explores the IP implications of 3D printing from the perspective of several major jurisdictions); Daly (n 28); R Ballardini, M Norrgård and J Partanen (eds), *3D Printing, Intellectual Property and Innovation* (Alphen aan den Rijn, Kluwer International, 2017) (examines 3D printing from a multidisciplinary perspective, looking at law, economics, and engineering); Chan, Choo, Osuji and Griffin (n 16) (based on empirical research, offers specific solutions and recommendations to tackle the IP challenges raised by 3D printing); J Griffin, *The State of Creativity: The Future of 3D Printing, 4D Printing and Augmented Reality* (Cheltenham, Edward Elgar, 2019); B van den Berg, S van der Hof and E Kosta E (eds), *3D Printing: Legal, Philosophical and Economic Dimensions* (The Hague, Asser Press, 2016).

Overview of Chapters

Chapter two begins with a contextual overview of the history and evolution of 3D printing. It explains how a once prohibitively expensive technology – that was exclusively confined to industrial use – has now reached the homes of individual users. It discusses the dichotomy between industrial and desktop 3D printing – an important distinction that is not always clearly addressed in the legal literature and media publications where the affordability of desktop machines is often conflated with the more sophisticated capabilities of industrial 3D printers. Next, the chapter discusses the core technology behind 3D printing and examines the production process in detail – from creating a digital 3D model and converting it into machine-readable code to manufacturing. While this aspect is often overlooked in the literature, it has direct implications for some pertinent legal issues addressed later in the book. Finally, the chapter discusses the wider socio-economic significance of the technology and considers whether it is likely to be as 'revolutionary' and groundbreaking as many commentators had initially predicted.[36]

Chapter three provides a general overview of the IP framework so that all readers – regardless of their professional background and specific field of expertise – can become familiar with its basic features, functions and the theoretical rationales behind it. First, the chapter outlines the remarkably diverse range of subject matter protected by this area of law. For example, copyright protects creative works such as books, music and paintings. Patents protect new inventions, such as medicines and technology. Trade marks protect signs that allow consumers to distinguish between competing products. While there are some notable differences between these rights, they share some essential basic features – most notably, they protect intangible assets and grant exclusive control over products of the human mind. That is, the right to *exclude* third parties from performing certain reserved acts without the owner's permission. Second, the chapter discusses the theoretical rationales underpinning modern IP law and explains how the granting of exclusive rights is justified from a normative perspective. Finally, it explores the practical value of 'theory' and highlights some of the key critiques of the IP framework.

Before exploring the application of specific legal provisions and principles in the context of 3D printing in subsequent chapters, chapter four first considers the challenges that the technology poses to IP theory and practice at a general and global level – that is, broader issues that cannot be confined to a specific jurisdiction and are likely to affect most IP systems around the world. First, the chapter notes that while the early days of digitisation were primarily concerned with copyright law and intangibles, 3D printing has the potential to change this dynamic as it, at least

[36] See, eg, 'The third industrial revolution' (*The Economist*, 21 April 2012) at www.economist.com/leaders/2012/04/21/the-third-industrial-revolution; Rimmer (n 11) 51; R Ballardini and M Norrgård, 'Digitising Patent Law: Challenges from 3D Printing Technologies' (2016) 38 *European Intellectual Property Review* 519, 521; Desai and Magliocca (n 10) 1719.

in theory, enables individual end users to reproduce various tangible products on a highly decentralised basis. The technology could therefore bring the full force of digitisation to other industries and areas of IP (such as patent and trade mark law) that have not yet experienced the full force of this process. Second, it considers the enforcement challenges posed by desktop 3D printing and argues that when considering possible measures to tackle piracy online, it is important to learn from the recent past (in particular, to look at the content industry's response to the arrival of the internet) and to try to avoid making the same mistakes again. Finally, drawing on Mark Lemley's theory of 'post-scarcity IP', the chapter considers some of the less immediate and more 'theoretical' long-term challenges posed by the technology.[37]

Chapters five, six and seven respectively examine the relationship between 3D printing and UK (and EU) copyright, patent and trade mark law, focusing on the application of specific legal provisions and doctrines in this context.[38]

Chapter five first looks at copyright law. It begins by discussing the copyright status of 3D printable files, an issue that would be especially important for rightsholders given that these files could carry substantial economic value.[39] It considers the issue in the context of a variety of different scenarios, including creating a new model from scratch and using 3D scanning. Moreover, it considers the issue of copyright infringement in the context of file sharing, manufacturing and 3D scanning.

Chapter six focuses on patent law. Although desktop 3D printing is not as sophisticated as its industrial counterparts, there are several patentable items that are certainly within the reach of individual users.[40] At the same time, the patent framework has not yet been exposed to the process of digitisation to the same extent as copyright law, and there are several uncertainties regarding the application of key provisions in this context.[41] For example, while there is little doubt that manufacturing a patented product through 3D printing may constitute infringement (as the specific type of technology used is irrelevant in this regard), more complex legal and policy questions arise where, for instance, users share *intangible* 3D printable versions of claimed physical inventions. There are further important questions concerning the private and non-commercial use exemption in patent law, a provision that may be a concern for rightsholders in light of the increasing availability of desktop 3D printing.

[37] See Lemley (n 33).

[38] As also explained above, while this monograph primarily focuses on UK law, despite Brexit, relevant EU principles continue to play an important role in UK IP law, so their application will be taken into account where relevant. The same applies to pertinent intergovernmental treaties of which the UK is a member state. Rather than attempting to provide a comprehensive 'guide' or an overview of each and every single aspect of IP that may be relevant to the operation of 3D printing, it focuses on select areas that are especially problematic from a legal or policy perspective.

[39] For example, 3D printable files may contain valuable works of art, sculptures and action figures from popular culture that may be subject to copyright. See the wide range of models available at www.thingiverse.com.

[40] For instance, Godtfred Christiansen was granted a US patent for the Lego toy building brick in the 1960s (now in the public domain); see US Patent No 3,005,282. 3D printable versions of items of this nature are commonly shared through file repositories online. See, eg, www.thingiverse.com/thing:615256.

[41] See Desai and Magliocca (n 10).

Chapter seven focuses on 3D printing and trade mark law. Amid concerns that 3D printing may dramatically increase counterfeiting and decrease demand for genuine goods (thus undermining rightsholders' economic interests),[42] the chapter explores the challenges that 3D printing poses to this area of law with a particular focus on the issue of infringement. We will explore the extent to which the use of 3D printing is likely to interfere with the core 'functions' of a trade mark and discuss the application of other relevant doctrines in this context, such as infringement action based on 'confusing similarities' and dilution.

Chapter eight is slightly different. While this book is primarily concerned with the extent to which 3D printing – *as a technology* – presents a challenge to IP theory and practice, the history behind the making of modern 3D printing is itself a fascinating case study which contributes to a more nuanced understanding of the complex relationship between exclusive rights, innovation and net social welfare in the digital age. In particular, a closer look at the development of the desktop sector indicates that key patents may have effectively kept the technology prohibitively expensive for decades and prevented valuable follow-on innovation in this area. Upon the expiry of these patents, an open-source hardware community utilised the existing technology and not only helped to dramatically increase the quality of 3D printing, but also reduced hardware costs by orders of magnitude – thus effectively shaping the modern desktop 3D printing sector. In this sense, it appears that the recent 3D printing 'boom' was not caused by the invention of a new and radically different technology but rather by existing technology being 'freed' from exclusive monopoly control.

Chapter nine outlines the findings of the empirical study, presenting the results from each stream of data collection in a thematically structured manner. The aim of this project was to provide insights into the experiences and perspectives of experts and users in the 3D printing community on a wide range of pertinent issues, which was essential not only to assess the extent to which law reform is likely to be necessary in the future, but also to better understand the norms and values that the community is based on.

The final chapter summarises the key points identified throughout the book and answers the central question of how, if at all, the law should respond to 3D printing.

[42] A Scardamaglia, 'Flashpoints in 3D Printing and Trade Mark Law' (2015) 23 *Journal of Law, Information and Science* 30, 50; see also B van Wiele, 'Decentralised, Democratised and Disruptive: How 3D Printing Challenges the Consumer Protection Rationale of Trade Marks' (2019) 41 *European Intellectual Property Review* 313, 319 ('3D printing … expands the range of products that can be counterfeited and eliminates the means for effective enforcement'); J Ammar and S Craufurd, 'When is a Trade Mark use not a Trade Mark Use? A 3D Perspective' (2015) 1 *International Journal of Law and Interdisciplinary Legal Studies* 4, 4 (arguing that 3D printing is 'likely to disturb the longstanding balance between the costs and frequency of infringement' in trade mark law); I Silverman, 'Optimising protection: IP rights in 3D printing' (2016) 38 *European Intellectual Property Review* 5, 6 (arguing that 3D printing 'may decrease demand for genuine goods and could devalue brands').

2

Understanding 3D Printing

Introduction

What is 3D printing, and how does it work? Why is it important? This chapter explores these key issues. It begins with a contextual overview of the history of the technology and explains how a once prohibitively expensive manufacturing process – which was exclusively confined to industrial use – has now reached the homes of individual users. Second, it considers the subtleties of the production process – from digital data creation and conversion to a machine-readable format to actual manufacturing. This is a critical aspect that is essential not only to understand how exactly 3D printing works, but also to fully appreciate some of the intricate legal issues explored later in the book. Third, the chapter highlights some of the key features and practical applications of the technology. Finally, it looks at the broader socio-economic impact of 3D printing and considers whether it is likely to evolve into a truly paradigm-shifting technology.

What is 3D Printing?

Manufacturing technologies generally fall into three main categories based on geometry and how they form objects: subtractive, formative and additive. In subtractive and formative manufacturing, the intended geometry is achieved by either removing material through cutting, milling and grinding, or by using external forces such as heat and forging to alter the original geometry of the object and transform it into the desired shape.[1]

In contrast, additive manufacturing, now commonly referred to as 3D printing,[2] successively deposits layers of material until the final geometry is achieved. There are several different additive manufacturing processes available and while each of them relies on a distinct technology, what they have in common is that they all make objects from 3D model data, typically layer by layer.[3] The use of digital

[1] A Gebhardt and J Hötter, *Additive Manufacturing: 3D Printing for Prototyping and Manufacturing* (Munich, Hanser, 2016).

[2] ibid 3.

[3] F Calignano and others, 'Overview on Additive Manufacturing Technologies' (2017) 105 *Proceedings of the IEEE* 593, 593.

computer-aided design (CAD) files is of critical importance here, as the hardware cannot function without these files.

In terms of terminology, we should note that 'additive manufacturing' is technically the formal umbrella term for a number of distinct additive processes, while '3D printing' is the brand name for a specific additive manufacturing process known as binder jetting, originally developed at MIT.[4] However, in recent years, the terms '3D printing' and 'additive manufacturing' have increasingly been used interchangeably to describe *any* additive manufacturing process.[5] In fact, 3D printing is now expected to become the dominant term for all additive processes and replace all other existing names:

> This is mainly because it is very easy to understand. Everyone who can operate a text editor … and a 2D office printer easily understands that he or she will be able to print a 3D object using a 3D design program (a part processor) and a 3D printing machine …[6]

Indeed, in very simple terms, 3D printing allows users to convert digital design files into physical objects and, in this sense, produces tangible matter in a similar fashion to regular printers, but in three dimensions.[7]

For the sake of simplicity, this book will use the term *3D printing* interchangeably with *additive manufacturing* to refer to any manufacturing technology of this nature, unless otherwise stated.

A Brief History of 3D Printing

3D printing is not a new technology. While a fictional article on the concept first appeared in *New Scientist* in 1974,[8] it was, among others, Wyn Kelly Swainson's and Charles Hull's important patents in the 1970s and 1980s that played a key role in bringing the first 'real' 3D printers into existence.[9] Hull invented stereolithography, a key additive manufacturing technology based on photopolymerisation, and went on to found 3D Systems, one of the major hardware manufacturers in the industry today (along with Stratasys). In the late 1980s, Scott Crump invented

[4] Li P and others, 'Intellectual Property and 3D Printing: A Case Study on 3D Chocolate Printing' (2014) 9 *Journal of Intellectual Property Law and Practice* 322. Some commentators have drawn a distinction between the two, arguing that *3D printing* refers to the process of making products 'at home or the community' while *additive manufacturing* involves a business-to-consumer supply chain; see, eg, D Mendis, D Secchi, and P Reeves, 'A Legal and Empirical Study into the Intellectual Property Implications of 3D Printing: Executive Summary' (Intellectual Property Office, 2015/41) 6, 10 at assets.publishing.service.gov.uk/government/uploads/system/uploads/attachment_data/file/549044/Legal-Empirical-_Executive-Summary.pdf.

[5] S Ford, L Mortara and T Minshall, 'The emergence of additive manufacturing' (2016) 102 *Technological Forecasting & Social Change* 156.

[6] Gebhardt and Hötter (n 1) 3.

[7] I Gibson, 'The Changing Face of Additive Manufacturing' (2017) 28 *Journal of Manufacturing Technology Management* 10, 14.

[8] D Jones, 'Ariadne' (1974) 64 *New Scientist* 80.

[9] A Daly, *Socio-Legal Aspects of the 3D Printing Revolution* (London, Palgrave Macmillan, 2016) 5.

an extrusion-based process called fused filament fabrication (also known as fused deposition modelling) whereby thermoplastic material is deposited layer by layer, which is also one of the most widely used additive manufacturing technologies in the more affordable 'personal' 3D printing sector today.[10] While much of this early innovation took place in the US, other top patent filers in this field include China, Germany, Japan and Korea.[11] Of course, it goes without saying that the quantity of patents granted is not necessarily indicative of quality and impact.

The adoption (and industrial use) of 3D printing has been a multi-layered process which corresponds to different uses determined by the capabilities and costs of the technology at a given time.[12] In its early days, 3D printing was a crude and expensive process with considerably limited applications. As primarily rough-looking objects made of plastic could be made at the time, one of its first applications was rapid prototyping. This enabled manufacturers to quickly test a new concept, design or process.[13] However, 3D printing's capabilities have grown tremendously since then. Technological advancements eventually enabled the entire manufacturing process to start with a digital model and end with a complete physical product without the need for any extra tools.[14]

While 3D printers were initially prohibitively expensive and limited to industrial use, this is no longer the case.[15] There is now a well-established market of affordable and compact hardware devices suitable for home and business use, which we will now explore in more detail.

The Desktop Sector

What exactly is 'desktop' or 'consumer' 3D printing? There is no clear consensus in the academic literature, let alone a stable and universally agreed formal definition.

[10] Gibson (n 7) 13; C Barnatt, *3D Printing: Third Edition* (CreateSpace, 2016); P Holzmann and others 'User Entrepreneur Business Models in 3D Printing' (2017) 28 *Journal of Manufacturing Technology Management* 75. For a recent patent lawsuit involving inventions related to fused deposition modelling (between Stratasys and Bambu Lab), see J Butts, '3D Printer Maker Bambu Lab Faces Patent Infringement Lawsuits That Could Threaten Hobbyist 3D Printing in General' (*Tom's Hardware*, 11 August 2024) at tomshardware.com/3d-printing/3d-printer-maker-bambu-lab-faces-patent-infringement-lawsuits-that-could-threaten-hobbyist-3d-printing-in-general.

[11] World Intellectual Property Organization, 'Breakthrough Innovation and Economic Growth' (2015) at www.wipo.int/edocs/pubdocs/en/wipo_pub_944_2015.pdf.

[12] See T Rayna and L Striukova, 'From Rapid Prototyping to Home Fabrication: How 3D Printing is Changing Business Model Innovation' (2016) 102 *Technological Forecasting and Social Change* 214, 216. It is important to note that each of these new stages does not render previous ones obsolete (for instance, the technology is still widely used for rapid prototyping in the industrial sector). Rather, each stage should be seen as an extension of the preceding ones which diversifies and expands the applications of the technology.

[13] C Weller and others, 'Economic Implications of 3D Printing: Market Structure Models in Light of Additive Manufacturing Revisited' (2015) 164 *International Journal of Production Economics* 43, 44.

[14] I Gibson, D Rosen and B Stucker, *Additive Manufacturing Technologies Rapid Prototyping to Direct Digital Manufacturing* (Cham, Springer, 2010).

[15] Rayna and Striukova (n 12).

These terms have been loosely used to refer to relatively affordable and compact additive manufacturing devices that are small enough to fit on a desk and are suitable for use in non-industrial environments, such as at home or in educational establishments and offices. For example, Wohlers Reports (a major additive manufacturing consultancy firm) uses the term 'desktop 3D printer' to refer to machines priced under $5,000, while Context Research describes additive manufacturing hardware priced under $2,500 as 'entry-level 3D printers'.[16] Desktop 3D printers are most commonly based on extrusion-based technologies, such as fused filament fabrication (as described above),[17] and typically have lower build volume and print quality compared to their more expensive industrial counterparts.

The unit costs of desktop 3D printers have decreased tremendously over the past decade (which, in turn, has contributed to their increasing popularity). Nowadays, a 'personal' 3D printer can be purchased for less than a few hundred US dollars.[18] A recent market report estimated that nearly one million 'entry-level' 3D printers were shipped in the last quarter of 2023 alone.[19] The mere fact that online discussion boards dedicated to 3D printing have nearly three million members as of early 2025 is also indicative of the growing interest in this technology.[20]

While desktop 3D printers are not yet as technologically sophisticated as industrial machines, they are nevertheless becoming increasingly accessible and have gained substantial popularity among passionate hobbyists, hardware enthusiasts, and individual users (also known as 'Makers') who are using the technology at home and as part of various educational, engineering and DIY hardware projects.[21] This community has also contributed to creating a vibrant ecosystem of 3D printable files that are shared online on a daily basis, typically by using licences that allow anyone to freely download these models and to create their own tangible products at home.[22]

Interestingly, the general public's (more specifically, individuals who do not necessarily qualify as hardware enthusiasts or engineers) interest in 3D printing

[16] Wohlers Associates, 'Wohlers Report 2016' (2016) 4 at www.wohlersassociates.com/wp-content/uploads/2016/05/2016-ExSum.pdf; see also C Schwaar, 'A 3D Printer On Every Desk? Why Companies Are Buying More 3D Printers' (*Forbes*, 2 May 2024) at www.forbes.com/sites/carolynschwaar/2024/05/02/a-3d-printer-on-every-desk-why-companies-are-buying-more-3d-printers. For the sake of simplicity, this book uses the term 'desktop 3D printer' to refer to any affordable 3D printer suitable for personal or domestic use.

[17] See Gibson (n 7) 13.

[18] J Kietzmann, L Pitt and P Berthon, 'Disruptions, Decisions, and Destinations: Enter the Age of 3-D Printing and Additive Manufacturing' (2015) 58 *Business Horizons* 209, 210.

[19] However, see Schwaar (n 16) ('But it's not the number of machines sold that's surprising; it's who's buying them: businesses').

[20] See, eg, www.reddit.com/r/3Dprinting.

[21] C Anderson, *Makers: The New Industrial Revolution* (London, Crown Business, 2012); C Doctorow, *Makers* (New York, Tor Books, 2010); M Hatch, *The Maker Movement Manifesto: Rules for Innovation in the New World of Crafters, Hackers, and Tinkerers* (New York, McGraw-Hill, 2013); M Rimmer, 'The Maker Movement: Copyright Law, Remix Culture and 3D Printing' (2017) 41 (2) *The University of Western Australia Law Review* 51; S Bradshaw, A Bowyer and P Haufe, 'The Intellectual Property Implications of Low-Cost 3D Printing' (2010) 7 *ScriptEd* 5.

[22] See, eg, www.thingiverse.com.

also appears to coincide with the emergence of the desktop sector, despite the fact that the core technology behind 3D printing has been quietly around for decades. This interest could be explained by the fact that personal 3D printing has, at least in theory, the potential to dramatically reduce existing barriers to product design and manufacturing (and therefore give consumers more than a merely passive role in production).

At the same time, there has also been sensational media coverage that has often failed to properly explain the dichotomy between industrial and desktop 3D printing, or has conflated the affordability of entry-level machines with the sophisticated capabilities of industrial printers:

> Based on popular articles, the public may create the impression that 3D printing is the Holy Grail; we are going to print everything as one piece, traditional manufacturing is at the brink of collapse, and exotic applications, such as cloning a human body by 3D bio-printing, are just around the corner.[23]

Finally, while 3D printing *as a whole* is a multibillion-dollar industry and the technology is already widely used in various high-cost commercial applications, it remains to be seen whether the desktop sector can achieve more mainstream adoption.[24] For the time being, owners of home 3D printers are still a relatively small fraction of the general population (a demographic that some commentators have compared to early adopters of personal computers).[25]

How Exactly Does 3D Printing Work?

Commentators have likened 3D printing to concepts previously depicted in science fiction, such as the Star Trek Replicator – a device that can create anything on demand out of pure energy (however, its mysterious mechanics were never fully explained).[26] In reality, 3D printing is a little more complicated.

The process typically starts with making a virtual model in computer-aided design (CAD) modelling software; second, converting it into a surface-mesh format such as STL (that describes the geometry of the object); third, using 'slicer'

[23] W Oropallo and L Piegl, 'Ten Challenges in 3D Printing' (2016) 32 *Engineers with Computers* 135, 135.

[24] Wohlers Associates, 'Wohlers Report 2024 Shows Metal AM Growth in New Report' (Wohlers Associates, 2024) at wohlersassociates.com/news/wohlers-report-2024-shows-metal-am-growth-in-new-report ('Meanwhile, the AM industry grew by 11.1% to $20.035 billion').

[25] H Lipson and M Kurman, *Fabricated: The New World of 3D Printing* (Indianapolis, Wiley, 2013) 49–50 ('Somewhat like software hackers, Makers tend to be affluent males from Europe or North America … Makers are highly educated'); T Birtchnell and others, '3D Printing and Intellectual Property Futures' (UK Intellectual Property Office, 2018/03) 11, at assets.publishing.service.gov.uk/government/uploads/system/uploads/attachment_data/file/757767/3D-printing.pdf.

[26] Daly (n 9) 4; I Budmen and A Rotolo, *The Book On 3D Printing* (CreateSpace, 2013); M O'Rourke, 'A 3D Printed Future' (2013) 60 *Risk Management* 1.

software to convert this file into machine-readable G-code (that directly sends instructions to the printer); and, finally, using the 3D printer to manufacture the intended physical object.

The industry standard and most commonly shared 3D printable file format online is STL, derived from stereolithography.[27] As neatly explained by Michael Weinberg:

> Physical objects can live in a digital form. For 3D printing, this digital form is often that of an .stl file. These files can be thought of as the object equivalent of a .pdf file – they are more or less universally printable by 3D printers …[28]

This file format encodes the geometry of the (tangible) three-dimensional object it represents by tessellating the model's outer surface into millions of triangles. By doing so, it records information about each triangle's coordinates and vectors and aims to approximate the skin of the CAD model with planar triangles.[29] STL files consist of both computer code and digital design drawings which users can view and edit prior to printing.

STL files can be obtained in several different ways. First, users can create their own model from scratch by using 3D modelling software, which allows them to customise the model exactly as they see fit (there are several freely available tools and web apps that are becoming increasingly accessible).[30] Second, files can be obtained by '3D scanning' existing physical objects.[31] In a sense, 3D scanners work in a similar fashion to regular cameras but generate 3D renderings of the object's position in three-dimensional space and collect data about their appearance and geometry (information that can then be further edited to make a 3D printable model and a physical replica of the original).[32] The technology can be used to capture various archaeological artefacts,[33] everyday objects, and even people's

[27] This book will generally use terms such as '3D printing design files' and '3D printable files' to refer to the STL format in particular, unless otherwise specified, and unless this is necessary to make a distinction. For a more detailed overview of the significance of the different file formats when it comes to assessing relevant legal issues, see L Osborn, *3D Printing and Intellectual Property* (Cambridge, CUP, 2019) 27. It is also worth noting that while there are several alternatives to STL, such as AMF (Additive Manufacturing Format), STL remains the industry standard file format; see G Navangul, R Paul and S Anand, 'Error Minimization in Layered Manufacturing Parts by Stereolithography File Modification Using a Vertex Translation Algorithm' (2013) 135 *Journal of Manufacturing Science and Engineering* 031006.

[28] M Weinberg, 'What's the Deal with Copyright and 3D Printing?' (*Public Knowledge*, 2013) 14 at michaelweinberg.org/docs/WhatstheDealwithCopyright_%20Finalversion2.pdf.

[29] W Oropallo and L Piegl, 'Ten Challenges in 3D Printing' (2016) 32 *Engineers with Computers* 135, 138. As this is only an approximation, it may result in imprecision, especially when it comes to curved surfaces.

[30] See, eg, www.tinkercad.com.

[31] See Lipson and Kurman (n 25) 95–96 (arguing that 3D scanning could allow us to 'edit the physical world' as easily as we can edit digital photos); see also P Oruc, '3D Digitisation of Cultural Heritage: Copyright Implications of the Methods, Purposes and Collaboration' (2020) 11 *Journal of Intellectual Property, Information Technology and E-Commerce Law* 149.

[32] Once a 3D scan is complete, users would typically still have to process the resulting data through modelling software and convert it into a printable format.

[33] See, eg, www.myminifactory.com/scantheworld and www.smk.dk/en/article/3d-models.

faces (which is why the technology also raises concerns about privacy and data protection).[34] Third, users can download files made by others from online repositories, which is especially valuable in cases where users do not have 3D modelling skills to make their own products.[35]

Next, prior to printing, digital models have to be 'sliced' into layers, generating machine-readable G-code that corresponds to each layer.[36] This code directly provides printer-specific instructions to the hardware and determines where and how material is to be deposited.[37]

Once conversion is complete, the actual manufacturing (or printing) process starts. The 3D printer deposits the raw material layer by layer until the intended tangible three-dimensional object is produced. 3D printing is therefore technically a 'two-and-a-half-dimensional' process, given that all additive models are built by joining single layers of equal thickness, as opposed to using continuous z coordinates (the third dimension effectively results from single layers being stacked on top of each other).[38]

It is also important to emphasise that the precise way in which the manufacturing process works will depend on the specific type of 3D printing technology used. For example, when it comes to fused filament fabrication, the printer extrudes molten or semi-liquid filament through a nozzle before the material cools and solidifies, continuously repeating this process until completion.[39] In many cases, this will typically take several hours to complete. Other processes (more commonly used in the industrial sector) are based on rather different additive technologies, such as binding powders or bonding sheets of material together.[40]

What Makes 3D Printing Different

There are several 'practical features' that make 3D printing an attractive technology for many, from individual users to small enterprises and large corporations.

[34] Daly (n 9) 6.

[35] For an overview of the different types of 3D printing online platforms and services, see T Rayna and L Striukova, 'A Taxonomy of Online 3D Printing Platforms' in B van den Berg, S van der Hof and E Kosta (eds), *3D Printing: Legal, Philosophical and Economic Dimensions* (The Hague, Asser Press, 2016) 158.

[36] G Ahn, H Kim and S Lee, 'Fabrication Direction Optimization to Minimize Post-machining in Layered Manufacturing' (2007) 47 *International Journal of Machine Tools and Manufacture* 593. Layer thickness is also linked to the 'stair-stepping' or 'staircase' effect, a topographical defect which is a typical characteristic of additive manufacturing; see L Carolo and R Cooper, 'A Review on the Influence of Process Variables on the Surface Roughness of Ti-6Al-4V by Electron Beam Powder Bed Fusion' (2022) 59 *Additive Manufacturing* 103103, 6; A Phatak and S Pande, 'Optimum Part Orientation in Rapid Prototyping using Genetic Algorithm' (2012) 31 *Journal of Manufacturing Systems* 395, 395.

[37] Machine-readable G-code files are less commonly shared online as these are hardware specific. Instead, users typically share STL files.

[38] Gebhardt and Hötter (n 1) 22; Calignano and others(n 3) 593.

[39] S Kalpakjian and S Schmid, *Manufacturing Engineering & Technology* (London, Pearson, 2013).

[40] R Mahamood, E Akinlabi and S Pityana, 'Revolutionary Additive Manufacturing: An Overview' (2014) *Lasers in Engineering* 161.

For example, it provides a high level of design freedom and customisation. Rather than being confined to mass-produced products that only partially fulfil individual needs, it allows users to have more tailored solutions.[41] As a digital model can be changed relatively quickly and inexpensively, 3D printing makes it easier for manufacturers to quickly adapt production strategies and respond to rapidly evolving market demands.[42] 3D printing dramatically lowers the cost of producing certain things (for example, complex shapes)[43] and enables volume-independent production, which makes small-production runs economically feasible.[44] In contrast, traditional manufacturing typically only becomes economically viable once goods are produced in sufficiently large quantities.[45] Moreover, since 3D printing requires little or no tooling, it also significantly reduces the initial start-up costs and lowers market entry barriers for small businesses or individuals who may lack the resources to invest in expensive facilities.[46] Finally, while 'traditional' manufacturing typically requires skilled labour for onsite production, and this process often takes place overseas to minimise costs, 3D printing enables goods to be produced closer to the point of consumption and could boost jobs and employment locally (this could, in turn, also have environmental benefits, as fewer goods may have to be shipped from overseas).[47]

All of those features make 3D printing an attractive technology that could diversify production methods and change the way a number of industries currently operate.[48] However, 3D printing is unlikely to replace traditional manufacturing techniques. Rather, these technologies are expected to co-exist and complement each other.[49] For example, there is little doubt that traditional manufacturing is more economically sensible for large-volume production runs where economies of scale play a key role. In contrast, 3D printing excels at low-volume production where customisation – rather than a one-size-fits-all approach – is essential.

Finally, it is worth noting that although 3D printing shares many similarities with other digital manufacturing technologies, such as computer numerical control

[41] D Teece, 'Business Models, Business Strategy and Innovation' (2010) 43 *Long Range Planning* 172.

[42] S Huang and others, 'Additive Manufacturing and its Societal Impact: A Literature Review' (2013) 67 *International Journal of Advanced Manufacturing Technology* 1191, 1194.

[43] Lipson and Kurman (n 25) 59.

[44] C Cozmei and F Caloian, 'Additive Manufacturing Flickering at the Beginning of Existence' (2012) 3 *Procedia Economics and Finance Volume* 457, 459.

[45] G Stigler, 'The Economies of Scale' (1958) 1 *The Journal of Law and Economics* 54.

[46] S Mellor, L Hao and D Zhang, 'Additive Manufacturing: A Framework for Implementation' (2014) 149 *International Journal of Production Economics* 194, 195.

[47] See, eg, The White House, 'President Barack Obama's State of the Union Address – As Prepared for Delivery' (12 February 2013) at obamawhitehouse.archives.gov/the-press-office/2013/02/12/president-barack-obamas-state-union-address-prepared-delivery.

[48] It goes without saying that adopting a good business strategy is essential, as technological innovation is not always the most important factor for businesses. In fact, many companies with superior products have failed throughout history because of poor business models. See T Rayna and L Striukova, 'Adaptivity and Rapid Prototyping: How 3D Printing Is Changing Business Model Innovation' in B van den Berg, S van der Hof and E Kosta (eds), *3D Printing: Legal, Philosophical and Economic Dimensions* (The Hague, Asser Press, 2016) 168.

[49] I Petrick and T Simpson, '3D Printing Disrupts Manufacturing: How Economies of One Create New Rules of Competition' (2013) 56 *Research-Technology Management* 12.

(CNC) milling, 3D printing has attracted significantly more attention in mass media (and in the IP literature). This could be explained by the fact that CNC milling relies on *subtractive* manufacturing, meaning that it is typically louder, 'messier', and requires more human intervention compared to desktop 3D printing.[50] In other words, the latter technology is generally more accessible and user-friendly, which also makes it more attractive to individual end users.

3D Printing in the Real World

3D printing is already widely used in several industries. For example, automotive manufacturers use the technology to get new products on the market more quickly. The aerospace sector (including companies such as General Electric, Boeing, Lockheed Martin, and SpaceX) relies on 3D printing to integrate internal functionality and complex structures that would be exceptionally difficult to produce otherwise.[51] In the medical sector, the technology is used to make dental devices, hearing aids and prosthetics.[52] Other prominent examples include 3D printing's use in biotechnology where it has been used to print human tissue.[53] For example, French cosmetics firm L'Oréal has used 3D-printed human skin for product tests.[54] Amid critical shortages during the COVID pandemic, a number of 3D printing companies worked with governments around the world to provide essential equipment such as face shields. Popular Czech company Prusa Research is but one such example.[55] What is more, the technology was used to quickly produce lifesaving equipment, such as oxygen valves, reportedly saving several lives.[56]

[50] Bradshaw, Bowyer and Haufe (n 21) 7–8; A Varotsis, '3D Printing vs. CNC machining' at www.3dhubs.com/knowledge-base/3d-printing-vs-cnc-machining. CNC is typically louder and not all CNC machines are fully enclosed, so there is risk of material dispersion. What is more, in CNC milling, an expert operator is typically required to make several decisions in terms of tooling, whereas 3D printing requires less human intervention once the printable file is ready.

[51] R Campbell, D Bourell and I Gibson, 'Additive Manufacturing: Rapid Prototyping Comes of Age' (2012) 18 *Rapid Prototyping Journal* 255, 256; V Petrovic and others, 'Additive Layered Manufacturing: Sectors of Industrial Application Shown Through Case Studies' (2011) 49 *International Journal of Production Research* 1061; Engineering.com, 'SpaceX Launches 3D Printed Parts to Space' (5 August 2014) at www.engineering.com/spacex-launches-3d-printed-parts-to-space.

[52] R D'Aveni, 'The 3-D Printing Revolution' (2015) May Issue, *Harvard Business Review*; J Flaherty, '3-D Printed Prosthetics That Look Fit for a Sci-Fi Warrior' (*Wired*, 7 January 2015) at www.wired.com/2015/01/3-d-printed-prosthetics-look-fit-sci-fi-warrior.

[53] D Freeman, 'Israeli Scientists Create World's First 3D-Printed Heart Using Human Cells' (*NBC*, 19 April 2019) nbcnews.com/mach/science/israeli-scientists-create-world-s-first-3d-printed-heart-using-ncna996031.

[54] S Murphy and A Atala, '3D Bioprinting of Tissues and Organs' (2014) 32 *Nature Biotechnology* 773, 773; *BBC News*, 'L'Oreal to start 3D-printing skin' (19 May 2015) at www.bbc.co.uk/news/technology-32795169.

[55] J Prusa, 'From Design to Mass 3D printing of Medical Shields in Three Days' (18 March 2020) at www.blog.prusaprinters.org/from-design-to-mass-3d-printing-of-medical-shields-in-three-days.

[56] F Brown, 'Firm 'refuses to give blueprint' for coronavirus equipment that could save lives' (*Metro News*, 16 March 2020) (reporting that an 'Italian hospital that ran out of life-saving equipment … was saved by a 'hero' engineer who used cutting-edge technology to design oxygen valves within a matter of hours') at

While these use cases are clearly impressive and demonstrate the immense potential of the technology, it is important to emphasise that many of them are high-cost *industrial* applications. As desktop 3D printers are relatively compact, size restrictions inherently limit the range of products that can be produced at home. What is more, their output quality is typically inferior to expensive industrial 3D printers.

Yet, the range of 'desktop' applications continues to expand and is becoming increasingly versatile. Files commonly shared online range from sculptures, artworks and items from popular culture, such as Stormtrooper helmets and Marvel action figures, to phone accessories, coffee grinder parts, TV wall mounts, cutlery holders, handles, and repair parts for household appliances.[57] Popular file-sharing platforms such as Thingiverse have therefore been described as 'the closest thing to teleportation', given the ease and speed with which digital models can be shared and turned into tangibles across the globe.[58]

The Dark Side of 3D Printing

There is also a dark side to 3D printing. The technology has already been used to create various dangerous items, such as guns, at home. For example, in 2014, a person who 3D printed a gun was sentenced to two years in jail in Japan.[59] Similar recent cases abound in the UK and US.[60] For instance, Luigi Mangione, the perpetrator charged with killing United Healthcare CEO Brian Thompson in December 2024, is suspected of having used a firearm that was at least partially 3D printed.[61]

One of the key concerns here is regulatory control and detecting the production of such items in the first place. For example, when Defense Distributed (an organisation that develops digital schematics of printable firearms) posted its original 3D printable gun design for the first time online, it was downloaded over 100,000 times in a matter of just two days before the file was taken down by law enforcement.[62]

www.metro.co.uk/2020/03/16/firm-refuses-give-blueprint-coronavirus-equipment-save-lives-12403815.

[57] See www.thingiverse.com; see also Mendis, Secchi and Reeves (n 4).

[58] J Peels, 'Shapeways interviews Bre Pettis of MakerBot Industries' (January 2010) at www.shapeways.com/blog/shapeways-interviews-bre-pettis-of-makerbot-industries.

[59] J Vincent, 'Japanese man jailed for two years for creating 3D printed guns' (*The Independent*, 21 October 2014) at www.independent.co.uk/life-style/gadgets-and-tech/japanese-man-jailed-for-two-years-for-creating-3d-printed-guns-9807765.html.

[60] *BBC News*, 'Man Who Used 3D Printer to Build Gun Jailed' (25 November 2024) at www.bbc.com/news/articles/crmz9dn941eo; see also C Lancaster, 'Man Jailed for 3D-Printed Gun and Terror Offences' (*BBC News*, 14 October 2024) at www.bbc.com/news/articles/c20myxlrrn1o.

[61] E Helmore, 'Suspect in UnitedHealthcare CEO shooting charged with murder by New York prosecutors' (*The Guardian*, 10 December 2024) at www.theguardian.com/us-news/2024/dec/09/brian-thompson-shooting-suspect-mayor.

[62] A Greenberg, '3D-Printed Gun's Blueprints Downloaded 100,000 Times In Two Days (With Some Help From Kim Dotcom)' (*Forbes*, 8 May 2013) at www.forbes.com/sites/andygreenberg/2013/05/08/3d-printed-guns-blueprints-downloaded-100000-times-in-two-days-with-some-help-from-kim-dotcom.

It goes without saying that copies of the file are likely available in various other darker parts of the internet.

Indeed, given the power of digital technology, once a certain file is uploaded online, attempts to prevent and effectively control its further dissemination may be simply futile. This applies not only to dangerous or defective goods, but also to various objects that may be protected by intellectual property rights. In this specific regard, 3D printable files are virtually indistinguishable from any other digitised content (including music, films and books) that continues to be pirated and shared online on a daily basis.

Socio-economic Impact – Or Why 3D Printing Matters

The wider socio-economic impact of 3D printing has become the subject of much academic discourse. Early scholarly views on the technology's potential to bring about major societal changes have generally ranged 'from cautiously optimistic to enthusiastic'.[63] Other commentators have been considerably more sceptical.[64]

This transformative potential has also not gone unnoticed by government officials and world leaders. As stated by former US President Barack Obama in a high-profile State of the Union speech:

> A once-shuttered warehouse is now a state-of-the art lab where new workers are mastering the 3D printing that has the potential to revolutionize the way we make almost everything.[65]

The European Commission has similarly identified 3D printing as one of the key technologies that 'will revolutionise how we produce, work, move and consume'.[66]

[63] S Bechtold, '3D Printing, Intellectual Property and Innovation Policy (2016) 47 *International Review of Intellectual Property and Competition Law* 517, 522; see also Anderson (n 21); G Dumitrescu and I Tanase, '3D Printing – A New Industrial Revolution' (2016) 8 *Knowledge Horizons – Economics* 32; J Koten, 'A Revolution in the Making' (*The Wall Street Journal*, 10 June 2013) at www.wsj.com/articles/SB10001424127887324063304578522812684722382; *The Economist*, 'The Third Industrial Revolution' (21 April 2012) at www.economist.com/node/21552901.

[64] A Daly, 'Don't Believe the Hype? Recent 3D Printing Developments for Law and Society' in D Mendis, M Lemley and M Rimmer (eds), *3D Printing and Beyond* (Cheltenham, Edward Elgar, 2019) 347 (arguing that although 3D printing is 'technically speaking' revolutionary, it appears that it is not fulfilling its potential in practice due to limited consumer uptake).

[65] The White House (n 47).

[66] Commission, 'Reflection Paper on Harnessing Globalisation' (Communication) COM (2017) 240 final. Australian government officials have similarly argued that 3D printing could introduce significant productivity gains to the economy and 'turn Australia's manufacturing industry on its head'; see C Pyne, '3D Printing Brings New Dimension to Australian Manufacturing' (19 November 2015) at www.pyneonline.com.au/media-centre/media-releases/3d-printing-brings-new-dimension-to-australian-manufacturing.

However, what exactly are these fundamental changes that 3D printing could potentially introduce? First, 3D printing has the potential to further decentralise manufacturing and introduce major changes to existing labour practices. Traditionally, manufacturing power has been in the hands of a select few. That is, those with substantial resources and access to factories and machinery.[67] 3D printing could disrupt this dynamic as it enables individual end users to have an active – as opposed to merely passive – role in manufacturing and product design, therefore blurring the well-established producer-consumer dichotomy.[68] The technology brings the decentralised power of the internet – a lateral entity that does not require central control – to the physical world.[69] What is more, by lowering market entry barriers, 3D printing may affect existing ownership structures, leading to a proliferation of smaller enterprises and startups as well as a transition from top-down to bottom-up innovation.[70] Matt Ratto and Robert Ree even argue that the existing conceptions of labour may dramatically change as a result of 3D printing and that skills such as computer-aided design modelling may become increasingly valuable in society.[71] Indeed, there is already a trend in educational institutions towards incorporating such skills into the curriculum.[72] What is more, many engineering jobs now require CAD skills.[73]

The next key issue here is linked to the digitisation of tangibles. Early digital technologies, such as computers and the internet, transformed creative works such as music, books and film into purely informational content that can now be consumed in an electronic format, without the need to ever have a physical copy of that item.[74] While this process of 'dematerialisation' introduced dramatic changes to the way several industries operate today, many other businesses have not experienced the full force of this process.[75] This is precisely where 3D printing may introduce substantial changes. By allowing a remarkably wide range of physical products to exist entirely as strings of binary digits, it places more emphasis on the

[67] E Keymolen, 'The Focal Practice of 3D Printing' in B van den Berg, S van der Hof and E Kosta (eds), *3D Printing: Legal, Philosophical and Economic Dimensions* (The Hague, Asser Press, 2016) 100.

[68] Anderson (n 21).

[69] P Troxler and C van Woensel, 'How Will Society Adopt 3D Printing?' in B van den Berg, S van der Hof and E Kosta (eds), *3D Printing: Legal, Philosophical and Economic Dimensions* (The Hague, Asser Press, 2016) 200.

[70] Keymolen (n 67) 102.

[71] M Ratto and R Ree, 'Materializing Information: 3D Printing and Social Change' (2012) 17 *First Monday* 1 ('[Also] disrupted are the professional roles of designers, the relationships between producers and consumers, and the nature of the work itself').

[72] H Steenhuis and L Pretorius, 'The Additive Manufacturing Innovation: A Range of Implications' (2017) 28 *Journal of Manufacturing Technology Management* 131.

[73] ibid.

[74] However, see L Barron, 'Back on record – the reasons behind vinyl's unlikely comeback' (*The Conversation*, April 2015) at theconversation.com/back-on-record-the-reasons-behind-vinyls-unlikely-comeback-39964.

[75] See also Rayna and Striukova (n 12) 214.

digital side of production.[76] It is easier than ever to transform digital models into physical products (and, vice versa, where 3D scanning is used to make a printable copy of an existing object). Bits, as opposed to atoms, are becoming increasingly valuable, and the strict delineation between the physical and the digital world is becoming increasingly fragile.[77]

Finally, 3D printing facilitates *mass customisation*.[78] The growing availability of manufacturing tools such as 3D printing coincides with recent shifts in consumer behaviour where people increasingly look for 'individualized experiences and expect that products be tailored to their specific needs, wants, contexts and tastes'.[79] For example, Nike allows consumers to create their own custom designs online and then manufactures and ships these products to customers.[80] 3D printing goes one step further by allowing *anyone* with access to modelling software to design and produce goods which match their precise individual preferences, exactly as they see fit, and without the assistance of an intermediary.

Is 3D Printing Really 'Disruptive'?

In light of its potential to bring about major socio-economic change, media outlets have frequently labelled 3D printing as 'disruptive' and 'revolutionary'. For example, in a 2012 article about the technology, popular weekly magazine *The Economist* wrote that 'a third revolution is under way':

> Like all revolutions, this one will be disruptive … Most jobs will not be on the factory floor but in the offices nearby, which will be full of designers, engineers, IT specialists … The manufacturing jobs of the future will require more skills … The revolution will affect not only how things are made, but where.[81]

[76] Anderson (n 21), 41; T Ebrahim, '3D Printing: Digital Infringement & Digital Regulation' (2016) 14 *Northwestern Journal of Technology and Intellectual Property* 37, 37; J Grimmelmann, 'Indistinguishable from Magic: A Wizard's Guide to Copyright and 3D Printing' (2014) 71 *Washington and Lee Law Review* 683.

[77] Ratto and Ree (n 71) 1 ('No longer does the term "digital media" automatically imply content that is both produced and consumed exclusively in digital form … Digital information … is becoming increasingly porous with physical representation … Thus the notions, assumptions and understandings of what constitutes "digital media" … are thrown in to question'); L Osborn, 'Regulating Three-Dimensional Printing: The Converging Worlds of Bits and Atoms' (2014) 51 *San Diego Law Review* 553 ('3D printing … is invading society, bringing with it the ability to 'print' objects (atoms) from computer files (bits). Posting a computer-assisted design … file of an object … to the Internet essentially makes the physical object available to the world').

[78] See Rayna and Striukova (n 12) 218 (arguing that one of the key aspects of direct manufacturing is that it facilitates large-scale mass customisation); D Mendis, 'In Pursuit of Clarity: The Conundrum of CAD Software and Copyright – Seeking Direction Through Case Law' (2018) 40 *European Intellectual Property Review* 694.

[79] Ratto and Ree (n 77); see also L Lessig, *Remix: Making Art and Commerce Thrive in the Hybrid Economy* (New York, Penguin Press, 2008).

[80] See, eg, www.nike.com/nike-by-you.

[81] *The Economist*, 'The third industrial revolution' (21 April 2012) at www.economist.com/leaders/2012/04/21/the-third-industrial-revolution.

Legal scholars have expressed similar sentiments. For example, in the words of Matthew Rimmer, '3D printing is a disruptive technology, which promises to transform art and design, science and manufacturing, and the digital economy'.[82] However, can 3D printing actually be classified as disruptive or revolutionary in strict economic terms? What do these terms actually mean?

Socio-economic change is generally linked to technological innovation.[83] For example, the economic growth and workforce changes introduced by the First Industrial Revolution can be directly attributed to the inventions that took place at the time, such as the introduction of steam power.[84] Economists thus divide technological innovation into several categories, depending on the level of its impact: incremental, radical, disruptive and revolutionary.[85] *Incremental* innovation involves subtle improvements that enhance existing capabilities in a given sector, typically related to quality, performance and speed.[86] *Radical* innovations concern breakthrough technologies that introduce novel capabilities that change the face of a certain industry (for example, the jet engine).[87] *Disruptive* innovation refers to inventions that established companies do not initially view as a threat and therefore fail to adapt their business strategies to on time.[88] When the new technology becomes viable, market entrants move up market and replace the incumbents, thus 'disrupting' the existing market. For instance, Apple's iPhone is a classic example of a disruptive technology (though it was technically disruptive in the sense that it replaced laptops as the primary access point to the internet, as opposed to being disruptive of other smartphones).[89] Lastly, *industrial* revolutions bring about a whole new magnitude of change and typically concern fundamental economic and societal shifts in terms of the nature of the work being done, its location, and the structure of the

[82] M Rimmer, 'The Maker Movement: Copyright Law, Remix Culture and 3D Printing' (2017) 41 *The University of Western Australia Law Review* 51, 51; see also D Desai and G Magliocca, 'Patents, Meet Napster: 3D Printing and the Digitization of Things' (2014) 102 *Georgetown Law Journal* 1691, 1703, 1719; R Ballardini and M Norrgård, 'Digitising Patent Law: Challenges from 3D Printing Technologies' (2016) 38 *European Intellectual Property Review* 519, 521 ('Disruptive technologies by definition distort social constructs. As IP law is the bridge connecting innovations to markets it is usually challenged by the advent of new technologies … 3D printing is but one of such developments').

[83] E Malecki, *Technology and Economic Development: The Dynamics of Local, Regional and National Competitiveness* (Essex, Longman, 1997); D Mowery and N Rosenberg, *Technology and the Pursuit of Economic Growth* (Cambridge, CUP, 1995).

[84] W Bernstein, *The Birth of Plenty, How the Prosperity of the Modern World Was Created* (New York, McGraw-Hill, 2004). See also Petrick and Simpson (n 49) 12.

[85] Steenhuis and Pretorius (n 72) 125; see also D Marquis, 'The Anatomy of Successful Innovations' (1969) 1 *Innovation* 28.

[86] Steenhuis and Pretorius (n 72).

[87] ibid.

[88] J Bower and C Christensen, 'Disrupting Technologies: Catching the Wave' (January-February Issue, 1995) *Harvard Business Review* 43 at hbr.org/1995/01/disruptive-technologies-catching-the-wave.

[89] C Christensen, M Raynor and R McDonald, 'What Is Disruptive Innovation? (December Issues, 2015) *Harvard Business Review* ('The iPhone's subsequent growth is better explained by disruption – not of other smartphones but of the laptop as the primary access point to the internet') at hbr.org/2015/12/what-is-disruptive-innovation.

workforce.[90] Although there is no scholarly consensus in the academic literature, three industrial revolutions have generally been identified so far. These can be directly linked to the introduction of steam power, electrification, and, more recently, the advent of digital technologies.[91]

Where does 3D printing fit within this spectrum of innovation? In their comprehensive economic analysis of the technology, Leon Pretorius and Harm-Jam Steenhuis argue that 3D printing has already had an incremental effect in some areas where it has replaced or complemented traditional manufacturing technologies – though the improvements have been relatively minor.[92] There are also some indications that 3D printing has the potential to be 'disruptive', as industries relying on larger production volumes may become vulnerable, if (or once) the technology becomes more sophisticated.[93] Some of the changes introduced by 3D printing, the argument goes, 'appear to be of the industrial revolutionary type':

> [They] have the potential for fundamental shifts in society. Among these are trends from factories back toward more household manufacturing, related changes in educational systems in terms of what and how the educational process is approached, and AM also presents severe challenges to the current legal system which is therefore undergoing change.[94]

While it therefore appears that 3D printing has the potential to be 'disruptive' or 'revolutionary' in strict economic terms, as explored in subsequent chapters, this does not necessarily mean that it will be 'disruptive' in the same sense in which the term is often used in the legal literature.

Conclusion

While the core technology behind 3D printing has been quietly around for a long time and is already widely used in several industries – from aerospace to biotechnology and medicine – it is the newly emerged desktop 3D printing sector that has recently captured the attention of academics, policymakers, hardware enthusiasts, mass media and the general public. One of the key reasons for this is that desktop 3D printing has the *potential* to democratise manufacturing. It enables consumers to play an active role in design and manufacturing and to make various

[90] P Stearns, *The Industrial Revolution in World History* (Boulder, Westview Press 2013); Steenhuis and Pretorius (n 72) 127.

[91] P Kurtz, 'The Industrial-technological Revolution' (2007) 27 *Free Inquiry* 4; G von Tunzelmann, 'Innovation and Industrialisation: A Long-term Comparison' (1997) 56 *Technological Forecasting & Social Change* 1; A Russell, 'Telecommunications Standards in the Second and Third Industrial Revolutions' (2006) 5 *The Journal of the Communications Network* 100; G Dosi and L Galambos L (eds), *The Third Industrial Revolution in Global Business* (Cambridge, CUP, 2013).

[92] Steenhuis and Pretorius (n 72) 137.

[93] ibid.

[94] ibid.

creative decisions. While it remains to be seen whether this transformative potential will truly materialise (as explored in subsequent chapters, there are several technological limitations that would have to be addressed first), it is important to ensure that the legal framework is not only compatible with 3D printing, but that it is also conducive to innovation and growth and that there are no unnecessary legal restrictions in place.

This is what the rest of the book will focus on. As we will see in the following chapters, the IP framework in particular will play a critical role in determining how free users will be to utilise the full potential of the technology.

3

The Role of Intellectual Property

Introduction

This chapter provides a general overview of the IP framework, with the aim of introducing the reader – regardless of their background and whether they are a 3D printing enthusiast, student or legal practitioner – to some core IP principles. This is essential to fully appreciate the risks and challenges that 3D printing poses to IP theory and practice, which the rest of the book will focus on. First, the chapter begins by defining the term 'intellectual property'. Second, it provides a brief introduction to some of the major categories of IP law and explains how and why these rights originally came into being. Third, it outlines the key theoretical rationales underpinning the modern IP system and discusses some of the main critiques in this area.

What is Intellectual Property?

The use of the collective term 'intellectual property' is a relatively recent phenomenon.[1] What was traditionally a category *of* laws has now become a category *in* law and while there is no clear consensus on the precise boundaries of IP, most modern definitions include at least copyright, patents and trade marks (other categories include designs and trade secrets).[2] Given the remarkably diverse subject matter that it covers, IP has thus been described as 'a loose cluster of legal doctrines that regulate the uses of different sorts of ideas and insignia'.[3]

Some commentators even argue that placing all of these distinct rights under the broad umbrella term 'IP' is unfounded and artificial. As put by open-source activist Richard Stallman:

> The term 'intellectual property' operates as a catch-all to lump together disparate laws. Nonlawyers who hear the term … applied to these various laws tend to assume they are instances of a common principle, and that they function similarly. Nothing could

[1] See Bently and others, *Intellectual Property Law* (Oxford, OUP, 2022) 2.

[2] ibid 2.

[3] W Fisher, 'Theories of Intellectual Property' in Munzer S (eds), *New Essays in the Legal and Political Theory of Property* (Cambridge, CUP, 2001) 168.

be further from the case … These laws originated separately, evolved differently, cover different activities, have different rules, and raise different public policy issues.[4]

Yet, while IP is clearly not a homogenous body of law, most of these rights share some key distinctive features. The IP framework grants exclusive rights (in the form of intangible assets) over products of the human mind.[5] That is, it enables proprietors to *exclude* others from performing certain acts without permission.

Historical Background and a Brief Introduction to the Key IP Rights

The first known use of rights resembling modern IP protection is often attributed to the Greek colony of Sybaris where chefs were granted exclusive rights to make certain culinary delights.[6] Historians have also found various references to ownership interests associated with intellectual works (for instance, the ownership of a painting) in the Roman world.[7] In the fifteenth century AD, the Florentine Republic passed a statute that 'not only recognized the rights of authors and inventors to the products of their intellectual efforts [but also] built in an incentive mechanism that became a prominent feature of Anglo-American intellectual property protection'.[8] Despite these early developments, however, more sophisticated and mature forms of exclusive rights (and, indeed, the modern IP framework itself) came into being significantly later.

Let's look at copyright law first. Prior to the invention of Johannes Gutenberg's printing press, the reproduction of books was so expensive, difficult and time-consuming that no legal protection was even necessary. As Lawrence Lessig puts it, 'nature itself protected that interest'.[9] Once the technology became more

[4] R Stallman, 'Did You Say 'Intellectual Property'? It's a Seductive Mirage' (2006) 4 *Policy Futures in Education* 334, 334 ('Copyright law was designed to promote authorship and art … Patent law was intended to encourage publication of ideas, at the price of finite monopolies over these ideas … Trademark law was not intended to promote any business activity, but simply to enable buyers to know what they are buying; however, legislators under the influence of 'intellectual property' have turned it into a scheme that provides incentives for advertising (without asking the public if we want more advertising').

[5] S Ghosh, 'Decoding and Recoding Natural Monopoly, Deregulation, and Intellectual Property' [2008] *University of Illinois Law Review* 1125. Unlike other forms of state regulation, however, the government cannot generally control the price and the number of copies produced. This is determined by rightsholders and the market. See also S Besen and L Raskind, 'An Introduction to the Law and Economics of Intellectual Property Stanley' (1991) 5 *The Journal of Economic Perspectives* 3; R Posner, 'Intellectual Property: The Law and Economics Approach' (2005) 19 *The Journal of Economic Perspectives* 57; M Lemley, 'IP in a World Without Scarcity' (2015) 90 *New York University Law Review* 460.

[6] A Moore and K Himma, 'Intellectual Property' in E Zalta and U Nodelman (eds), *The Stanford Encyclopedia of Philosophy* (2022) at plato.stanford.edu/archives/fall2022.

[7] ibid.

[8] ibid.

[9] L Lessig, *Code: And Other Laws of Cyberspace, Version 2.0*, 2nd edn (New York, Basic Books, 2006) 172; see also P Torremans, *Intellectual Property Law* (OUP 2019) 8.

widespread, however, this necessitated the development of a more robust framework to address the issue – namely, copyright law. Indeed, the rationale behind the enactment of the Statute of Anne 1709 (widely regarded as the world's first modern copyright statute)[10] is quite clear:

> Whereas printers, booksellers, and other persons have lately frequently taken the liberty of printing, reprinting, and publishing books without the consent of the authors and proprietors ... to their very great detriment, and too often to the ruin of them and their families: for preventing therefore such practices for the future, and for the encouragement of learned men to compose and write useful books ...[11]

Under the Copyright, Designs and Patents Act 1988 – the key copyright statute in the UK today – copyright law protects a wide range of subject matter, from 'conventional' creative works, such as sculptures, music and novels, to more modern types of creations such as computer software. While protection arises automatically, a certain work will only be protected if it satisfies the relevant subsistence criteria. For example, authorial works, such as literature and music, must be 'original' and recorded in writing or otherwise to qualify for protection (we will contextually explore all of these requirements in chapter five). The term of protection for authorial works is limited to the life of the author plus 70 years after their death. Upon expiry, these works enter the 'public domain', meaning that anyone can then use them without permission (for example, this would apply to the works of William Shakespeare and Jane Austen). What is more, the protection conferred by copyright only extends to the *expression* of an idea, as opposed to the idea itself.

Second, although the history of 'monopolies' goes back a long way,[12] modern patent law is a more recent phenomenon. Patents have traditionally served as a mutually beneficial instrument between the inventor and the state, known as the 'patent bargain'. That is, while the patent owner gets a set of temporary exclusive rights over the invention, the technical information disclosed in their application can be utilised by competitors and the general public upon expiry (it could therefore be assumed that society benefits in the long term).[13]

[10] See Bently and others (n 1).

[11] L Patterson and C Joyce, 'Copyright in 1791: An Essay Concerning the Founders' View of Copyright Power Granted to Congress in Article 1, Section 8, Clause 8 of the US Constitution' (2003) 52 *Emory Law Journal* 910, 919; L Bently, U Suthersanen and P Torremans, *Global Copyright: Three Hundred Years since the Statute of Anne, from 1709 to Cyberspace, Proceedings of the ALAI Congress London 2009* (Cheltenham, Edward Elgar, 2009); S Karapapa and L McDonagh, *Intellectual Property Law* (Oxford, OUP, 2019) 7.

[12] The statutory roots of UK patent law (or England, as it was then) can be traced back to the Statute of Monopolies 1624, which offered fourteen-year monopolies to inventors.

[13] See, for instance, *Asahi Kasei Kogyo* [1991] RPC 485, 523 (HL), per Lord Oliver (arguing that the overarching purpose of patent law is to encourage improvements and innovation and that in return for disclosing an invention to the public, the inventor receives limited monopoly control over the invention); see also E Mansfield, 'Patents and Innovation: An Empirical Study' (1986) 32 *Management Science* 173; P Dinev, 'Machine Inventorship' (2025) 141 *Law Quarterly Review* 43, 47.

Under the Patents Act 1977 – the key statute in the UK today – the current legislative framework protects products and processes that are novel, involve an inventive step (that is, the invention must not be obvious to the average expert in the field) and are capable of industrial application (meaning that they can be used in any industry).

Patents can be of great commercial value.[14] For example, patentable subject matter includes inventions essential to products such as drugs and medicines (including products such as the weight loss drug semaglutide, marketed under the brand name Ozempic) and various engineering breakthroughs (such as Bluetooth technology).

Third, and finally, let's look at trade mark law. Traders have attached marks to their goods to indicate ownership since early times.[15] Following the Industrial Revolution, individuals increasingly began using marks to indicate the *origin* of various products. As these marks also served as an indicator of quality, they gradually became even more influential in guiding purchasing decisions.[16] Over the years, marks became an asset in their own right, as the mark itself now carried some important emotional meaning. It evolved from a mere 'signal' (that merely performs source-indicating functions) to a 'symbol' (that evokes meanings).[17] While the original rationale behind trade mark law was to primarily help customers identify the source of the goods (and, therefore, to reduce their search costs), modern trade marks thus increasingly act as a 'silent sales person' that is capable of selling products irrespective of origin considerations.[18]

Under the Trade Marks Act 1994 – the key statute in UK law today – modern trade mark law protects signs that enable consumers to distinguish between the goods or services of one undertaking from those of another. Whether it is Apple's distinctive logo or the famous shape of the Coca-Cola bottle, it is clear that these rights play a fundamental role in the modern economy.

[14] It is also worth noting that although the UK is an economy primarily based on services, and grants fewer patents per capita compared to other jurisdictions that are more reliant on manufacturing, patent activity in the UK remains high. See World Intellectual Property Organization, 'World Intellectual Property Indicators 2023' (2023) at www.wipo.int/edocs/pubdocs/en/wipo-pub-941-2023-en-world-intellectual-property-indicators-2023.pdf.

[15] Bently and others (n 1) 853.

[16] B Pattishall, 'Trade Marks and the Monopoly Phobia' (1952) 42 *TM Rep* 588, 590–1; S Diamond, 'The Historical Development of Trademarks' (1975) 65 *TM Rep* 265, 281, as cited in Bently and others (n 1) 854.

[17] T Drescher, 'The Transformation and Evolution of Trademarks: From Signals to Symbols to Myth' (1992) 82 *TM Rep* 301. Modern trade marks may even have a 'mythical' status which helps consumers to build their identity (for example, creating an 'image' as a Porsche driver or Marlboro smoker). See also L McDonagh, 'From Brand Performance to Consumer Performativity: Assessing European Trade Mark Law after the Rise of Anthropological Marketing' (2015) 42 *Journal of Law and Society* 611, 632–3; D Gangjee, 'Property in Brands: The Commodification of Conversation' in Howe H and Griffiths J (eds), *Property Concepts in Intellectual Property Law* (Cambridge, CUP, 2013).

[18] Bently and others (n 1) 856; S Dogan and M Lemley, 'Trademarks and Consumer Search Costs on the Internet' (2004) 41 *Houston Law Review* 777, 799; B Beebe, 'Semiotic Analysis of Trademark Law' (2004) 51 *UCLA Law Review* 621, 623.

Justifying Exclusivity

Why do we need IP rights? What is the normative basis for their existence? There are distinct theoretical rationales for the different categories of IP, and these vary between jurisdictions. However, the justifications typically given for 'IP' as a whole, if loosely considered as a general category of law, tend to fall into the following main categories.[19]

First, scholars have drawn on moral and ethical justifications. According to personality-based rationales, based on the works of philosophers such as Georg Hegel and Immanuel Kant, and commonly found in continental European traditions, IP is regarded as an extension of individual personality.[20] Individuals, the argument goes, have moral claims to their talents, feelings and experiences. Therefore, control over physical and intellectual objects is necessary to achieve self-actualisation (that is, fulfilment of our talents and potential):

> [B]y expanding our selves outward beyond our own minds and mixing these selves with tangible and intangible items, we both define ourselves and obtain control over our goals … [B]y controlling and manipulating objects … our will takes form in the world and we obtain a measure of freedom … [I]n some cases our personality becomes fused with an object …[21]

Second, there is John Locke's 'labour' or 'natural rights' theory (also commonly referred to as 'Lockean' justifications in the literature):

> When an individual labors on an unowned object, her labor becomes infused in the object and for the most part, the labor and the object cannot be separated. It follows that once a person's labor is joined with an unowned object … rights to control are generated. The idea is that there is an expansion of rights: we each own our labor and when that labor is mixed with objects in the commons, our rights are expanded to include these goods.[22]

In other words, as thinking and producing are voluntary acts, those who engage in these activities should have rights over the things they have created. When our labour is mixed with objects or resources belonging to the whole community, we should be entitled to rights in the goods in question.[23]

[19] Bently and others (n 1) 6; see also P Menell, 'Intellectual Property: General Theories' (1999) at www.sfu.ca/~allen/intellectual.pdf.

[20] Moore and Himma (n 6); see also J Hughes, 'The Philosophy of Intellectual Property' (1998) 77 *Georgetown Law Journal* 287.

[21] Moore and Himma (n 6) (further explaining that, according to this rationale, given that our personality becomes intertwined with the relevant object, 'thus moral claims to control feelings, character traits, and experiences may be expanded to intangible work').

[22] ibid; see also Hughes (n 20); W Gordon, 'A Property Right in Self-Expression: Equality and Individualism in the Natural Law of Intellectual Property' (1993) 102 *Yale Law Journal* 1533; A Yen, 'Restoring the Natural Law: Copyright as Labour and Possession' (1990) 51 *Ohio State Law Journal* 517.

[23] Moore and Himma (n 6).

Third, modern Anglo-American IP systems are primarily modelled as incentive-based and utilitarian.[24] Utilitarianism is concerned with maximising net social welfare, which entails striking:

> an optimal balance between, on one hand, the power of exclusive rights to stimulate the creation of inventions and works of art and, on the other, the partially offsetting tendency of such rights to curtail widespread public enjoyment of those creations.[25]

It is important to emphasise that once information (or an intellectual work) is disclosed, it becomes vulnerable to freeriding given that it is cheaper to be an imitator than a creator.[26] In the absence of exclusive rights, therefore, there is a possibility that individuals (aware of the risk that others may copy their work without incurring the costs they had to incur) may simply lack the incentive to produce socially valuable intellectual works.[27] Through the lens of utilitarianism, IP therefore enables creators to recoup the sunk costs spent in creating and inventing.[28] While granting exclusive rights does not necessarily mean that there will be an optimal amount of works being produced, proponents of this theory argue that 'failure is inevitable if those who incur no investment costs can seize and reproduce the intellectual effort of others'.[29] This justification has played a key part in modern US and UK intellectual property law – for example, an expression of this rationale can even be found in the Constitution of the US which explicitly states that Congress should have the power 'to promote the progress of science and useful arts, by securing for limited times to authors and inventors the exclusive right to their respective writings and discoveries'.[30]

[24] F Machlup, *Production and Distribution of Knowledge in the United States* (New Jersey, Princeton University, 1962); C Oppenheim, 'An Approach to Evaluation of the American Patent System' (1951) 33 *Journal of the Patent and Trademark Office Society* 555; E Hettinger, 'Justifying Intellectual Property' (1989) 18 *Philosophy and Public Affairs* 31, as cited in Moore and Himma (n 6).

[25] Fisher (n 3) 169; see also F Scherer and D Ross, *Industrial Market Structure and Economic Performance* (Boston, Houghton Mifflin, 1990); Hettinger (n 24); see also Moore and Himma (n 6) (further noting that according to this rationale, relying on systems of protection such as copyright, patents and trade marks results not only in an optimal amount of intellectual works being created, but also in a corresponding optimal amount of social utility).

[26] P Menell and others, *Intellectual Property in the New Technological Age 2023 Vol. I: Perspectives, Trade Secrets and Patents* (Berkeley, Clause 8 Publishing, 2023).

[27] Lemley (n 5) 460, 482.

[28] W Landes and R Posner, *The Economic Structure of Intellectual Property Law* (Cambridge, MA, Harvard University Press, 2003), as cited in Lemley (n 5).

[29] Moore and Himma (n 6); see also Torremans (n 11) 17 (noting that while copyright has traditionally developed on a different basis from the more industrially-focused patents and trade marks, 'copyright has increasingly been used to protect the commercial exploitation of the work and new, more technologically oriented, types of work have been protected'); J Reichman, 'Charting the Collapse of the Patent-Copyright Dichotomy: Premises for a Restructured International Intellectual Property System' (1995) 13 *Cardozo Arts and Entertainment Law Journal* 475; R Watt, *Copyright and Economic Theory: Friends or Foes?* (Cheltenham, Edward Elgar, 2000), as cited in Torremans (n 11) 17.

[30] US Constitution, Art I, § 8, cl 8, available at www.archives.gov/founding-docs/constitution-transcript. See also *E Mishan & Sons v Hozelock* [2020] EWCA Civ 871, [76], per Lord Justice Arnold in the Court of Appeal of England and Wales (arguing that patent law aims to encourage technical innovation, as well as investment in such innovation, by conferring time-limited monopoly control to inventors).

Having discussed these key rationales, what practical value, if any, does IP 'theory' really have? Should it play any role in the debate on the regulation of 3D printing? Advocates of IP theories often claim to provide answers to a range of questions. Indeed, some even view them as guides that should be used to shape or modify legal principles.[31] Commentators have argued that, for example, utilitarianism has been used (and should be used) to create specific doctrines in the field.[32] Yet, all theoretical rationales suffer from ambiguities, internal inconsistencies and a lack of empirical data to support key premises, which inevitably limits their prescriptive power.[33] Moreover, the lawmaking process is inherently complex and it is often driven by a variety of pragmatic and political considerations. In other words, some argue that theory rarely dictates positive law.[34]

Despite this, William Fisher argues that IP theory nevertheless retains important practical value as it can not only help us identify attractive solutions to particular problems, but it also catalyses important conversations between scholars, lawmakers, and the general public, which could in turn enhance accountability.[35] What is more, others argue that reliance on theory can help to enhance the legitimacy of the legal framework. As put by Adam Moore, '[to] be justified – to warrant coercion on a worldwide scale – systems of intellectual property should be grounded in theory'.[36]

Critiques of Intellectual Property

While theorists have offered several justifications in support of IP law, not everyone finds these arguments convincing. In fact, not everyone even agrees that we need IP rights in the first place. For instance, commentators have argued that since intellectual works are non-rivalrous and multiple individuals can consume a certain work without depleting the resource, maximum access should be granted.[37] Indeed, while consuming a scarce resource, such as an apple, would naturally prevent others from doing the same, information can be used infinitely

[31] Fisher (n 3) (arguing that some commentators view these arguments as guides that lawmakers can use to modify or extend doctrines in response to changing circumstances).

[32] ibid 169 ('This utilitarian rationale, they argue, should be – and, for the most part, has been – used to shape specific doctrines within the field'), referring to Landes and Posner's work; see W Landes and R Posner, 'An Economic Analysis of Copyright Law' (1989) 18 *Journal of Legal Studies* 325.

[33] Fisher (n 3).

[34] See G Austin, 'Copyright's Modest Ontology: Theory and Pragmatism in *Eldred v. Ashcroft*' (2003) 16 *The Canadian Journal of Law & Jurisprudence* 163, 163 ('[T]he realities of intellectual property lawmaking are such that there are few instances where theory dictates … positive law').

[35] Fisher (n 3).

[36] A Moore, 'Intellectual Property: Theory, Privilege, and Pragmatism' (2003) 16 *Canadian Journal of Law & Jurisprudence* 191, 191.

[37] Moore and Himma (n 6).

without loss. Others have emphasised the undesirable restrictions that IP imposes on free speech:

> It restricts methods of acquiring ideas (as do trade secrets), it restricts the use of ideas (as do patents), and it restricts the expression of ideas (as do copyrights) – restrictions undesirable for a number of reasons.[38]

Yet another prominent critique derives from the argument that information is a social product and individuals typically create new things by building upon existing works made by others. That is, they utilise the shared knowledge of society (as famously put by Bernard of Chartres and Isaac Newton, by 'standing on the shoulders of giants').[39] On this basis, some commentators argue that granting exclusive rights to the last person to 'place a brick in a public works dam' is unprincipled, unnecessary and unjust.[40]

Perhaps the most significant critique of IP law comes from empirical evidence. While such data used to be scarce, there is now a wealth of studies on the efficiency of the IP system from a wide range of fields, including economics, business and psychology.[41] The problem is that much of this evidence has not been particularly favourable to the IP framework. As put by Mark Lemley, money and exclusive IP rights are not necessarily the prime drivers behind creativity, and a great number of people are perfectly happy to share their work for free, now that the internet has given them the means to do so.[42] What is more, the efficiency of the patent system seems to depend greatly on the specific industry concerned, and while patents may have a positive 'net social welfare' effect in some areas, this would not necessarily be the case in other fields.[43]

In light of some of these concerns, critics of the IP system, such as Michele Boldrin and David Levine, have even argued that certain areas (such as patent law) should be abolished altogether:

> Our preferred policy solution is to abolish patents entirely and to find other legislative instruments, less open to lobbying and rent seeking, to foster innovation when there is clear evidence that laissez-faire undersupplies it.[44]

[38] Hettinger (n 24) 35.

[39] The phrase is commonly attributed to Bernard of Chartres, later popularised by Isaac Newton. See Historical Society of Pennsylvania, 'Isaac Newton letter to Robert Hooke, 1675', available at discover.hsp.org/Record/dc-9792/Description ('In this letter, Newton also writes his famed remark "if I have seen further, it is by standing on the shoulders of giants"').

[40] Moore and Himma (n 6), citing I Shapiro, 'Resources, Capacities, and Ownership: The Workmanship Ideal and Distributive Justice' (1991) 19 *Political Theory* 47; J Boyle, *Shamans, Software, and Spleens: Law and the Construction of the Information Society* (Cambridge, MA, Harvard University Press 1997); A Simmons, *The Lockean Theory of Rights* (New Jersey, Princeton University Press, 1992).

[41] M Lemley, 'Faith-Based Intellectual Property' (2015) 62 *UCLA Law Review* 1333–4.

[42] ibid, 1334. See also K Darling and A Perzanowski, *Creativity without Law: Challenging the Assumptions of Intellectual Property* (New York, NYU Press, 2017) (arguing that incentives for creativity often exist in the absence of formal legal protection and that some 'communities rely on evolving social norms and market responses – sensitive to their particular cultural, competitive, and technological circumstances – to ensure creative incentives').

[43] Lemley (n 41) 1333–4.

[44] M Boldrin and D Levine, 'The Case Against Patents' (2013) 27 *Journal of Economic Perspectives* 3.

Several 'alternatives' to IP have been proposed in the literature, including governmental support of intellectual labour (for example, funded research projects where the results automatically become public property)[45] or a different reward framework that does not come with exclusive rights.[46]

Conclusion

This chapter aimed to provide a brief introduction to some essential principles of intellectual property law. As explored above, the range of subject matter protected by this category of law is remarkably wide – from sculptures and artworks to technological inventions and brand logos. While these rights have different features and function differently, they do have some common essential features – most notably, they give proprietors the right to *exclude* others. When it comes to the justifications provided in support of IP law, commentators have offered various normative arguments – from more philosophical theories (focused on individuals' spiritual interests) to more economically-oriented and incentive-based utilitarian rationales (that are primarily concerned with maximising net social welfare). Moreover, while there are several critiques of the IP framework (and, indeed, not everyone agrees that these rights are even necessary), IP law continues to play a fundamental role in modern society.

Having outlined these basic principles, we will now explore the fascinating relationship between IP law and 3D printing in the upcoming chapters.

[45] S Calandrillo, 'An Economic Analysis of Intellectual Property Rights: Justifications and Problems of Exclusive Rights, Incentives to Generate Information, and the Alternative of a Government-Run Reward System' (1998) 9 *Fordham Intellectual Property, Media, & Entertainment Law Journal* 301.

[46] S Shavell and T van Ypersele, 'Rewards versus Intellectual Property Rights' (2001) 44 *Journal of Law and Economics* 525, as cited in Moore and Himma (n 6).

4

An Unfamiliar Challenge to IP Theory and Practice

Introduction

As a natural extension of early digital technologies, 3D printing has the *potential* to replicate and amplify many of the legal challenges brought about by digitisation in the recent past. The IP framework in particular, as 'the bridge connecting innovations to markets', has been identified as a particularly vulnerable area in this regard.[1] However, before we explore the application of specific legal provisions, case law and doctrines in the context of 3D printing (which the next three chapters will focus on), it is important to consider some of the challenges that the technology poses to IP theory and practice at a more general and global level. That is, issues that cannot be confined to a specific jurisdiction and are likely to affect most systems of IP globally.

First, this chapter examines the issue of piracy in the context of 3D printing. While the early days of digital media were primarily concerned with copyright and intangibles, the technology has the potential to change this dynamic as it enables individual users to reproduce various tangible products on a decentralised basis. It could, therefore, bring the full force of digitisation to other industries and areas of IP law that have not yet fully experienced this process. Second, it discusses the closely related issue of IP enforcement, drawing parallels to the so-called Napster era, and explores the implications of potential approaches to tackling piracy online. Third, and finally, drawing on Mark Lemley's theory of 'post-scarcity IP', the chapter considers some of the less immediate and more 'theoretical' challenges that the technology may pose to core IP tenets and rationales in the long term.[2]

[1] R Ballardini and M Norrgård, 'Digitising Patent Law: Challenges from 3D Printing Technologies' (2016) 38 *European Intellectual Property Review* 519, 521.

[2] M Lemley, 'IP in a World Without Scarcity' (2015) 90 *New York University Law Review* 460.

A New Kind of Piracy

In the early days of digital media and mass internet access, users most commonly pirated creative works such as music, books and films (content that is now predominantly consumed in digital form). Naturally, copyright took centre stage. However, 3D printing has the potential to change this as it enables individual users to reproduce a remarkably wide range of physical goods on a decentralised basis.[3] As explored in previous chapters, files commonly shared online include sculptures, artworks, action figures, phone accessories, coffee grinder parts, TV wall mounts, and various items bearing the logos of well-known brands.[4] Given the creative freedom that the technology facilitates, there is certainly a risk that it may allow users to interfere with virtually all major categories of IP rights, including copyright, patents and trade marks. Indeed, the entire IP framework may be exposed to the digitisation and piracy issues that were previously experienced predominantly in the field of copyright.[5]

Consider the 'patent bargain' (the rationale that while the inventor gets a set of exclusive rights for disclosing the invention, the product or process can be utilised by the general public and competitors upon expiry). Patentees have traditionally relied on the assumption that the cost to infringe a patent, even when information is disclosed, is generally too high.[6] Indeed, even if a home DIY project happened to reproduce an invention, this would be difficult to replicate on a sufficiently large-scale basis. However, 3D printing, at least in theory, allows anyone with access to a printer and a digital design file containing the necessary information to replicate the patented product as many times as they wish. The effect of this could be cumulatively significant. As stated by Geertrui Van Overwalle and Reinout Leys:

> The upsurge of 3D printing … does challenge the foundational premise of centralized, singular infringement in patent law, allowing as it does decentralized, frequent and low-cost infringement and leads to interesting comparisons with (digital rights problems) in copyright.[7]

[3] B van Wiele, 'Decentralised, Democratised and Disruptive: How 3D Printing Challenges the Consumer Protection Rationale of Trade Marks' (2019) 41(5) *European Intellectual Property Review* 313, 314.

[4] See www.thingiverse.com.

[5] D Desai and G Magliocca, 'Patents, Meet Napster: 3D Printing and the Digitization of Things (2014) 102 *Georgetown Law Journal* 1691, 1697.

[6] D Doherty, 'Downloading Infringement: Patent Law as a Roadblock to the 3D Printing Revolution' (2012) 26 *Harvard Journal of Law & Technology* 353, 354 (arguing that, historically, even if hobbyists happened to infringe a patent, this was difficult to replicate on a large-scale basis and, therefore, unlikely to be a major concern for proprietors); see also D Brean, 'Patenting Physibles: A Fresh Perspective for Claiming 3D-Printable Products' (2015) *55 Santa Clara Law Review* 837. It should be noted that in jurisdictions such as the United Kingdom, there is a private and non-commercial use exemption to patent infringement (see s 60(5)(a), Patents Act 1977). We will explore this issue in more detail in subsequent chapters.

[7] G van Overwalle and R Leys, '3D Printing and Patent Law: A Disruptive Technology Disrupting Patent Law?' (2017) 48 *International Review of Intellectual Property and Competition Law* 504, 530.

Although desktop 3D printing is clearly not yet as sophisticated as its industrial counterparts (and, therefore, reproductions of high-value patents are likely to be rare), there are several 'simple' patentable items that are certainly within its reach. For instance, users commonly share models of Lego bricks (formerly patented) through online platforms.[8]

Other commentators have identified trade mark law as a particularly problematic area in the context of 3D printing. For example, Iona Silverman argues that home 3D printing 'may decrease demand for genuine goods and could devalue brands'.[9] Similarly, Bram van Wiele contends that '3D printing … expands the range of products that can be counterfeited and eliminates the means for effective enforcement'.[10]

Concerns about 3D printing-induced piracy are not merely theoretical. There have already been a number of early legal skirmishes between proprietors and users. For example, in 2015, Katy Perry performed at the Super Bowl's halftime show, upstaged by a dancer wearing a shark costume.[11] When a user made a printable file based on the costume and uploaded it online, Perry's lawyers sent a letter to the online service hosting the model, arguing that it violated copyright law (a claim widely criticised by commentators as lacking substance).[12] In 2019, Lego initiated takedown orders targeting a number of repositories hosting 3D printable files that allegedly infringed their rights, 'including but not limited to the famous LEGO word mark, the famous red-square LEGO logo and the Minifigure figurine'.[13] In one of the last publicly available transparency reports published by

[8] See US Patent US3005282A. See also www.thingiverse.com/thing:3461554.

[9] I Silverman, 'Optimising Protection: IP Rights in 3D Printing' (2016) 38 *European Intellectual Property Review* 5, 6.

[10] van Wiele (n 3) 319; see also A Scardamaglia 'Flashpoints in 3D Printing and Trade Mark Law' (2015) 23 *Journal of Law, Information and Science* 50 (arguing that 3D printing could democratise objects and thus lead to a further increase in counterfeit items, while also noting that this would depend on future improvements in output quality); V Elam, 'The Transfer of Computer-Aided Design Files in the Era of 3D Printing: Trademark Infringement Under the Current European Framework' in *Building a European Digital Space: 12th International Conference on Internet, Law & Politics* (Barcelona, 7–8 July 2016) at cadmus.eui.eu/handle/1814/60440; J Ammar and R Craufurd-Smith, 'When is a Trade Mark use not a Trade Mark Use? A 3D Perspective' (2015) 1 *International Journal of Law and Interdisciplinary Legal Studies* (2015) 4, 4 (arguing that the technology is 'likely to disturb the long-standing balance between the costs and frequency of infringement' in trade mark law).

[11] T Dagne, 'The Left Shark, Thrones, Sculptures and Unprintable Triangle: 3D Printing and its Intersections with IP' (2015) 25 *Albany Law Journal of Science & Technology* 573, 580.

[12] M Rimmer, 'The Maker Movement: Copyright Law, Remix Culture and 3D Printing' (2017) 41 *The University of Western Australia Law Review* 51, 58.

[13] M Weinberg, 'Lego's IP Grab Bag' (2019) at michaelweinberg.org/blog/2019/10/10/lego-ip-grab-bag; see also M Petch, 'LEGO 3D Printing Takedowns: A Lawyer Responds and LEGO Replies' (9 October 2019) at www.3dprintingindustry.com/news/lego-3d-printing-takedowns-a-lawyer-responds-and-lego-replies-163104 ('LEGO says that issuing takedown notices and challenges is necessary to ensure that the "LEGO wordmark or IP protected elements" does not erode over time'). There have also been IP disputes involving 3D scanning. For example, the technology was recently used to make a copy of a sixteenth-century Michelangelo's Moses replica statue held at Augustana College in South Dakota, which led to allegations of copyright infringement; see M Weinberg, 'Cultural Institutions Behaving Badly: Stupid Reactions to 3D Scanning' (*Public Knowledge*, 22 January 2015) at www.publicknowledge.org/cultural-institutions-behaving-badly-stupid-reactions-to-3d-scanning.

Shapeways – one of the leading 3D printing marketplaces – the company reported that they received a total of 638 infringement claims in 2018 (down from 1,622 in the previous year).[14] Interestingly, while comments made by users who were targeted by such infringement claims indicate that factors such as the cost of litigation often acted as a deterrent to submitting a counternotice (even where they believed that they had not actually committed infringement), those who objected to the claims tended to be successful.[15]

These disputes are indicative of the challenges lying ahead. They have the potential to escalate and turn into larger legal battles, especially if the technology gains more mainstream adoption and 3D-printed goods are of sufficiently high quality so as to act as a substitute for the 'original' product (and, therefore, rightsholders and manufacturers start incurring more significant economic losses as a result). As put by Michael Weinberg, '[t]hese skirmishes will attempt to wed existing intellectual property protections to new realities, and in doing so will slowly change the state of the law … In aggregate, these changes will decide how free we will be to use disruptive new technologies like 3D printing'.[16]

Enforcement Challenges

Enforcement action is likely to be especially challenging in the context of desktop 3D printing, given that manufacturing takes place in individuals' private homes.[17] As put by John Hornick:

> The [other] reason is what I call 3D printing "away from control," which means the ability to make almost anything without anyone knowing about it or being able to control it.[18]

While manufacturing industries have always had issues with enforcement, 3D printing presents an unfamiliar challenge as it enables individual users to directly make the infringing articles themselves, without the assistance of a centralised

[14] Shapeways, '2018 Transparency Report' (2018) at www.shapeways.com/legal/transparency/2018 ('This year we received 638 claims, down significantly from the previous year [when 1,622 claims were received]. Shapeways attributes this to the bursty nature of takedown requests … 291 (46%) of those claims involved copyright, 2 (0.3%) involved patent, and 331 (52%) involved trademark … 5 claims combined trademark and copyright claims').

[15] Shapeways, '2017 Transparency Report' (2017) at www.shapeways.com/legal/transparency/2017.

[16] M Weinberg, 'When 3D Printing and the Law Get Together, Will Crazy Things Happen?' in B van den Berg, S van der Hof and E Kosta (eds), *3D Printing: Legal, Philosophical and Economic Dimensions* (The Hague, Asser, 2016) 28.

[17] L Osborn, 'Of PhDs, Pirates and the Public: Three-Dimensional Printing Technology and the Arts' (2014) 1 *Texas A&M Law Review* 811, 824 (arguing that as desktop 3D printers would often be used in private or domestic settings, detecting the actual manufacturing will be especially difficult).

[18] J Hornick, '3D Printing and IP Rights: The Elephant in the Room' (2015) 55 *Santa Clara Law Review* 801, 802–3; see also J Hornick, *3D Printing Will Rock the World* (CreateSpace, 2015).

entity.[19] This can be contrasted with traditional manufacturing practices where products are typically made at a more centralised level and unauthorised use is easier to detect (for example, when goods cross borders).[20]

Moreover, given the decentralised nature of the internet, the dissemination of infringing 3D printable files online is itself difficult to effectively monitor and control. In this sense, 3D printing 'anonymises' manufacturing.[21] It would be especially difficult to determine who is sharing what and how frequently infringement takes place. Discussing this issue in the context of patent law, Deven Desai and Gerard Magliocca even argue that it is 'unclear why personal 3D printing should be unlawful, especially given the futility of enforcement'.[22]

It goes without saying that rightsholders only have limited resources to enforce their rights. The greater the pool of potential infringers, the less effective and cost-efficient enforcement action is likely to be.[23] Peer-to-peer file sharing websites such as The Pirate Bay are a prime example of this. After decades of trying to shut the website down, including lobbying, police raids and confiscating hardware, it is up and running under an endless list of proxy domains (or 'mirrors' of the original website).[24] This is a shining example of 'code' overpowering law and traditional enforcement methods.[25]

In light of this, how should IP aim to deal with the risk of piracy in this context? In answering this question, it would be sensible to look at how rightsholders responded to the advent of the internet and try to avoid making the same mistakes again.

[19] B Depoorter, 'Intellectual Property Infringements & 3D Printing: Decentralized Piracy' (2014) 65 *Hastings Law Journal* 1483, 1486 (also noting that 3D printing presents some of the same challenges that digitisation brought to the creative industries (music, books, and films) in the past); see also A Daly, *Socio-Legal Aspects of the 3D Printing Revolution* (London, Palgrave Macmillan, 2016) 15 ('3D printing exhibit[s] elements which frustrate the effective control of the technology by centralised forces such as the nation-state and large private sector actors').

[20] I Silverman, 'Optimising protection: IP rights in 3D printing' (2016) 38 *European Intellectual Property Review* 6 (argues that unlike traditional manufacturing – which is typically costly and often requires overseas factories – 3D printing is more affordable and enables counterfeiters to make such products closer to the point of consumption, which in turn means that counterfeits are less likely to cross borders and be detected).

[21] L Osborn, '3D Printing and Intellectual Property' in F Xavier Olleros and Majlinda Zhegu (eds), *Research Handbook on Digital Transformations* (Cheltenham, Edward Elgar, 2016) 265 ('As with patents, however, 3D printing will disintermediate and largely anonymize the manufacture of trademarked goods. Instead of going to a store to buy a name-brand item … consumers will have a third option: obtain a CAD file and print it at home').

[22] D Desai and G Magliocca, 'Patents, Meet Napster: 3D Printing and the Digitization of Things (2014) 102 *Georgetown Law Journal* 1691, 1716 (arguing that the inability of proprietors to prevent individual users from infringing patents could lead policymakers to take the opposite approach and rely on punitive measures to address such conduct). It should also be noted that this comment has been made in the context of US patent law, which, unlike UK law, does not provide a private and non-commercial use exemption.

[23] Depoorter (n 19) 1497.

[24] See K Zetter, 'Pirate Bay Has Been Raided and Taken Down: Here's What We Know' (*Wired*, 9 September 2014) www.wired.com/2014/12/pirate-bay-raided-taken-down.

[25] See also, more generally, R Giblin, 'The P2P Wars: How Code Beat Law' (2012) *IEEE Internet Computing*, May/June, 92.

Lessons from the Napster Era

Given that IP owners have the most to lose from large-scale piracy, they may resort to a wide range of punitive measures to set examples and try to deter further infringement:

> As 3D printing away from control erodes IP rights, rights owners will react, drawing from their traditional arsenal, by filing patent applications, licensing digital blueprints, filing IP lawsuits, lobbying … to change the law, and employing DRM.[26]

This is exactly how the content industry responded to piracy during the early days of widespread internet access and the so-called 'Napster era' (Napster, often seen as an existential threat to the record industry, was a controversial file-sharing platform that enabled users to disseminate pirated music).[27] However, commentators argue that despite the intensity and scope of these aggressive IP enforcement measures, efforts to lock down the internet have largely failed to prevent mass infringement.[28] Moreover, the campaign against file sharing resulted in a significant public backlash:

> Media reports that a single mother and a college student were each charged with six-figure damage awards for copyright infringements involving a handful of songs likely undermined the public support for the enforcement of copyright law and might have contributed to a public belief that the campaign against file sharing was excessive.[29]

Such action could even be counterproductive. The enormous damages sought by the content industry – seen by many as excessive and unjustified – have contributed to calls for radical proposals to reform copyright law.[30]

On a technological level, proprietors are likely to rely on various digital locks, rights management (DRM) systems, and other hardware restrictions in order to stem piracy (DRM is an access-control technology which restricts unauthorised access to devices and content, whether it is music, films or books).[31] In fact, a

[26] Hornick (n 18) 801, 815.

[27] T Lamont, 'Napster: The Day the Music Was Set Free' (*The Guardian*, 24 February 2013) at www.theguardian.com/music/2013/feb/24/napster-music-free-file-sharing; see also A Greene, 'The 50 Worst Decisions in Music History' (*Rolling Stone*, 29 November 2022) at au.rollingstone.com/music/music-lists/the-50-worst-decisions-in-music-history-44119 ('Metallica weren't wrong to see Napster as an existential threat to the record industry as it had existed up until that point in time … But in the eyes of many fans, they crossed a huge line when they delivered the names of over 30,000 Metallica fans to Napster and asked them to be banned by the service. The backlash was almost universal, and it dogged them for years').

[28] Lemley (n 2) 460.

[29] Depoorter (n 19) 1499.

[30] ibid 1497–8 (arguing that when the content industry adopted a punitive approach to set examples, the damage awards were seen as arbitrary and excessive by many and led to proposals to reform copyright); see also P Samuelson and T Wheatland, 'Statutory Damages in Copyright Law: A Remedy in Need of Reform' (2009) 51 *William & Mary Law Review* 439.

[31] Regarding DRM more generally, see L Bently and others, *Intellectual Property Law* (Oxford, OUP, 2022) 401. Moreover, manufacturers and rightsholders have already considered placing restrictions on 3D printers to only work with proprietary materials (that is, only materials that are approved by the original manufacturer, as opposed to 'unauthorised' filament made by third parties); see M Weinberg, 'Keep 3D Printers Unlocked (the win! 2023)' (1 November 2024) (discussing 'DRM that prevents them from using materials of their choice in 3D printers') at michaelweinberg.org/blog/2024/11/01/1201-win.

patent has been granted for 'a system in which a 3D printer assesses whether a 3D design file has an authorization code that grants access for printing'.[32] As further explained by Dinusha Mendis, this system is designed to 'look for a licensing agreement or evidence of payment. Where none exists, the printer will not print a 3D object'.[33]

While restrictions of this nature are often employed amid genuine concerns about piracy, there is a risk that they may be deployed in an indiscriminate manner and that they unduly restrict legitimate use of 3D printing, harming honest consumers. Indeed, Stephanie Santoso and Stephen Wicker argue that based on past experience, DRM 'has not been able to distinguish between legitimate and illegal uses of content'.[34] Critics even argue that there is insufficient evidence to demonstrate that DRM is actually an effective tool for preventing infringement.[35] Reliance on such measures should therefore be approached with caution.

Artificial Scarcity and the Digitisation of Tangibles

Beyond the more immediate and practical challenges that 3D printing poses to the IP system, the increasing digitisation of tangibles may challenge some of the core tenets underpinning the legal framework in the long term.

The concepts of abundance and scarcity play a key role in the modern economy. The rarer something is or the more resources it takes to produce (whether it is time, money, physical or intellectual labour), the more it usually costs.[36] However, the economics of physical goods are different from the economics of information. Consuming a rivalrous resource, such as an apple, naturally prevents others from doing the same. This does not apply to information.[37] Unlike an apple, an idea has infinite capacity and can simultaneously be consumed by others without depleting the resource. The marginal costs of allowing each additional person to use it are zero.[38] Once information is disclosed, it becomes vulnerable to freeriding, meaning that others can copy or sell it without incurring the costs that the original creator had to incur.[39] Viewed through utilitarian lenses, individuals may

[32] S Bechtold, '3D Printing, Intellectual Property and Innovation Policy (2016) 47 *International Review of Intellectual Property and Competition Law* 517, 531, referring to US Patent US8286236.

[33] D Mendis, 'Clone Wars: Episode I – The Rise of 3D Printing and its Implications for Intellectual Property Law: Learning Lessons from the Past?' (2013) 35 *European Intellectual Property* 155, 161.

[34] S Santoso and S Wicker, 'The Future of Three-dimensional Printing: Intellectual Property or Intellectual Confinement?' (2016) 18 *New Media and Society* 138, 148.

[35] Electronic Frontier Foundation, 'DRM', at www.eff.org/issues/drm.

[36] Lemley (n 2) 466 (discusses the supply-and-demand graph in economics whereby the supply curve slopes up given that resources are scarce, and demand goes down because money is scarce).

[37] B Frischmann, 'An Economic Theory of Infrastructure and Commons Management' (2005) 89 *Minnesota Law Review* 917, 946; see also W Landes and R Posner, 'An Economic Analysis of Copyright Law' (1989) 18 *Journal of Legal Studies* 325.

[38] D Desai and G Magliocca, 'Patents, Meet Napster: 3D Printing and the Digitization of Things (2014) 102 *Georgetown Law Journal* 1691, 1697; see also Frischmann (n 37) 27.

[39] P Menell and others, *Intellectual Property in the New Technological Age 2023 Vol. I: Perspectives, Trade Secrets and Patents* (Berkeley, Clause 8 Publishing, 2023).

therefore have little incentive to produce things that cost a lot to develop but little to copy.[40]

This economically inefficient outcome can be avoided if we grant exclusive rights so that individuals can recoup their sunk costs spent in creating or inventing.[41] IP is therefore designed to '[make] ideas scarce because then we can bring them into the economy and charge for them, and economics knows how to deal with scarce things'.[42]

However, this approach is being increasingly challenged by new technologies.[43] In the analogue age, creating and distributing content required substantial facilities and resources.[44] Even when videocassette recorders and tapes were first invented (and they enabled individuals to carry out unauthorised activities on a small scale more easily), they did not fundamentally alter the broader counterfeiting landscape.[45] The reason for this is that these technologies provide an 'inferior' analogue method of copying that cannot match modern digital power.

Besides providing instant access to most of the world's publicly available media and knowledge, the internet has now democratised the distribution of content by separating the act of creation from the acts of production and distribution.[46] Copies of a film or an entire music album can now be made and shared across the globe in the blink of an eye – by anyone. Crucially, by dramatically reducing the cost of distribution of informational content, the internet has effectively eliminated *scarcity* for a wide range of goods.[47]

3D printing makes its own very important contribution to this ongoing process of digitisation. By enabling various tangible goods – whether it is a sculpture, vase, or Lego brick – to exist as informational content that can be made and stored in purely digital form, it could dramatically reduce the costs associated with producing and distributing a wide range of physical goods. As put by Mark Lemley:

> A world in which sophisticated 3D printers are widely available would change the economics of things in a fundamental way. 3D printers, like the Internet, separate

[40] W Landes and R Posner, *The Economic Structure of Intellectual Property Law* (Cambridge, MA, Harvard University Press, 2003); see also F Scherer and D Ross, *Industrial Market Structure and Economic Performance* (Boston, Houghton Mifflin, 1980), as cited in Lemley (n 2) 467.

[41] W Fisher, 'Theories of Intellectual Property' in Munzer S (eds), *New Essays in the Legal and Political Theory of Property* (Cambridge, CUP, 2001) 168; see also M Lemley, 'The Economics of Improvement in Intellectual Property Law' (1997) 75 *Texas Law Review* 989, 993–97.

[42] Lemley (n 2) 462.

[43] ibid 504.

[44] M Lemley and R Reese, 'Reducing Digital Copyright Infringement Without Restricting Innovation' (2004) 56 *Stanford Law Review* 1345, 1373–74, as cited in Lemley (n 2) 469.

[45] Lemley (n 2) 469 (argues that the mass reproduction of certain types of content, such as film and music, was exceptionally difficult until the invention of videocassette and audiocassette recorders, and that while these technologies led to 'dire warnings', they are an analogue method of copying that had the same inherent limitations as previous (analogue) technologies).

[46] ibid 469; see also L Lessig, *The Future of Ideas* (New York, Random House, 2002) 265.

[47] Lemley (n 2) 460, 471.

> things into their information content and their manufacturing. By doing so, they eliminate the cost of distribution … and substantially reduce the cost of manufacturing …[48]

In other words, 3D printing could do for tangible products what the internet has already done for music, films and books – that is, it could gradually eliminate scarcity for an ever-expanding range of goods.[49] In the long term, this may be an increasing problem for the IP framework – a system that is inherently designed to artificially replicate scarcity.

Conclusion

By digitising tangibles and lowering barriers to reproducing various physical products, 3D printing has the potential to disrupt some fundamental IP norms and policies. There is little doubt that we need a broader conversation on how to adapt the existing framework to face these new digital realities in the long term. When it comes to the more immediate and pressing challenges raised by 3D printing (such as the risk of decentralised infringement and piracy), it would be essential to look at how the content industry responded to the arrival of digital media and try to avoid making the same mistakes again. Attempting to apply the same aggressive and punitive enforcement measures to stem piracy may not only be ineffective, but it may also be counterproductive and further undermine public support for IP rights. It goes without saying that such an approach could deprive 3D printing of its immense potential and social value.

[48] ibid 474–5 ('[A] world in which manufactured goods no longer have to be produced in bulk and are no longer scarce. But it is also a world in which the manufacture and sale of newly-designed things becomes harder and harder to control. All someone needs to do is download a design from the Internet and they can print that design without paying'); see also N Gershenfeld, 'How to Make Almost Anything: The Digital Fabrication Revolution' (2012) 91 *Foreign Affairs* 43, 56; J Grimmelmann, 'Indistinguishable from Magic: A Wizard's Guide to Copyright and 3D Printing' (2014) 71 *Washington and Lee Law Review* 683, 696.

[49] Lemley (n 2).

5

3D Printing, Creativity and Copyright Law

Introduction

Despite the ubiquity of digital media, core intellectual property acts – including the Copyright, Designs and Patents Act (CDPA) 1988 – remain 'rooted in the analogue world'.[1] And while copyright has already faced the issue of digitisation and mass infringement following the Napster era, patent and trade mark law have not yet experienced the full force of this process.[2]

3D printing could change this dynamic – as the technology equips individual end users with access to manufacturing tools, it also enables them to interfere with all major IP rights on a potentially highly decentralised basis. Indeed, a quick look at any major 3D printing file sharing platform reveals that there is a remarkably diverse range of printable files being shared online on a daily basis, ranging from lucrative sculptures and artworks (protectable by copyright) to Lego bricks (formerly patented) and items bearing the logos of well-known brands (that may be subject to trade mark law).[3]

Yet, the legal framework has not yet fully caught up with these new digital realities, and there is no scholarly consensus on how existing IP principles would apply in the context of 3D printing. What is more, there is a scarcity of case law on point, which has fuelled speculation in the academic literature. Is the IP framework – as far as specific provisions and doctrines are concerned – ready to tackle the transformation of tangibles into digital files? What are the key 'problem areas', either from a legal or policy perspective? Is reform necessary?

[1] R Arnold, 'The Need for a New Copyright Act: a Case Study in Law Reform' (2015) 5 *Queen Mary Journal of Intellectual Property* 110, 123–4 ('There are at least seven reasons why we now need a new Copyright Act. The first is the passage of time. During that period, technological change relevant to copyright has accelerated and has become more transformative. We have had the advent of the world wide web, the whole online world including Internet television and social media, smart phones, tablet computers, and now 3D printing').

[2] D Desai and G Magliocca, 'Patents, Meet Napster: 3D Printing and the Digitization of Things' (2014) 102 *Georgetown Law Journal* 1691; see also T Lamont, 'Napster: the day the music was set free' (*The Guardian*, 24 February 2013) at www.theguardian.com/music/2013/feb/24/napster-music-free-file-sharing.

[3] See www.thingiverse.com.

We will explore these questions over the course of the next few chapters, starting with copyright law (the present chapter focuses on copyright, while chapters six and seven respectively deal with patents and trade marks).[4]

First, this chapter will look at the copyright status of 3D printable files – an issue that would be of particular importance for rightsholders, given that these models could carry significant economic value. It will assess the issue both in the context of models designed from scratch (through computer-aided design software) and those created through 3D scanning. It will critically discuss some controversial recent disputes involving ownership claims in 3D scans of ancient artworks, such as the Bust of Nefertiti, and highlight the wider policy and ethical issues in this area. Second, the chapter will focus on the issue of infringement and the application of relevant principles in this context – including scenarios involving the sharing of 3D printable files online, the act of manufacturing tangibles, and the issue of 3D scanning. Before looking at each of these questions, however, I will provide a brief overview of some general copyright principles.

The General Scope of Copyright Protection

The key copyright statute in the UK is the Copyright, Designs and Patents Act (CDPA) 1988. The CDPA operates an exhaustive list of protected works, including (among other things) authorial literary, dramatic, artistic and musical works. As the list is 'closed', there has traditionally been little room for courts to protect new forms of less 'conventional' types of creativity.[5] Following harmonisation at the EU level, however, the Court of Justice of the European Union (CJEU) has seemingly put an end to the exhaustive list through its interpretation of various directives.[6] Its recent jurisprudence indicates that in order to qualify for protection, the work in question must be original; an expression of an idea; and identifiable with sufficient clarity and precision.[7] As long as these requirements are met, a work that does not strictly fall under one of the categories explicitly recognised in CDPA may

[4] Other relevant rights such as designs (and the intersection between copyright and design law, in particular) will be taken into account where relevant. For an overview of the existing literature, see ch 1.

[5] For example, the 'artistic' arrangement of objects around a swimming pool was found not to be an artistic or dramatic work in *Creation Records v News Group* [1997] EMLR 444; see also L Bently and others, *Intellectual Property* (Oxford, OUP, 2022) 63.

[6] L McDonagh, 'UK Patent Law and Copyright Law after Brexit: Potential Consequences' (Centre for International Governance Innovation Paper No 3, 2017) at www.cigionline.org/sites/default/files/documents/Brexit%20Series%20Paper%20no3.pdf 9.

[7] Case C-393/09 *Bezpečnostní softwarová asociace* [2010] ECR I-13971 ('BSA'); Case C-683/17 *Cofemel – Sociedade de Vestuário SA v G-Star Raw CV* EU:C:2019:721 [29]; Case C-310/17 *Levola Hengelo BV v Smilde Foods BV* EU:C:2018:899 [40]–[42]; see also J McCutcheon, 'Levola Hengelo BV v. Smilde Foods BV: The Hard Work of Defining a Copyright Work' (2019) 82 *Modern Law Review* 936.

therefore now be protected by copyright. As stated by Eleonora Rosati, 'exhaustive lists of protectable subject matter [are] incompatible with EU law'.[8]

'Originality' is an essential element of copyright law, as any authorial work must satisfy this requirement in order to qualify for protection. This criterion is concerned with the relationship between the author and the work, the latter being an expression of the author's idea. There is no requirement for novelty or uniqueness here. Rather, the term derives from 'origination'.[9] Under the 'traditional' UK approach to originality, the threshold for considering a work original has, historically, been rather low. As long as the work was not copied and the author was able to exercise sufficient skill, labour and judgment in its creation, the requirement would be satisfied.[10]

However, this standard has now been effectively replaced with the 'intellectual creation' test developed under EU law.[11] Under this approach, the work must reflect the author's personality in the sense that they are able to exercise 'free and creative' choices and 'stamp the work with a personal touch' which reflects their personality.[12] Mere choice is not sufficient – the choice must also be creative. For example, in *Infopaq*, the Court of Justice held that words as such, considered in isolation, are not subject to copyright protection, and that it is 'only through the choice, sequence and combination of those words that the author may express his creativity in an original manner and achieve a result which is an intellectual creation'.[13] Similarly, in *Painer*, a case involving portrait photography, the court held that choosing the appropriate background, subject's pose, and lighting are relevant factors that may be sufficient to render a work original for the purposes of EU copyright law.[14] As further held in *Football Dataco*, choices 'dictated by

[8] E Rosati, 'CJEU Rules That Copyright Protection for Designs Only Requires Sufficient Originality' (2019) 14 *Journal of Intellectual Property Law and Practice* 931, 932; see also Bently and others (n 5) 66–7 ('Whatever a literal reading of any of the categories might now be, henceforth they should be offered a broad reading so as to ensure protection of anything that constitutes the expression of an intellectual creation').

[9] Bently and others (n 5) 104.

[10] *University of London Press v University Tutorial Press* [1916] 2 Ch 601 Ch D.

[11] See, eg, *THJ Systems Ltd v Sheridan* [2023] EWCA Civ 1354, [23] (arguing that in the previous instance, the judge had incorrectly applied the old 'skill and labour' test, as opposed to the new 'intellectual creation' standard established by the Court of Justice following *Infopaq*); see also, McDonagh (n 6) 9 ('The ECJ's intellectual creation standard has become part of the common law through its interpretation in cases such as *Meltwater*').

[12] Case C-5/08 *Infopaq International v Danske Dagblades* Forening [2009] ECR I-6569 [45]; Case C-145/10 *Eva-Maria Painer v Standard Verlags GmbH* [2012] ECDR 6. While this harmonised standard was initially only applicable to computer programs, databases and photos, the CJEU has interpreted this test to apply to all copyright works through its case law; see also *The Newspaper Licensing Agency v Meltwater Holding* [2010] EWHC 3099 Ch; Case C-406/10 *SAS Institute Inc v World Programming Ltd* [2013] Bus LR 941; E Rosati, 'Originality in a Work, or a Work of Originality: The Effects of the Infopaq Decision' (2011) 33 *European Intellectual Property Review* 746.

[13] *Infopaq* (n 12) [45].

[14] *Painer* (n 12) [91]; [99].

technical considerations, rules or constraints' leave no room for such creative freedom (in other words, they would not meet the originality threshold).[15]

What is the difference between the two approaches? The 'intellectual creation' standard imposes a higher threshold compared to the traditional UK test in the sense that works which require mere labour and skill but no 'creative choices' may no longer be protected.[16]

Finally, even with the ability of courts to depart from EU law following Brexit, recent cases such as *THJ v Sheridan* indicate that UK judges continue to follow the 'intellectual creation' standard.[17]

The Copyright Status of 3D Printing Design Files

Since a 3D printer is unable to function without a design file as a starting point – and such files could potentially carry considerable economic value – the ability to exercise control over their dissemination would be critical for rightsholders. In fact, there have already been several controversial disputes involving allegations of copyright infringement in this context, which further illustrates the need for legal certainty in this area.[18] It is therefore essential to consider whether, and when, such files would be subject to copyright protection.

STL, originally derived from stereolithography, is the industry standard and most commonly shared 3D printing file format.[19] An STL file describes the geometry of the three-dimensional object it represents by 'tessellating' its outer surface, recording information about its coordinates and vectors in the form of computer code.[20] It also contains a graphic model of the physical object that users can view

[15] Case C-604/10 *Football Dataco Ltd v Yahoo! UK Ltd* [2012] 2 CMLR 24, [38]–[39].

[16] C Handig, 'Infopaq International A/S v Danske Dagblades Forening (C-5/08): is the Term 'Work' of the CDPA 1988 in line with the European Directives?' (2010) 32 *European Intellectual Property Review* 53. However, for the most part, it is unclear whether this new approach will lead to different results in practice in the majority of cases; see Bently and others (n 5) 111.

[17] *THJ Systems Ltd v Sheridan* [2023] EWCA Civ 1354.

[18] See M Rimmer, 'The Maker Movement: Copyright Law, Remix Culture and 3D Printing' (2017) 41 *Western Australia Law Review* 51.

[19] See M Weinberg, 'What's the Deal with Copyright and 3D Printing?' (*Public Knowledge*, 2013) 14 at www.michaelweinberg.org/docs/WhatstheDealwithCopyright_%20Finalversion2.pdf; M Antikainen and D Jongsma, 'The Art of CAD: Copyrightability of Digital Design Files' in R Ballardini, M Norrgård and J Partanen (eds), *3D Printing, Intellectual Property and Innovation* (Alphen aan den Rijn, Kluwer Law International, 2017) 258, citing K Dickson and A Coles, 'Textile Design Protection: Copyright, CAD and Competition' (2000) 20 *Technovation* 47 (CAD models are not exclusive to 3D printing and have, in fact, been used for decades in various fields, including video games, automotive, textile, architecture and animation).

[20] In the early literature, scholars argued that these files could be protected as original computer programs, part of the literary works category, on the basis that they contain code describing the geometry of the object; see S Bradshaw and others, 'The Intellectual Property Implications of Low-Cost 3D Printing' (2010) 7 *SCRIPTed* 1, 22 (arguing that a 3D printable file 'may be protected by literary copyright in the same manner as computer software (which, as a series of instructions, it resembles)'); I Silverman, 'Optimising protection: IP rights in 3D printing' (2016) 38 *European Intellectual Property*

on a computer screen (prior to converting it into machine-readable G-code and, finally, 3D printing the item).[21]

When it comes to copyright, files of this nature effectively serve as the medium of expression where an original work may be recorded, much like any other media file that may contain protectable text, images or videos.[22] An original artistic work, such as a sculpture,[23] created through modelling software and recorded in STL form or equivalent – which can subsequently be utilised to 3D print a tangible copy – should not be treated any differently than the same work produced in physical form, just as a photo or painting created by using digital software should not receive any less protection than its tangible instantiation.[24] The fact that these works have been created through digital means (as opposed to, for example, making a sculpture by using more 'conventional' methods) is of little significance in this regard. As stated by Birss J in *Abraham Moon*, 'artistic copyright must relate to the content of the work of the artist and not the medium in which it is recorded'.[25]

As always, the originality requirement will play a critical role in determining whether copyright subsists here. Just like with any other 'real' (or tangible) creative work, the user of the modelling software would be expected to exercise free

Review 5, 6; D Mendis, 'Clone Wars Episode II – The Next Generation: The Copyright Implications relating to 3D Printing and Computer-Aided Design (CAD) Files' (2014) 6 *Law, Innovation and Technology* 265, 271. However, a computer program will only be protected to the extent it is an original expression, which would generally not be the case here; see Antikainen and Jongsma (n 19) 267–8 ('There is little reason to look at the computer-generated code in the case of CAD files any more than there is in the case of a Word file … [The] graphical and visual elements … are the main parts of the work's originality'); V Elam, 'CAD files and European Design Law' (2016) 7 *Journal of Intellectual Property, Information Technology and Electronic Commerce Law* 146, 148; L Osborn, '3D Printing and Intellectual Property' in Olleros F Xavier and Zhegu M (eds), *Research Handbook on Digital Transformations* (Cheltenham, Edward Elgar, 2016) 169–171 ('[A] draftsperson uses a CAD program to draw the image, and the computer translates the shapes into textual code using algorithms directed to utilitarian goals, not creative ones … [T]he literal code does not reflect creativity as to its wording. The only creativity attributable to the draftsperson would correspond to the creativity in the CAD drawing itself … Although a JPEG file is a "computer program" … and can be represented in code format, this fact alone cannot transform the text, generated by a digital camera, into a protectable work').

[21] For more details regarding the technological process, see ch 2. The analysis here will primarily focus on STL files, as this is the most commonly shared file format online.

[22] Elam (n 20) 146, 148; P Malaquias, 'Consumer 3D Printing: Is the UK Copyright and Design Law Framework Fit for Purpose' (2016) 6 *Queen Mary Journal of Intellectual Property* 321.

[23] See www.thingiverse.com/search?q=sculpture.

[24] Antikainen and Jongsma (n 20) 264.

[25] *Abraham Moon & Sons Ltd v Andrew Thornber Ltd & Ors* [2013] FSR 17 [105]–[106] (discussing the protection of a fabric design recorded on a 'ticket' and comparing this to David Hockney's works that were created on an iPad before physical 'copies' were hanged at the Royal Academy: 'The only thing which makes sense to be referred to as the artist's work in that case is the computer file recording the image. The same images, hanging on the wall of the Royal Academy … are not the actual pictures drawn by the artist, they are "copies" produced from the computer file. Although Mr Hockney … uses a [different] technique … in both cases the only record fixed in a material form of the visual image the artist created is an organised table of essentially numerical data which, when looked at directly by a layman, means nothing … The visual image of Skye Sage if it was fixed in a material form as a drawing would be protected … It seems to me that to deny artistic copyright in this case … is to confuse the medium with the message'); Osborn (n 20) 145–6.

and creative choices and stamp the work with a personal touch, so as to render it original for the purposes of copyright law.[26]

The 'closed list' of categories under the Copyright, Designs and Patents Act 1988 will be of limited significance in light of recent harmonising action at the EU level (and, indeed, what would matter is whether the work is the author's intellectual creation, not whether it strictly falls within a certain category of works). For example, cases such as *Lucasfilm* (where protection was denied on the basis that a Stormtrooper helmet did not qualify as a 'sculpture' under the exhaustive list) may be decided differently today.[27] This would be especially important for designers and users in the 3D printing community, given that printable files of this nature are commonly made and shared online.[28]

What about 3D printable models of purely functional or utilitarian objects? It is clear that copyright can subsist in original drawings.[29] An STL model certainly fits this description, given that it contains a digital design drawing describing the geometry of the physical object that is meant to be printed.[30] Moreover, drawings of a technical nature can, in principle, still be protected by copyright, as long as the originality requirement is satisfied.[31] However, the process of creating a work of this nature would typically leave significantly less room for free and creative choices. For example, a simple drawing of an exclusively functional object, such as a pipe, would have to follow specific rules and guidelines, which means that the process is more likely to be dictated by technical constraints.[32] While UK copyright law has traditionally imposed a relatively low originality threshold (whereby as long as the work was not copied and there was sufficient judgment and skill involved in its creation, it could be protected), the higher standard now imposed under the 'intellectual creation' test may prove to be a more significant hurdle in this regard.[33] As a general rule, the less room for creative freedom there is in the process, the less likely it is that a 3D printable file containing an object of a purely

[26] *Infopaq* (n 12); *Painer* (n 12); T Dagne and C Dubeau, '3D Printing and the Law: Are CAD files Copyright-protected?' (2015) 28 *Intellectual Property Journal* 101, 123–4; Mendis (n 20) 265, 274.

[27] *Lucasfilm Ltd v Ainsworth* [2011] UKSC 39, [45]–[46] (arguing that it would not be in accordance with the normal use of language to refer to a military helmet used in the making of a film as a sculpture and that the Stormtrooper helmet was 'utilitarian' instead); see also E Rosati, 'CJEU Rules That Copyright Protection for Designs Only Requires Sufficient Originality' (2019) 14 *Journal of Intellectual Property Law & Practice* 931, 932 (arguing that the decision in *Lucasfilm* is 'even more questionable' following recent EU jurisprudence).

[28] See www.thingiverse.com/search?q=stormtrooper+helmet&page=1.

[29] CDPA, s 4(1)-(2). Under the statutory list, the artistic works category includes a 'graphic work' (which itself encompasses 'any painting, drawing, diagram, map, chart or plan'); *Autospin (Old Seals) Ltd v Beehive Spinning* [1995] RPC 683, 694.

[30] See Malaquias (n 22); see also Osborn (n 20) 146 (argues that, under US copyright law, a 3D printable file can simultaneously be a copy of multiple types of works, including a pictorial work).

[31] See Antikainen and Jongsma (n 20) 265, and the case law cited therein.

[32] See *Football Dataco* (n 15), [39]; see also Antikainen and Jongsma (n 20) 265, citing U Loewenheim and G Schricker, *Urheberrecht. Kommentar* (Munich, C H Beck, 2010) §2 [201].

[33] Antikainen and Jongsma (n 20) 264.

functional nature will qualify for protection.[34] As argued by Lionel Bently, albeit in a different context:

> [It] seems unlikely that the requirement of an "own intellectual creation" will be reducible to the "not copied" test that was widely appealed to in the heyday of industrial copyright. Some of the trivia – drawings of nuts, bolts and even exhaust pipes – might well not pass muster.[35]

What if a 3D printable file is obtained by using 3D scanning instead, as opposed to creating a model from scratch through modelling software? We will now explore this issue in detail below.

Are 3D Scans 'Original'?

3D scanning allows users to turn a wide range of physical objects – from sculptures and other artworks to various functional objects – into digital models suitable for 3D printing.[36] For example, *Scan the World* is one such initiative aimed at archiving culturally significant artworks.[37] Similarly, Denmark's Statens Museum for Kunst (The National Gallery of Denmark) has digitised and released thousands of high-quality 3D scans of (public domain) classical artworks – from the busts of Athena, Plato and Orfeus to the Discobolus and the Horse of Selene – in a format that allows anyone to freely download a digital copy and 3D print their own version of these items.[38] The technology is clearly of immense social value, especially as cultural artefacts of this nature are often damaged in natural disasters, or may even be intentionally wiped from existence. For instance, the terrorist group ISIS has recently destroyed several such artefacts in Palmyra and other locations in the Middle East.[39]

[34] See Antikainen and Jongsma (n 20) 265. There may also be compelling normative arguments *not* to extend protection to these files from a policy perspective. For instance, Osborn argues that these models 'do not implicate the core aesthetic and creative expression that is at the heart of copyright. Rather, they implicate overwhelmingly (if not exclusively) utilitarian concerns'; see Osborn (n 20) 143.

[35] L Bently, 'The Return of Industrial Copyright?' (2012) 34 *European Intellectual Property Review* 654, 670 (discussing the implications of recent CJEU jurisprudence for the copyright-design interface); see also Case C-168/09 *Flos SpA v Semeraro Casa e Famiglia SpA* EU:C:2011:29, [2011] ECDR 8; see also Antikainen and Jongsma (n 20) 265–6; Osborn (n 20) 168.

[36] M Rimmer, '3D printing Jurassic Park: Copyright Law, Cultural Institutions, and Makerspaces' [2016] *Pandora's Box* 1 (arguing that 3D scanning could play an important role in helping institutions recover various objects of cultural significance).

[37] See www.myminifactory.com/scantheworld.

[38] See the Statens Museum's collection at www.open.smk.dk/en/art?q=*&filters=has_3d_file%3Atrue.

[39] K Shaheen, 'Isis fighters destroy ancient artefacts at Mosul museum' (*The Guardian*, 26 February 2015) at www.theguardian.com/world/2015/feb/26/isis-fighters-destroy-ancient-artefacts-mosul-museum-iraq; K Shaheen, 'Isis destroys tetrapylon monument in Palmyra' (*The Guardian*, 20 January 2017) at www.theguardian.com/world/2017/jan/20/isis-destroys-tetrapylon-monument-palmyra-syria; A Curry, 'Here Are the Ancient Sites ISIS Has Damaged and Destroyed' (*National Geographic*, 1 September 2015) at www.nationalgeographic.com/history/article/150901-isis-destruction-looting-ancient-sites-iraq-syria-archaeology.

Unsurprisingly, the copyright status of 3D scans has attracted considerable attention among IP scholars (we will explore the infringement implications of the technology separately below).[40] Who, if anyone, is the owner of these scans? Does the act of 3D scanning itself involve sufficient free and creative choices so as to satisfy the 'originality' criterion? Can a 3D scan of a public domain or otherwise unprotectable work ever work qualify for protection? To answer these questions, it is essential to provide some more context regarding the 3D scanning process first.

There are different types of 3D scanning technologies (for example, photogrammetry, laser scanning and contact scanning), each of which functions differently and has its own specific features and limitations.[41] Generally, 3D scanning enables users to record information about the shape and dimensions of the physical object being scanned as sets of three-dimensional coordinates.[42] The data can then be modified and 'cleaned up' through modelling software in order to ensure that the model is represented accurately, and to create a fully-functioning 3D printable model.[43] In the vast majority of cases, 3D scanning is used to make a *faithful reproduction* of the original. In other words, the aim is to capture the physical object as accurately as possible and to produce a technically excellent copy of the original, also known as a 'representational' scan.[44]

When it comes to copyright law, it is beyond doubt that there is substantial skill and effort involved in creating a quality 3D scan. For example, the process may include preparing the scan itself, processing the resulting data, and ensuring that the final model is depicted correctly. Yet, no matter how labour-intensive and time-consuming the process is, it is unlikely that the 'intellectual creation' standard will be satisfied where the goal is to merely make a perfect copy of the original.[45] In cases involving pure reconstructions, the decision-making process would leave little room for free and creative choices that may allow the user to stamp the work with a personal touch that 'reflects their personality'.[46] Precision is key here – the process is driven by technical and practical considerations, not creative ones.

Some commentators have drawn analogies between 3D scanning and photography, arguing that 'selecting particular views of the physical object when a 3D

[40] Infringement liability could arise where the object being 3D scanned is subject to copyright protection.

[41] For more details regarding the different processes, see P Oruç, '3D Digitisation of Cultural Heritage: Copyright Implications of the Methods, Purposes and Collaboration' (2020) 11 *Journal of Intellectual Property, Information Technology and E-Commerce Law* 149.

[42] Antikainen and Jongsma (n 20) 261; see also H Lipson and M Kurman, *Fabricated: The New World of 3D Printing* (Indianapolis, Wiley, 2013) 95–6.

[43] M Weinberg, 'Copyright Implications of 3D Scanning' in R Ballardini, M Norrgård and J Partanen (eds), *3D Printing, Intellectual Property and Innovation: Insights from Law and Technology* (Alphen aan den Rijn, Kluwer Law International, 2017) 219, 227.

[44] ibid 228; see also Antikainen and Jongsma (n 20) 260–1.

[45] Antikainen and Jongsma (n 20) 269–71; see also Weinberg (n 43) 228–31 (discussing the issue from the perspective of US law).

[46] Antikainen and Jongsma (n 20) 269 (arguing that the use of a 3D scanner would not generally involve sufficient creativity to qualify for copyright protection); Osborn (n 20) 156.

digital model is created by scanning an object is sufficient to make the 3D digital model an 'intellectual creation of the author'.[47] For example, they have drawn on *Painer* to support this argument, where the Court of Justice held that factors such as choosing the background, subject's pose, lighting, angle of view and atmosphere may qualify as 'free and creative choices' so as to render a photo original and, therefore, a work protectable by copyright.[48]

However, copyright only subsists in *some* photographs. Not all instances where a photo is taken will meet the relevant originality criteria.[49] Crucially, the choices and formative freedom that are typically present in creative photography would simply be absent or insignificant from a creative standpoint when it comes to 3D scanning. As stated by Mikko Antikainen and Daniël Jongsma, '[a]nalogies with photography will in principle fail, since the creative options available to the photographer (composition, angle, lighting, etc.) are typically absent in the case of using a 3D scanner'.[50] Similarly, from the perspective of US copyright law, Lucas Osborn argues that:

> Photographs are only copyrightable to the extent that the photographer includes creative choices like angle, perspective, and lighting. But where … the photograph is nothing more than a slavish copy of an unprotected work, it contains no protectable creativity … Detailed 3D scans of useful objects represent nothing more than slavish copying of the object's shape.[51]

In this sense, 3D scanning is rather more similar to traditional image scanning techniques, such as photocopying, as opposed to creative photography.[52]

Having said that, this does not mean that 3D scans will never attract copyright. Beyond pure reconstructions, 3D scanning can also be used to make an 'expressive' scan where the goal is to produce something new and achieve some creative impact or to make an expressive statement by using an initial scan of the original

[47] Mendis (n 20) 278.

[48] ibid; see *Painer* (n 12) [91]–[92].

[49] J Hughes, 'The Photographer's Copyright – Photograph as Art, Photograph as Database' (2012) 25 *Harvard Journal of Law and Technology* 339, 368, as cited in Weinberg (n 43) 226 (while this concerns US law, the outcome is likely to be the same under the 'intellectual creation' standard).

[50] Antikainen and Jongsma (n 20) 269.

[51] Osborn (n 20) 156–7 (noting that the user of a 3D scanner is not making creative choices as to lighting, perspective or angles and that there is no creativity in the initial scan). The outcome is likely to be the same if instead of 3D scanning, users create a 3D printable model of an unprotected work through modelling software. For a relevant US case, see *Meshwerks, Inc. v Toyota Motor Sales U.S.A., Inc., 528 F.3d 1258* (10th Cir. 2008) (copyright was denied where a 3D model of a car aimed to capture it as accurately as possible).

[52] Weinberg (n 43) 229–30 (arguing that using a photocopier to scan a document requires no creative decision-making, given that the few decisions that the user makes in this context are driven by technical considerations directly linked to the quality of the copy); see also A Rahmatian, 'Copyright Protection for the Restoration, Reconstruction and Digitisation of Public Domain Works' in E Derclaye (ed), *Copyright and Cultural Heritage: Preservation and Access to Works in a Digital World* (Cheltenham, Edward Elgar, 2010) 51, 71 (though in a different context and drawing on the traditional UK approach to originality, argues that if the derivative work is exclusively mechanical, like in cases involving traditional photocopying, it would not qualify as original and, therefore, it would not be subject to protection).

object as a starting point.[53] In these scenarios, some post-scan editing would typically be necessary to transform the initial scan into an expressive one – that is, to interpret the physical object in a different manner. For example, Michael Weinberg notes that artists such as Sophie Kahn and Geoffrey Mann use scanning techniques to deconstruct sculptures and to create models that are *deliberately* distortive, incomplete, or otherwise different from the original.[54] To the extent that there are free and creative choices involved in this process, copyright could certainly subsist in these cases. Likewise, the originality standard may be satisfied where, for example, users scan an action figure and add a new feature or attribute that did not exist in the original.[55]

Why the Bust of Nefertiti Should Stay in the Public Domain

Beyond the more 'mundane' technical legal questions that have captured the attention of academics and lawyers, 3D scanning also raises some important policy issues that may have far-reaching implications for the general public. In fact, there have already been several controversial attempts to drag public domain works into the realm of exclusive rights by 3D scanning them and attaching a copyright licence to the resulting digital model. That is, to try to bring copyright back from the dead and to enforce it in relation to works that are no longer subject to protection.

The wider policy issues in this area can be neatly illustrated with a recent dispute involving a 3D scan of the Bust of Queen Nefertiti, a famous limestone statue believed to have been created in 1345 BC by sculptor Thutmose. Despite its global recognition, and despite being one of the most treasured (and copied) works of Ancient Egypt, the artwork was only discovered a century ago by German archaeologist Ludwig Borchardt, and is currently located in the Neues Museum in Berlin.[56]

[53] Weinberg (n 43) 231.

[54] ibid 232; see also www.sophiekahn.net and geoffreymann.com.

[55] Antikainen and Jongsma (n 20) 269–70; see also M Weinberg, '3D Scanning: A World Without Copyright' (2016) 7–11 at www.michaelweinberg.org/docs/white-paper-3d-scanning-world-without-copyright.pdf. In cases where there is alteration or entirely new added elements, works based on pre-existing materials can be independently protected as derivative works under UK copyright law, regardless of whether this act of alteration also infringes copyright in the original. See *Interlego v Tyco Industries* [1989] AC 217 (stating that in order to be protected as a derivative, the work must not only be original, but it must also have some quality or character which the raw material did not possess and which differentiates the product from the raw material); see also *Macmillan v Cooper* (1924) 40 TLR 186; *Redwood Music v Chappell* [1982] RPC 109; Bently and others (n 5) 101 (noting that any copyright that arises in relation to a derivative work will be distinct from the copyright in the prior original work and that as long as the original work is still 'apparent' in the derivative, the licence of the original owner would still be needed); see also Berne Convention for the Protection of Literary and Artistic Works, Art 2(3) (stating that adaptations of a literary or artistic work shall be protected as original without prejudice to any copyright in the original work).

[56] S Conrad, 'The Making of a Global Icon: Nefertiti's Twentieth-Century Career' (2024) *Global Intellectual History* 1.

In 2016, reports emerged that two artists managed to smuggle 3D scanning equipment into the Museum (allegedly hidden under a scarf) before making a scan of the bust.[57] However, the scan was of such high quality that it raised suspicions among experts that this may have been made by someone who had prolonged access to the sculpture.[58] In other words, that this may have been a leak. When experts within the community asked the institution to release an official 3D printable model of the artwork to the public, the Museum shared a file that had a copyright licence attached to it, digitally carved into the bottom of the 3D model itself.

The problem with this is that the Bust of Nefertiti is a public domain work. IP rights did not even exist at the time when it was created. If there was ever any doubt as to the copyright status of faithful reproductions of *public domain* works, Article 14 of the Digital Single Market Directive[59] now explicitly states that where the term of protection of a work of visual art has expired, any material resulting from an act of reproduction would not be subject to copyright unless the new material is the 'author's own intellectual creation' (while the UK was not required to implement the Directive in full due to Brexit, it is likely that the same general principles will apply under UK copyright law today).[60] As outlined in Recital 53 of the Directive, the policy rationale behind this provision is clear:

> In the field of visual arts, the circulation of faithful reproductions of works in the public domain contributes to the access to and promotion of culture, and the access to cultural heritage. In the digital environment, the protection of such reproductions through copyright … is inconsistent with the expiry of the copyright.[61]

[57] M Weinberg, 'The Bust of Nefertiti is Free (With One Strange Caveat)' (13 November 2019) at www.michaelweinberg.org/blog/2019/11/13/nefertiti-scan-nc-license.

[58] T Machemer, '3-D Scans of the Bust of Nefertiti Are Now Available Online' (*Smithsonian Magazine*, 22 November 2019) at www.smithsonianmag.com/smart-news/3-d-scans-bust-nefertiti-are-now-available-online-180973628.

[59] Directive (EU) 2019/790 of the European Parliament and of the Council of 17 April 2019 on copyright and related rights in the Digital Single Market and amending Directives 96/9/EC and 2001/29/EC, PE/51/2019/REV/1 OJ L 130. While Art 14 of the Directive seemingly leaves some possibility for protection where public domain works are reproduced, this is only likely to be the case in a very limited set of circumstances.

[60] It is evident that domestic (English) courts continue to apply the 'intellectual creation' standard after Brexit; see *THJ v Sheridan* (n 11). For a (pre-harmonisation) case involving the recreation of a public domain *musical* work, see *Hyperion Records v Sawkins* [2005] EWCA Civ 565. Here, Sawkins created new performance editions of music by a seventeenth century composer. The court held that the combination of effort and skill exercised by Sawkins was sufficient to make the works original, despite the fact that he simply made the original music playable through modern means and created no 'new' works as such (in particular, the skill exercised in adding the information had an impact on the tonality of the sounds). While Sawkins's skills as a music expert are unlikely to be relevant under the new 'intellectual creation' standard, we should note that Sawkins did succeed in similar proceedings in France (which has applied a test similar to that of the CJEU) where the national court stated that the defendants had not proven a degree of strict faithfulness. See *Sawkins v Harmonia Mundi* (2006) 37 IIC 116, 119. However, Bently and others argue that if the case had been one of *pure reconstruction*, 'it seems difficult to imagine that either court could now describe the work as an 'intellectual creation' bearing the 'personal touch' of its author'; see Bently and others (n 5) 115–6.

[61] While the concept of 'visual art' is not fully defined in the Directive, the Commission's press release on the issue explains that users 'will be completely free to share copies of paintings, sculptures and other works of art in the public domain with full legal certainty' (therefore, works relevant to 3D scanning, such as sculptures, would be covered under these provisions); see European Commission, 'Digital

What does this mean for the Nefertiti scan? As far as copyright law is concerned, anyone should be able to freely photograph and reproduce the artwork as they see fit, without the need for permission. As long as the 3D scan is a faithful reproduction of the original (which appears to be the case here), there will be no copyright to enforce in the first place, and the licence will be legally meaningless.[62] From a policy perspective, denying protection in such cases is also essential to ensure that we avoid an overextension of copyright and monopolies over otherwise unprotected works.[63]

Yet, the mere act of attaching a licence to such works may be all that matters in practice, given that this could still deter the general public from using the 3D model. Many individuals are simply not accustomed to verifying whether a certain licence is in fact valid, or may simply not have the knowledge or resources to do so. This could prevent artists, designers, educators and students from using the model for educational purposes, or as part of various art projects. While museums should be facilitating access to culturally important works, as argued by Michael Weinberg, '[etching] scary legal words in the bottom of a work in your collection in the hopes of scaring people away from engaging with it is the opposite of that'.[64] This is even more concerning when it is done by a powerful and well-funded public institution:

> When a large, well lawyered institution carves legally meaningless lawyer language into the bottom of the scan of a 3,000 year old bust to suggest that some uses are illegitimate, it is getting dangerously close to committing copy fraud …[65]

Although the risk of 'copyfraud' is part of a much broader issue,[66] if (or when) 3D scanning becomes more accessible and widespread and it allows anyone to easily digitise various public domain works, the technology could significantly

Single Market: EU negotiators reach a breakthrough to modernise copyright rules' (13 February 2019) at www.ec.europa.eu/commission/presscorner/detail/en/ip_19_528. For more details regarding the operation of Article 14 of the DSM Directive, see also A Wallace and E Euler, 'Revisiting Access to Cultural Heritage in the Public Domain: EU and International Developments' (2020) 51 *IIC – International Review of Intellectual Property and Competition Law* 823; see also European Copyright Society, 'Comment of the European Copyright Society on the Implementation of Art.14 of the Directive (EU) 2019/790 on Copyright in the Digital Single Market' (26 April 2020) at europeancopyrightsociety.org/wp-content/uploads/2020/04/ecs_cdsm_implementation_article_14_final.pdf. For a comprehensive overview of the Digital Single Market Directive more generally, see also E Rosati, *Copyright in the Digital Single Market* (Oxford, OUP, 2021).

[62] M Weinberg, 'The Nefertiti Bust Meets the 21st Century: When a German Museum Lost Its Fight Over 3D-Printing Files of the 3,000-Year-Old Artwork, It Made a Strange Decision' (*Slate*, 15 November 2019) at www.slate.com/technology/2019/11/nefertiti-bust-neues-museum-3d-printing.html.

[63] See also Weinberg (n 43) 233–4 ('Courts have rightly raised concerns about the threat that over-extending copyright can create 'a weapon for harassment in the hands of mischievous copiers' by allowing them to monopolize the public domain or impinge on the ability of rights holders of the underlying scanned object to fully exercise their own rights').

[64] ibid.

[65] ibid.

[66] J Mazzone, 'Copyfraud' (2006) 81 *New York University Law Review* 1026, 1028; J Mazzone, *Copyfraud and Other Abuses of Intellectual Property Law* (Stanford, Stanford Law Books, 2011) (such claims are often coupled with the threat of litigation on the basis that the work is allegedly being used

exacerbate this problem. Indeed, the controversy over the Bust of Nefertiti is far from an isolated incident. Examples abound. In 2014, the act of 3D scanning a centuries-old Michelangelo statue (a replica) led to questionable allegations of copyright infringement.[67] As of early 2025, there is a pending legal dispute in France involving 3D scans of the works of Auguste Rodin.[68]

While it is clear that the law alone cannot fully address this risk, policymakers and cultural institutions should play a more active role in informing the general public about the issue through educational campaigns and similar initiatives. For example, Denmark's Statens Museum clearly informs users that its entire web collection of 3D scanned public domain works is free to use and no permission is required – information that is prominently displayed on each individual webpage.[69] Moreover, there is certainly a good normative basis for requiring museums and cultural heritage institutions using 3D scanning to digitise their collections to make such scans freely available to the public, especially as these projects are often publicly funded.[70]

Finally, while the issue of repatriation is well beyond the scope of this book, the dispute surrounding the Bust of Nefertiti highlights some important ethical issues in this context.[71] We do not need to recount the controversies surrounding the transfer of cultural artefacts during colonial times. The Parthenon Marbles dispute has dominated the mainstream for decades.[72] Amid growing pressure to 'decolonise' these collections, evolving cultural norms, and a rise in opinion in favour of repatriation, relying on 3D scanning to digitise these works *and* illegitimately using IP as a vehicle to exercise monopoly control over their digital instantiations only

without the 'owner's' consent, or, alternatively, prospective users may be asked to obtain a licence or pay a fee in order to use the said work).

[67] Rimmer (n 18); A Bogle, 'Good News: Replicas of 16th-Century Sculptures Are Not Off-Limits for 3-D Printers' (*Slate*, 26 January 2015) at www.slate.com/technology/2015/01/3-d-printing-and-copyright-replicas-of-16th-century-sculptures-are-not-off-limits.html; B O'Neal, 'Sioux Falls Maker Accused of Infringing on Copyright Laws with 3D Models of Michelangelo's Statues' (*3DPrint*, 21 January 2015) at www.3dprint.com/38631/michelangelo-copyright-models; M Weinberg, 'Cultural Institutions Behaving Badly: Stupid Reactions to 3D Scanning' (*Public Knowledge*, 22 January 2015) at www.publicknowledge.org/cultural-institutions-behaving-badly-stupid-reactions-to-3d-scanning.

[68] C Wenman, 'Secret 3D Scans in the French Supreme Court' (29 September 2024) at cosmowenman.substack.com/p/secret-3d-scans-in-the-french-supreme.

[69] See www.open.smk.dk/en/art?q=*&filters=has_3d_file%3Atrue.

[70] See, for instance, Commission Recommendation (EU) 2021/1970 of 10 November 2021 on a common European data space for cultural heritage C/2021/7953 OJ L 401.

[71] On the issue of repatriation and 3D scanning, see P Oruç, 'Rethinking Who "Keeps" Heritage: 3D Technology, Repatriation and Copyright' (2022) 71 *GRUR International* 1138.

[72] A Marshall, 'After 220 Years, the Fate of the Parthenon Marbles Rests in Secret Talks' (*The New York Times*, 17 January 2023) at www.nytimes.com/2023/01/17/arts/design/parthenon-sculptures-elgin-marbles-negotiations.html; L Bursey, 'The Parthenon Marbles dispute – is the end in sight?' (*LSE Blogs*, 26 September 2024) at www.blogs.lse.ac.uk/europpblog/2024/09/26/the-parthenon-marbles-dispute-is-the-end-in-sight. On the Parthenon Marbles more generally, see Y Hamilakis, 'Stories from Exile: Fragments from the Cultural Biography of the Parthenon (or "Elgin") Marbles' (1999) 31 *World Archaeology* 303; J Merryman, 'Thinking about the Elgin Marbles' (1985) 83 *Michigan Law Review* 1881.

adds insult to injury.[73] 3D scanning should instead be used to produce quality replicas as a replacement for the original artefact, if (or once) it is repatriated.[74]

General Infringement Principles

Copyright infringement involves the appropriation of the intangible right in the *expression* of an idea. The idea itself is not subject to copyright – a core principle known as the idea-expression dichotomy.[75] For a finding of primary infringement, the defendant must carry out one of the activities reserved for the rightsholder, including, but not limited to, copying the work, issuing copies to the public, and adapting the work.[76] The work must be derived from the original, meaning that there must be a causal connection between the two, and the restricted act must be carried out in relation to the work or a 'substantial part' of it.[77] Infringement is therefore not confined to exact copying, as otherwise individuals could easily avoid liability by merely making minor changes to the original.

When assessing the question of whether the part that has been taken is 'substantial' under the pre-harmonised UK approach,[78] the inquiry focused on the part's importance and whether what was appropriated was original, a matter of impression judged qualitatively on a case-by-case basis, taking into account copying in its entirety.[79] However, following harmonisation at the EU level, the question now focuses on whether the defendant has reproduced *any* part of the work, as opposed to a substantial part.[80] As stated by the Court of Justice in the case of *Infopaq*, 'the various parts of a work … enjoy protection … provided that they contain elements which are the expression of the intellectual creation of the

[73] For a recent poll on the repatriation of the Parthenon Marbles, see K Razzall, 'Parthenon Sculptures: Pressure growing on British Museum' (*BBC News*, 21 July 2023) at www.bbc.co.uk/news/entertainment-arts-66239150.

[74] See G Hitch and M Fennell, 'Parthenon marbles recreated from 3D scans to sway British Museum to return them to Greece' at www.abc.net.au/news/2024-06-17/parthenon-elgin-marbles-greece-british-museum/103969352; see also C Wilder, 'Swiping a Priceless Antiquity … With a Scanner and a 3-D Printer' (*New York Times*, 1 March 2016) at www.nytimes.com/2016/03/02/arts/design/other-nefertiti-3d-printer.html.

[75] *IPC Media Ltd v Highbury-Leisure Publishing Ltd (No. 2)* [2005] FSR 20.

[76] CDPA 1988, s 16(1).

[77] CDPA 1988, s 16(3); see also Bently and others (n 5) 216–7.

[78] This still applies to some unharmonised rights, such as adaptation; see *England & Wales Cricket Board & Sky UK v Tixdaq & Fanatix* [2016] EWHC 575 (Ch) [67].

[79] *Designers Guild v Williams* [2000] 1 WLR 2416, 2431; *Ladbroke v William Hill* [1964] 1 WLR 273, 276; *Autospin* [1995] 697; *Newspaper Licensing Agency v Marks & Spencer plc* [2001] Ch 257, 268.

[80] For instance, see Article 2 of Directive 2001/29/EC of the European Parliament and of the Council of 22 May 2001 on the harmonisation of certain aspects of copyright and related rights in the information society OJ L 167; see also *Infopaq* (n 12). The new test has effectively widened the scope of protection. For a more detailed discussion of the differences between the two approaches, see Bently and others (n 5) 226–7.

author of the work'.[81] Following recent decisions such as *Meltwater* and *SAS*, UK courts have followed this harmonised approach.[82]

In contrast with primary infringement, secondary infringement typically targets accessories that facilitate or assist in the making or distribution of infringing copies in a commercial context.[83] While the state of mind of the defendant is irrelevant in the context of primary infringement, a finding of secondary infringement also requires that the defendant knows (or it would be reasonable to believe) that the activities in question are unlawful.[84]

New Technology, Old Rules – 3D Printing and Copyright Infringement

How would primary infringement rules apply in relation to the sharing of 3D printable files? While these doctrines would clearly be a critical remedial tool for rightsholders, there are no uniquely problematic or major novel legal issues worth exploring in great detail here. There is no doubt that, for example, making a copy of a 3D printable file containing a protected authorial work may amount to reproduction and, therefore, infringement. In this regard, files of this nature are virtually indistinguishable from other digital files containing music, film or software. Likewise, when it comes to secondary infringement, 3D file repositories may be liable if they knowingly host or continue to host infringing files in the course of business.[85]

It is worth noting that Article 14(1) of the e-Commerce Directive provides safe harbour provisions in relation to the storing of 'information' (formulated in broad terms).[86] In particular, it states that the provider shall not be liable for storing content where it does not have actual knowledge of illegal activity and is not

[81] *Infopaq* (n 12) [38] [39].

[82] *SAS Institute* (n 12) [38]–[39]; *Meltwater* (n 12) (stating that the correct test should now focus on assessing whether the reproduced parts are the author's own intellectual creation).

[83] CDPA 1988, ss 22–26.

[84] ibid.

[85] For a detailed analysis of how secondary infringement rules would apply in this context, see D Mendis, 'Back to the Future: From Engravings to 3D Printing – Implications for UK Copyright Law' in D Mendis, M Lemley and M Rimmer (eds), *3D Printing and Beyond: Intellectual Property and Regulation* (Cheltenham, Edward Elgar, 2019) 75.

[86] Directive 2000/31/EC of the European Parliament and of the Council of 8 June 2000 on certain legal aspects of information society services, in particular electronic commerce, in the Internal Market OJ L178. For more recently enacted EU provisions (not implemented by the UK as a result of Brexit) concerning the regulation of content-sharing online more generally, see Article 17 of Directive (EU) 2019/790 of the European Parliament and of the Council of 17 April 2019 on copyright and related rights in the Digital Single Market and amending Directives 96/9/EC and 2001/29/EC, PE/51/2019/REV/1 OJ L130 (concerning online content-sharing service providers); see also Regulation (EU) 2022/2065 on a Single Market For Digital Services (Digital Services Act).

aware of the facts or circumstances from which such activity is apparent.[87] Once again, the same general rules that apply to other digital media will generally also apply here.

When it comes to the act of 3D printing itself (or, essentially, manufacturing tangible items), it is irrelevant whether users rely on 3D printing or any other manufacturing technology to reproduce a certain item. Here, it is important to emphasise that the relevant statutory provisions explicitly cover the reproduction of two-dimensional artistic works in three dimensions and vice versa and it is also clear that copying a work includes reproduction in *any* material form.[88] Infringement could therefore arise both where a tangible object is manufactured through 3D printing, and also where an existing physical item is 3D scanned in order to obtain a design file containing a digital representation of that object. For example, scanning a modern art sculpture (as opposed to an unprotected work), such as Louise Bourgeois' 'Maman' (a giant spider)[89] or Yayoi Kusama's 'Pumpkin' (self-explanatory)[90] is likely to infringe copyright.[91] In contrast, 3D scanning a public domain work such as the Bust of Nefertiti would not amount to infringement, given that the original object is no longer subject to copyright protection.

Conclusion

How do existing copyright principles apply in the context of 3D printing? When it comes to the status of 3D printable files, there is little doubt that an original authorial work (such as a sculpture) designed through 3D modelling software and recorded in STL form or equivalent – which can subsequently be utilised to make a tangible copy of that item – could be eligible for protection. To the extent that users

[87] The provision further explains that once the provider obtains such knowledge, they should act expeditiously to remove the infringing content. However, according to Art 15(1) of the Directive, there is no general obligation on websites to actively monitor whether illegal activity is taking place on their platform.

[88] CDPA, ss 17(2)–(3); see also Case C-117/13 *Technische Universität Darnstadt v Eugen Ulmer KG*, EU:C:2014:2196 [37] ('[T]he digitisation of a work, which essentially involves the conversion of the work from an analogue format into a digital one, constitutes an act of reproduction'); see also *Autospin* [1995] 698.

[89] See www.guggenheim.org/artwork/10856.

[90] See www.serpentinegalleries.org/whats-on/yayoi-kusama-pumpkin-2024.

[91] For an analysis of the overlap between copyright and designs in the context of 3D printing and scenarios where users make a copy to a design which records a non-artistic work, see Bradshaw and others (n 20) 24–6 (discussing the operation of s 51(1) CDPA, which states that it is not an infringement of any copyright in a 'design document' for anything other than an artistic work to make an article to the design); see also Silverman (n 20) 8 ('By way of illustration, a counterfeiter who steals … a design file for a pair of sunglasses and uses that file to print an unauthorised copy of the sunglasses has not infringed copyright in the design file. He has, however, infringed copyright in the design file by making a copy of the design file itself, and may also have infringed design rights in the sunglasses if any exist'); D Mendis, 'Clone Wars: Episode I – The Rise of 3D Printing and its Implications for Intellectual Property Law: Learning Lessons from the Past?' (2013) 35 *European Intellectual Property* 155, 167; Malaquias (n 22).

are able to exercise free and creative choice in the modelling process (and this is not dictated by technical considerations), such works would certainly fall within the remit of copyright protection.

Of course, modelling software is not the only way to obtain a 3D printable file. Users can also rely on technologies such as 3D scanning to capture a physical object and to subsequently transform the resulting data into a printable file. However, given that 3D scans are typically pure reconstructions of the original, it is unlikely that the scanning process would, by itself, entail sufficient free and creative choices so as to satisfy the relevant originality criteria in the vast majority of cases.

While there have been several controversial attempts to drag public domain works into the realm of exclusive rights through 3D scanning, as explored throughout this chapter, there are strong legal and normative grounds to deny protection in such cases. In particular, there is a risk that treating these 3D scans as original could result in copyright overreach and thus stifle creativity.

Finally, when it comes to the question of infringement, 3D printing neither appears to be uniquely problematic in this regard, nor does it fundamentally challenge existing principles in this area. It is clear that reproducing a two-dimensional artistic work in three dimensions may constitute infringement and vice versa (which would also cover the act of 3D scanning a protected authorial work). In this respect, the specific type of technology used is irrelevant.

6

Analogue Laws in the Digital Age: 3D Printing and Patents

Introduction

Unlike copyright, patent law has not yet experienced the full force of digitisation. Yet, as 3D printing digitises tangibles and enables users to easily disseminate files containing patented inventions online, it is likely to expose the patent framework to new digital realities that were previously largely confined to the realm of copyright.

While desktop 3D printing is not yet as technologically sophisticated as its industrial counterparts, there are several patentable (or formerly patented) items that are certainly within its reach. For example, users commonly share printable models of items such as Lego bricks (formerly patented), components of coffee grinders, headphones and similar products online (which may, in principle, be subject to patent protection).[1] There is also little doubt that as 3D printing's capabilities continue to expand, the range of products that are possible to reproduce at home will continue to expand accordingly. At the same time, the patent framework was largely designed in the analogue world, and it is unclear whether existing principles mesh well with the very notion of digitised 3D printable inventions.

Do 3D printable files constitute patentable subject matter under existing doctrine? Are the relevant infringement principles adequate in this context? In light of the increasing availability of desktop 3D printing, should patent law interfere with activities occurring within the private sphere (that is, instances where users manufacture patented products at home)?[2] We will explore each of these issues in detail, beginning with the question of patentability before moving to infringement and, finally, exceptions to infringement.

[1] See, eg, US Patent US3005282A (Lego bricks were formerly patented); see also www.thingiverse.com/thing:3461554.

[2] This is especially important in light of the private and non-commercial use exemption in UK patent law.

The General Scope of Patent Protection

The key patent statute in the UK is the Patents Act 1977. While there is no complete harmonisation in this area at the European or international level, treaties and initiatives such as the European Patent Convention (EPC) and the Trade-Related Aspects of Intellectual Property Rights Agreement (TRIPS) have made important contributions to this process. The EPC, for example, of which the UK is a Member State, is an intergovernmental treaty that established the European Patent Office (EPO) and is primarily responsible for the granting of 'European' patents (or, essentially, a bundle of national patents).[3]

The general scope of protection conferred by a patent is determined by the 'patent claims'. That is, the subject matter that the applicant regards as their invention.[4] Patents are granted for products and processes that are novel, involve an inventive step, and are capable of industrial application.[5] To qualify as new, the invention must not form part of the state of the art, a term which includes all matter made available to the public. To satisfy the inventive step requirement, the invention must not be obvious to the average person skilled in the art.[6] The invention also must be capable of being used in 'any kind of industry'[7] and must have a 'useful purpose'.[8] In terms of patentability, the Act also specifically excludes certain subject matter from protection, including (but not limited to) discoveries, computer programs and methods for performing mental acts, though they are only excluded *as such*.[9]

When a patent is granted, the patentee receives a set of exclusive rights over the invention for a period of 20 years. This allows the rightsholder to prevent others from, for instance, reproducing the invention without authorisation during this period.[10] Upon expiry, competitors and the general public can utilise the invention without permission.

[3] Regarding the EPC's role in modelling the (UK) Patents Act 1977, see P Johnson, 'Mr Skemp's Preposterous Provision: The Drafting of the Patents Act 1977 and Harmonization in the 1970s' (2015) 5 *Queen Mary Journal of Intellectual Property* 367, as cited in L Bently and others, *Intellectual Property Law* (Oxford, OUP, 2022) 410, 416. Regarding the separate and newly created Unified Patent Court, see L McDonagh, *European Patent Litigation in the Shadow of the Unified Patent Court* (Cheltenham, Edward Elgar, 2016).

[4] See Patents Act 1977, ss 14(5) and 125; see also EPC, Art 84.

[5] See Patents Act 1977, ss 1–2.

[6] Patents Act 1977, s 1(1)(b). This refers to a notional interpreter equipped with the attributes, skills, background knowledge, and qualifications relevant to the field in which they work; see *Technograph Printed Circuits v Mills & Rockley (Electronics)* [1972] RPC 346, 355; see also *Pozzoli SpA v BDMO SA* [2007] EWCA Civ 588, [2007] FSR (37) 872 (under the *Pozzoli* approach, when assessing whether the invention is obvious, the inquiry focuses on identifying the average person skilled in the art; determining their general knowledge; the inventive concept of the claim; the difference between the inventive concept and the state of the art; and asking whether these differences would have been obvious).

[7] Patents Act 1977, s 4(1).

[8] *Chiron v Murex (No 12)* [1996] RPC 535, 607 (there must be some practical application or concrete benefit).

[9] Patents Act 1977, s 1(2)(a)–(d).

[10] Patents Act 1977, s 60(1)(a) (acts such as, among other things, making and using the invention without permission may amount to infringement).

Patentability and 3D Printing

Patents play a key role in protecting various 3D printing processes, hardware components, materials, and other inventions related to the technology.[11] It is also clear that a patent may be granted for any novel and inventive product that is intended to be manufactured through 3D printing, as long as all the other relevant patentability requirements are satisfied. In this regard, the type of manufacturing technology used is immaterial, and there are no novel or uniquely problematic legal or policy issues worth discussing in great detail.

Ideally, rightsholders would like to exercise control over *both* physical products and their 3D printable digital instantiations (this is important given that, as explored above, patents only protect what is covered by the claims). However, do files of this nature constitute patentable subject matter under existing doctrine?

In his thorough analysis of patentability and 3D printable files under EPC rules,[12] Lucas Osborn argues that the answer to this question depends on the specific file format involved and the way existing rules on excluded subject matter are interpreted.[13] While the EPC (and the Patents Act) excludes from protection computer programs 'as such',[14] a computer program may nevertheless constitute patentable subject matter as long as it has a technical character in the sense that it produces a 'technical effect', defined as an 'effect going beyond the 'normal' interactions between the software and the hardware'.[15]

[11] For an overview of key patents related to 3D printing generally, see S Bechtold, '3D Printing, Intellectual Property and Innovation Policy' (2016) 47 *IIC – International Review of Intellectual Property and Competition Law* 517; see also S Bechtold, '3D Printing and the Intellectual Property System' (Economic Research Working Paper No 28, World Intellectual Property Organization 2015) at www.wipo.int/edocs/pubdocs/en/wipo_pub_econstat_wp_28.pdf.

[12] The analysis here focuses on EPC rules for the sake of simplicity, and to make it relevant to other jurisdictions. However, please note that there have been some divergences in approaches between the UK and EPO in this area. Nevertheless, the two approaches are generally expected to lead to the same results in practice; see *Lenovo (Singapore) v Comptroller General of Patents* [2020] EWHC 1706 (Pat), [2020] RPC (18) 757, [9], per Birss J (noting that despite the fact that in methodological terms the approaches of the UK and the EPO appear different, they typically lead to the same results in practice); *HTC v Apple* [2013] EWCA Civ 451, [41], per Kitchin LJ ('[Whichever] route is followed, one ought to end up at the same destination'); see also Bently and others (n 3) 469; *Aerotel Ltd v Telco Holdings Ltd* [2006] EWCA 1371; *Symbian v Comptroller-General of Patents* [2008] EWCA Civ 1066, [2009] RPC 1; Intellectual Property Office, 'Manual of Patent Practice' (19 February 2016, updated 2 January 2025) at www.gov.uk/guidance/manual-of-patent-practice-mopp/section-1-patentability.

[13] L Osborn, *3D Printing and Intellectual Property* (Cambridge, CUP, 2019) 76; see also G van Overwalle and R Leys, '3D Printing and Patent Law: A Disruptive Technology Disrupting Patent Law?' (2017) 48 *The International Review of Intellectual Property and Competition Law* 504; D Brean, 'Patenting Physibles: A Fresh Perspective for Claiming 3D-Printable Products' (2015) 55 *Santa Clara Law Review* 837.

[14] EPC, Art 52(c), 52(3); Patents Act, s 1(2).

[15] Case T-1173/97 *Computer Program Product/IBM*, Technical Board of Appeal 1/7/1998 [13]; see also European Patent Office, 'Guidelines for Examination' (3.6) at www.epo.org/law-practice/legal-texts/html/guidelines/e/g_ii_3_6.htm. As specific examples of further technical effect, the EPO lists a program which 'specifies a method of controlling an anti-lock braking system in a car, determining emissions by an X-ray device, compressing video, restoring a distorted digital image'; see

Therefore, there are two questions that need to be addressed here. First, does a 3D printable file qualify as a 'computer program'? Second, if 3D printable files qualify as computer programs, do they nevertheless have a 'technical character' so as to fall outside of this exception? It has been argued that a broad interpretation of a computer program is likely to include both STL files (which describe the geometry of the object that is meant to be 3D printed) and the subsequently converted machine-readable G-code files (that tell the printer where to deposit material).[16] However, when it comes to the second question, it appears that only machine-readable files would satisfy the technical effect requirement. The reason for this is that these files provide direct instructions to the manufacturing device and effectively control a piece of hardware – that is, the 3D printer.[17] As stated in the *IBM* case, a patent can be granted 'where a piece of software manages, by means of a computer, an industrial process or the working of a piece of machinery'.[18] In contrast, an STL file is likely to be regarded as excluded subject matter on the basis that it is merely a geometrical representation which users can view as a two-dimensional image on a computer screen prior to printing.[19]

If this understanding of patentability is followed, a person who invents a novel physical product could therefore also obtain protection over a machine-instruction file representing that item.[20] However, this would be of more limited practical significance, given that these files are printer-specific.

In contrast, protection is unlikely to extend to STL files – the most commonly shared and most economically valuable 3D printing file format. This is likely to have important implications for rightsholders, given that individuals primarily share, sell and buy STL files, not G-code files.[21]

From a policy perspective, there may be a good normative case for treating the two file formats as interchangeable for the purposes of patentability in the future, given that conversion could be relatively simple (of course, depending on the expertise of the user).[22] Moreover, it could also be assumed that as the technology continues to improve, the process will gradually become more automated.

European Patent Office, 'Guidelines for Examination' (3.6.1) at www.epo.org/en/legal/guidelines-epc/2024/g_ii_3_6_1.html.

[16] Osborn (n 13) 77.

[17] ibid.

[18] Case T-1173/97 *IBM* [6.5].

[19] Osborn (n 13) 77–8.

[20] ibid 80.

[21] ibid 74.

[22] ibid 101.

General Infringement Principles

There are different types of patent infringement. Direct patent infringement requires some immediate engagement with the patented product or process.[23] This includes, for example, making, importing or disposing of a patented item without permission.[24] In contrast, indirect infringement involves facilitation.[25]

If the question of infringement arises, it may be necessary to compare the claimed invention to the defendant's product or process. If the two are identical, infringement is likely to be found. If they are completely different, there will be none. However, if there is a variation or the defendant uses different or alternative methods, the interpretation of the patent claims will play a key role.[26]

The Patents Act states that the scope of patent protection is 'taken to be that specified in a claim of the specification of the application or patent'.[27] Traditionally, claims have been interpreted purposively.[28] This inquiry focuses on what a person skilled in the art would have understood the patentee to have used the language in the claims to mean, and whether strict compliance with a particular word was intended to be an essential requirement of the invention. For example, in *Catnic*, infringement was found where the claims referred to a vertical lintel, whereas the defendant's product was only a few degrees away from being fully vertical.[29]

In the recent case of *Actavis*, the UK Supreme Court held that the issue of infringement is best approached by addressing two questions: first, whether the variant infringes the claims as a matter of normal interpretation; and if not, whether the variant differs in a way which is immaterial (if yes, there will be infringement).[30] When it comes to addressing the second part of the test, the Court reformulated the so-called 'Improver questions'[31] to read: notwithstanding that it is not within the literal meaning of the claims, does the variant achieve substantially the same result in substantially the same way as the invention; would it be obvious to a person skilled in the art that it does so in substantially the same way; and would they have concluded that the patentee nonetheless intended that strict compliance with the literal meaning of the claim was an essential requirement of

[23] Patents Act 1977, s 60(1). Infringement will only be found where the relevant act is carried out without permission. The burden of proof is on the patentee to show that the alleged infringer has performed one of the exclusive acts reserved for her on the balance of probabilities.

[24] ibid.

[25] Patents Act 1977, s 60(2).

[26] See Bently and others (n 3) 666–7.

[27] Patents Act 1977, s 125 (as interpreted by the description and any drawings).

[28] *Catnic v Hill & Smith* [1982] *RPC* 183; see also *Improver Corp v Remington* [1990] FSR 181; *Kirin-Amgen v Hoechst Marion Roussel* [2004] UKHL 46, [2005] RPC (9) 169. For a more detailed discussion of recent developments in this area, see P Torremans, *Intellectual Property Law* (Oxford, OUP, 2019) 150.

[29] *Catnic* (n 28).

[30] *Actavis UK Limited v Eli Lilly and Company* [2017] UKSC 48; see also Torremans (n 28) 155.

[31] *Improver* (n 28).

the invention?[32] The Court therefore clearly distinguished between 'normal' claim interpretation and the issue of 'equivalents'.[33]

Having briefly outlined some of the general principles governing patent infringement, let's see how they are likely to apply in the context of 3D printing.

Direct Patent Infringement Meets Digitisation

The application of existing rules on direct infringement is reasonably clear where the claimed invention is a tangible item and the relevant object is 3D printed in physical form. However, as explored above, a patent only protects what is covered by the patent claims. Can the mere act of making a digital 3D printable file containing the claimed physical product, therefore, nevertheless amount to infringement? This question would be of great importance to patentees, as they would also like to control the digital precursor to the physical product.[34]

Yet, this appears unlikely under existing doctrine, given that an *intangible* 3D printable file (regardless of whether this concerns an STL or machine-readable file) is completely different in form and function from its claimed tangible counterpart.[35] In this regard, patent law can be clearly distinguished from copyright, which specifically covers acts of reproduction in any material form.[36]

In order to address the potential remedial gap here and ensure that the law reflects modern digital realities, commentators have proposed a new theory of 'digital patent infringement' that would give rightsholders greater control over printable files:

> This theory bucks the historical trend that requires or assumes direct infringement must involve physical instantiations of inventions. It recognizes that digital technologies like 3D printing erode the barrier between the tangible world of atoms and the intangible world of bits and asks how patent law should react to a world where buying and selling a DMF of an object is regarded as buying or selling the physical object.[37]

[32] *Actavis* (n 30) [66].

[33] For a more detailed overview of the doctrine of equivalents, see Torremans (n 28) 156.

[34] Osborn (n 13) 91.

[35] ibid 90–1 (argues that there would be no literal infringement in these cases and that even under the doctrine of equivalents, it is unlikely that a proprietor would be able to prevent a competitor from making something that is 'categorically different' from the claimed item); see also M Mimler, '3D Printing and Patent Law – a UK Perspective: Apt and Ready?' in D Mendis, M Lemley and M Rimmer (eds), *3D Printing and Beyond* (Cheltenham, Edward Elgar, 2019) 122.

[36] Copyright, Designs and Patents Act 1988, s 17(2); see also Mimler (n 35).

[37] Osborn (n 13) 92–3 (arguing that as the technology progressively becomes more advanced, society may regard the sale of a 3D printable file as equivalent to the sale of the relevant tangible object); see also T Holbrook and L Osborn, 'Digital Patent Infringement in an Era of 3D Printing' (2015) 48 *UC Davis Law Review* 1319, 1373–5.

While 3D printing a physical product from a digital file is certainly not as straightforward as simply pressing a button,[38] it could be assumed that the process will progressively become more streamlined and automated. Therefore, there might be a good normative case for considering the adoption of such measures in the future.

Repair and 3D Printing

There is no doubt that manufacturing a patented physical product through 3D printing may constitute 'making' and thus infringement. Once again, the type of manufacturing technology used is immaterial in this regard.

What is more complicated – and particularly important in the context of *desktop* 3D printing – is drawing the line between 'making' (which would typically amount to infringement) and merely 'repairing' a product (which is likely to fall outside the scope of infringement). Indeed, one of the key benefits of 3D printing is the ability to 'print objects when and where needed',[39] and the technology is already widely used to make repair parts for various items (that may in theory be subject to patent protection).[40]

In *United Wire*, Lord Hoffmann explained that 'repair is one of the concepts (like modifying or adapting) which shares a boundary with "making" but does not trespass on its territory'.[41] This means that as long as individuals do not completely manufacture a product anew, their act would not constitute 'making'.[42] When it comes to the precise delineation between these two concepts, the question is to be assessed on a case-by-case basis, taking into account all of the relevant circumstances.[43] This may include both quantitative (such as the amount being repaired) and qualitative (such as whether the inventive part has been replaced and the importance of the specific part being repaired) factors.

[38] See, eg, R Ballardini, M Norrgård and T Minssen, 'Enforcing Patents in the Era of 3D Printing' (2015) 10 *Journal of Intellectual Property Law & Practice* 856 ('[P]rinting out a physical object from a CAD file is not a 'simple click of a button', but a rather tedious work that requires considerable technical expertise (both in the pre- and post- printing phase). Considering CAD files as same as physical objects and, this way, equating the making of a CAD file on a protected object to direct patent infringement, appears … improper and inaccurate at the least').

[39] Ballardini, Norrgård and Minssen (n 38) 850, 856; see also D Mendis, 'Clone Wars: Episode I – The Rise of 3D Printing and its Implications for Intellectual Property Law: Learning Lessons from the Past?' (2013) 35 *European Intellectual Property* 155, 160.

[40] See, more generally, the discussion in, ch 9. See also www.thingiverse.com.

[41] *United Wire v Screen Repair Services* [2000] 4 All ER 353 (HL), 358 (noting that this is a residual right or, in other words, it forms part of the right to do whatever does not qualify as 'making' the product).

[42] See *Solar Thomson Engineering v Barton* [1977] RPC 537, as cited in Bently and others (n 3) 651 (noting that while patent law has aimed to ensure that third parties can repair or modify a patented product without committing infringement, a line has to be drawn where this amounts to making the product anew).

[43] *Schütz v Werit* [2013] UKSC 16; see also Bently and others (n 3) 653.

Provided that 3D printing users do not completely remanufacture a certain product, therefore, they may be able to utilise this rule to avoid infringement.

Indirect Infringement in the 3D Printing World

Patentees may find it difficult to effectively utilise direct infringement rules in an environment where production is highly decentralised and, to a considerable extent, 'anonymised'.[44] In these instances, facilitation doctrines could play a key role. Under the Patents Act, a person will be liable as an indirect infringer if they supply or offer to supply in the UK 'any of the means, relating to an essential element of the invention, for putting the invention into effect'.[45] In exploring the application of this provision in the present context, let's assume that the claimed invention is a physical product and users share a 3D printable file containing this item online, which would allow others to download the model and print the claimed invention (or, essentially, to 'put it into effect' and commit an act of direct infringement).[46]

First, 'supplying or offering to supply' simply requires transferring the relevant means to a third party or offering to do so.[47] While the relevant statutory provisions indicate that the supply must originate from the UK, courts have given this requirement a broad interpretation. In *Menashe*, the claimant sued William Hill for operating a gaming system. The claimed invention concerned an interactive system with remote control, including a host computer, terminal computer and computer software, which allowed communication between devices.[48] The defendant claimed that their act fell outside the scope of the infringement provision on the basis that the host computers were technically located *outside* the UK. Yet, as the supply of the computer program was also available to UK customers, the court was satisfied that it was 'of no relevance to … the user, nor the patentee as to whether or not [the software] is situated in the United Kingdom'.[49] When it comes to 3D printing, as printable files uploaded online can be accessed from virtually anywhere in the world, this condition is likely to be satisfied in the vast majority of cases.

Second, the means supplied by the user must relate to an essential element of the invention. This will be the case where the supplied product is neither of

[44] L Osborn, '3D Printing and Intellectual Property' in F Xavier Olleros and Majlinda Zhegu (eds), *Research Handbook on Digital Transformations* (Cheltenham, Edward Elgar, 2016) 265.

[45] Patents Act 1977, s 60(2).

[46] See Osborn (n 13) 105 (noting that a finding of indirect infringement would depend on the claims in the patent and that where the claim is to a physical item, suppliers of 3D printable files may be liable on the basis that they assist those who manufacture the object).

[47] *Menashe Business Mercantile Ltd v William Hill Organization Ltd* [2002] EWCA Civ 1702, [2003] RPC (31) (concerning the supply of a gaming system through a computer situated in Antigua); Mimler (n 35) 352.

[48] *Menashe* (n 47).

[49] ibid [32].

subordinate importance nor trivial or of low value, and it cooperates functionally with the other integers of the claims.[50] While the definition of 'means' is not completely clear, commentators have argued that since this element has been previously interpreted to include supplying a kit of parts, a 3D printer, raw materials and printable files could *together* constitute the requisite means.[51] Conversely, a less restrictive approach to interpretation may allow 3D printable files alone to qualify as 'means' for the purposes of the provision.[52] Although commentators have argued that the legislature appears to have intended the term to only encompass objects of a 'tangible and physical nature' (therefore excluding abstract and digital matter),[53] software stored on a CD has previously been held to constitute 'means'.[54] While there is no direct precedent here, an argument could therefore be made that 'means' should also include 3D printable files, especially considering courts' willingness to accommodate new digital realities when it comes to interpreting this statutory provision more generally.[55]

Third, for liability to arise, the infringer must know, or it must be obvious to a reasonable person in the circumstances, that the means are suitable for putting, and are intended to put, the invention into effect. To satisfy this requirement, it is sufficient that at the time of supply, the supplier knows or it would have been obvious that some 'ultimate users' may intend to use or adapt the means in order to infringe.[56] This criterion is based on an objective standard, and the reference to intention is not linked to any specific person. As put by Ballardini and others, in the context of 3D printing, the question would be 'whether the supplier of the CAD file knew, or whether it would have been obvious from the circumstances,

[50] *Hazel Grove Limited v Euro-League Leisure* [1995] RPC 529, 541; see also Ballardini, Norrgård and Minssen (n 38) 858–9; Bently and others (n 3) 664.

[51] Bradshaw and others, 'The Intellectual Property Implications of Low-Cost 3D Printing' (2010) 7 *ScriptEd* 5 27, citing *Rotocrop v Genbourne* [1982] FSR 241 (selling infringing compost bins in the form of parts and instructions).

[52] Bradshaw and others (n 51) 27.

[53] Mimler (n 35).

[54] ibid, citing *Menashe* (n 47); Ballardini, Norrgård and Minssen (n 38) 858. However, see Osborn (n 13) 115 (arguing that the case is not directly on point as software was one of the explicitly claimed elements (while a 3D printing design file would not be if the claim is to a physical object) and that the court assumed without deciding that the software constitutes means).

[55] *Menashe* (n 47), [32] (in the context of the territorial scope of the provision and the requirement that the infringer must supply the means in the United Kingdom, the court held that in a digital environment, it is immaterial where the host computer is situated and that its location is not important to the user of the invention, nor to the claimed gaming system: 'it would be wrong to apply the old ideas of location'). While made in a different context, the statement demonstrates the court's flexibility and willingness to interpret the law in a flexible manner and take into account recent technological developments; see also Osborn (n 13) 115–6 ('The case stands for the proposition that something can constitute a "means relating to an element" even if some further manipulation of the means is required to produce the claimed element. In *Actavis*, the solid chemical needed to be manipulated (dissolved) to transform into its ionic (dissolved) form. That is somewhat different from the manipulation required to turn a DMF into a tangible object, but, as a matter of the statute's wording, it can be viewed as a difference in degree').

[56] *Grimme Maschinenfabrik v Derek Scott* [2010] EWCA Civ 1110, [2011] FSR (7) 193, [107], [131]; see also Bently and others (n 3) 664-5; P Johnson, 'Contributing to the Wrong: Indirect Infringement of Patents' (2010) 5 *Journal of Intellectual Property Law & Practice* 514.

that such a CAD file would be intended to be used in an infringing way by the person downloading that file'.[57] Putting into effect simply means that the means must be capable of making the invention work.

Finally, it is important to emphasise that under UK patent law, no act of direct infringement has to ever take place for indirect infringement liability to arise[58] (this can be contrasted with US patent law, where an underlying act of infringement would be required for contributory liability).[59] This principle would therefore be especially valuable for rightsholders as it allows them to take *preventive* action:

> Whereas it is often difficult and expensive to track every individual direct infringer, having a remedy against the supplier for the direct infringer as the "spider in the web" can become an advantage. Provisions against indirect infringement are meant to prevent direct patent infringement before it can occur.[60]

Should Patents Interfere in the Private Sphere?

Once it has been established that the defendant has performed one of the activities reserved for the patent owner, they will have the opportunity to demonstrate that the act falls under one of the relevant exceptions. While there is a scarcity of academic discussion on defences to patent infringement and their application,[61] these doctrines generally aim to provide a balance between the competing interests of rightsholders and other relevant groups, including competitors, users and research organisations.[62] UK patent law, in particular, provides several such exceptions, including, for example, private and non-commercial use, experimental use, and prior use.[63]

The most significant exemption in the context of desktop 3D printing is non-commercial use,[64] given that most users who use the technology at home typically do so for purely private purposes, or, essentially, without the intention of selling printed products for profit.[65] This section will therefore exclusively focus on this specific provision.

[57] Ballardini, Norrgård and Minssen (n 38) 865.

[58] ibid 857, citing *Grimme* (n 56) ('[I]n the UK … as well as in most jurisdictions in Europe … indirect infringement can be committed even where no direct infringement has occurred').

[59] *Aro Mfg Co v Convertible Top Replacement Co*, 365 U.S. 336, 341 (1961), as cited in Osborn (n 13) 110.

[60] M Mimler, '3D Printing, the Internet and Patent Law – A History Repeating?' (2013) 6 SSRN at papers.ssrn.com/sol3/papers.cfm?abstract_id=2482551.

[61] Bently and others (n 3) 679; see also R Eisenberg, 'Patents and the Progress of Science: Exclusive Rights and Experimental Use' (1989) 56 *University of Chicago Law Review* 1017; J Karp, 'Experimental Use as Patent Infringement' (1991) 100 *Yale Law Journal* 219, as cited in Bently and others (n 3) 679.

[62] Bently and others (n 3) 679.

[63] See, eg, Patents Act 1977, ss 60(5)(a), 60(5)(b), 60(5)(i), 64(1).

[64] Patents Act 1977, s 60(5)(a).

[65] See ch 9.

Generally, non-commercial use exemptions reflect the industrial nature of patents and intentionally leave certain private acts beyond the reach of the law. Historically, private reproductions of patented products have been relatively rare:

> [H]obbyists' and DIYers' activities have traditionally attracted little attention from patent holders because these types of use of patented inventions are usually a one-time use only and, as such, do not fall within the targeted market of patent owners in the value chain.[66]

Since the reproduction of a certain invention on a major scale has traditionally required resources, machinery and expertise (assets that most individuals would not have), it has been assumed that the economic harm to the patentee would not be significant enough to justify intervening in the private sphere.[67] In principle, it is best to limit the reach of patents where possible and to prevent a potential over-extension of the law, especially since this could disrupt the balance between public and private interests.[68] Furthermore, from a purely pragmatic perspective, taking action against private use would be exceptionally difficult in practice:

> As, both technically and legally, it is nearly impossible to know or monitor when an end user works out a patented invention for their own enjoyment at home, allowing such use … would make logical sense in the law.[69]

While this doctrine is not part of an internationally harmonised regime, and it is notable that major jurisdictions such as the US do not have such a provision in place, most EU Member States have incorporated a non-commercial use exemption to patent infringement in their legal systems.[70]

In the UK, the Patents Act explicitly states that an act that is 'done privately and for purposes which are not commercial' would be exempt from infringement.[71] However, what is the specific meaning of these terms?

[66] R Ballardini and N Lee, 'The Case of 3D Printing Technologies' in Ballardini, Norrgård & Partanen (eds), *3D Printing, Intellectual Property and Innovation: Insights from Law and Technology* (Alphen aan den Rijn, Kluwer Law International, 2017) 173 (arguing that discussions over the private and non-commercial use exception have been relatively scarce as such use has generally been rare due to technological and economic reasons).

[67] Ballardini and Lee (n 66) 174 ('[I]t is not necessary for a patent right to cover private and non-commercial uses of protected inventions in order to achieve the ultimate goal of the patent system – that is, to promote economic and technological development for the benefit of society as a whole'), citing World Intellectual Property Organization, 'Standing Committee on the Law of Patents, Exceptions and Limitations to Patent Rights: Private and/or Non-commercial Use' (2014) SCP/20/3 at www.wipo.int/edocs/mdocs/patent_policy/en/scp_20/scp_20_3.pdf; see also www.wipo.int/scp/en/exceptions/replies/germany.html (discussing the argument that acts carried out for private and non-commercial purposes are excluded from the scope of patent protection on the basis that patents are not intended to intervene in the private sphere); www.wipo.int/scp/en/exceptions/replies/netherlands.html.

[68] Ballardini and Lee (n 66) 173–4.

[69] Ballardini and Lee (n 66) 174–5; see also www.wipo.int/scp/en/exceptions/replies/portugal.html; W Gordon, 'Fair Use as Market Failure: A Structural and Economic Analysis of the "Betamax" Case and Its Predecessors' (1982) 82 *Columbia Law Review* 1600.

[70] Ballardini and Lee (n 66) 173.

[71] Patents Act 1977, s 60(5)(a).

While there is little statutory guidance on the issue, in *Smith, Kline & French (SKF) v Evans*, Aldous J held that 'private' does not require secrecy or confidentiality. Rather, it is the opposite of 'public' and refers to acts carried out solely for an individual's personal use or enjoyment.[72] 'Non-commercial' use simply means that there is no economic benefit for the user.[73] In assessing whether this criterion is satisfied, it is necessary to determine the subjective intention of the infringer.[74] This means that even if there is eventually some commercial benefit, as long as the user did not intend this, the exemption could still apply. In line with the wording of the statute, it is also clear that the two conditions are cumulative, meaning that the act must be both private *and* non-commercial.

When it comes to 3D printing, there is little doubt that using the technology at home for purely private purposes would typically be exempt from patent infringement. Moreover, given the way the statutory criteria have been interpreted, the exemption is also likely to extend to scenarios where users share 3D-printed products with friends or family, as long as there is no commercial benefit in mind.

While the exemption does not appear to be particularly problematic from a doctrinal perspective, it may, at least in theory, have far-reaching policy implications. As desktop 3D printing removes key barriers to making various (patented) products on a decentralised basis, it may pose a significant threat to the economic interests of rightsholders, especially considering the potential cumulative effect of such one-off reproductions. For example, proprietors may argue that consumers would be less inclined to buy a product from them if they can simply 3D print the same item at home.[75]

Some commentators even contend that since patent applicants are required to disclose how their invention works and there is a non-commercial use exemption in place (meaning that 3D printing users can hypothetically reproduce these inventions without the risk of infringement):

> [P]atent law, in its current form, is in danger of becoming irrelevant in respect of 3D printing … [T]he monopoly that patent holders currently enjoy will be eroded.[76]

[72] *Smith, Kline & French Laboratories Ltd v Evans Medical Ltd* [1989] 1 FSR 513, 518 (carrying out experiments in order to invalidate a patent); see also *McDonald v Graham* [1994] RPC 407.

[73] *Smith, Kline & French Laboratories* [1989] 1 FSR 513, 514 (commercial use includes 'any commercial purpose').

[74] ibid 514 (where the purpose is both commercial *and* non-commercial, the exception will not apply).

[75] See the discussion regarding users' motivations for using 3D printing in ch 9.

[76] P Twomey, 'A New Dimension to Intellectual Property Infringement: An Evaluation of the Intellectual Property Issues Associated with 3D Printing' (2014) 17 *Trinity College Law Review* 14, 21–2 (argues that the current patent model should be rethought 'to ensure both increased protection for patent holders and the continued development of consumer-level 3D printing'). Twomey refers to Irish patent law, which offers a virtually identical exemption; see Patents Act 1992 (Ireland), as amended, s 42(a). For a similar argument, see Ballardini and Lee (n 66) 187 (arguing that the advent of 3D printing may dramatically increase the private working of an invention and may therefore 'disturb the balance that patent law aims to strike by contemplating the exception').

While there is clearly a hypothetical risk that the original rationale behind the exception may become increasingly fragile in the future, there is an important 'if' here. Given the current technological limitations of desktop 3D printing in terms of ease of use, output quality (including the ability of goods printed at home to act as a substitute for the original product), and consumer uptake more generally, it is unclear whether these risks will actually materialise.

Should this change in the future and there is compelling empirical and economic evidence to reform the exemption, what specific measures should be adopted? Would abolishing the provision, so as to practically align UK patent law with US law, be sensible?[77] The issue with such an approach is that attempting to take enforcement action against infringers in a highly decentralised environment is unlikely to be effective. Even if rightsholders are able to detect infringing use, enforcement action is likely to often target individuals who may not even be aware that the object they are reproducing is subject to protection. Indeed, patent claims are highly complex, and the risk of infringement here may be less obvious than, for instance, downloading a song or a film, where users would typically know that copyright liability may arise.[78]

In light of these concerns, some commentators have suggested a more subtle recalibration of the existing doctrine. For example, modifying the provision to only apply where the infringer does not have 'actual knowledge' that they are infringing a patent.[79] Alternatively, policymakers could implement an 'actual or constructive' knowledge standard. That is, an objective test where the exemption will only apply if the person performing the relevant act does not know, or it would not be obvious to a reasonable person, that their action is infringing.

Conclusion

There is little doubt that manufacturing a patented tangible invention through 3D printing may constitute infringement. The specific technology used is irrelevant in this regard. However, patents only protect what is covered by the claims, which means that the act of making an *intangible* 3D printable version of a certain invention (where the claimed product is a physical item) is unlikely to fall within the scope of the monopoly conferred by patents. While applicants may try drafting claims so as to include the 3D printable instantiation of the relevant physical invention in order to circumvent this problem, there is no scholarly consensus on whether files of this nature constitute patentable subject matter under existing doctrine.

[77] Twomey (n 76) 32.

[78] Osborn (n 13) 118 (noting the highly technical nature of patent documents).

[79] ibid 86–7 (argues that a balance could be achieved by modifying the exemption to only apply where the user did not have actual knowledge of the patent, and that such knowledge could be derived from a stamp on the product or its digital version to indicate that it is subject to patent protection).

When it comes to the issue of infringement, given that individual instances of reproduction would be especially difficult to effectively monitor in a highly decentralised manufacturing environment, facilitation (indirect infringement) doctrines would play a key role in this context. Indeed, these principles would be a critical remedial tool for rightsholders, especially as there is no need to demonstrate that direct infringement has ever taken place in order for indirect infringement liability to arise under UK patent law. However, as explored throughout this chapter, this is an area where some further judicial clarifications would be necessary.

Finally, patent law expressly exempts private and non-commercial use from the scope of infringement. While this exception has traditionally not been a major concern for rightsholders (given that private reproductions have been relatively rare), 3D printing has the potential to change this dynamic and undermine some of the core policy rationales underpinning this doctrine. Indeed, *if* the technology achieves more mainstream adoption in the future and individual end users are able to easily interfere with high-value patents, it may be necessary to revisit the exception so as to enhance the protection afforded to patent holders. This is an area of the law that should continue to be closely monitored.

7

Brands, Trade Marks and the Decentralisation of Manufacturing

Introduction

There is a wide range of printable models bearing the logos of well-known brands that are shared online on a daily basis. Moreover, users commonly make 3D printable designs for action figures and fictional characters from popular culture – items that are often subject to trade mark protection.[1] There is thus little doubt that 3D printing enables users to interfere with this major category of IP rights, and, indeed, several commentators have expressed serious concerns about the impact of the technology on the trade mark system and on proprietors' economic interests.[2]

This chapter will explore the application of existing trade mark doctrines in the context of 3D printing. It will start by outlining the boundaries of trade mark infringement and discuss the different circumstances where liability is most likely to arise in this context, with a particular emphasis on *desktop* 3D printing. It will explore the implications of 3D printing for different trade mark 'functions' and consider the application of confusion- and dilution-based doctrines which would be critical in a world where, as some academic commentators have theorised, 'almost anyone may be able to make almost anything'.[3]

[1] A Scardamaglia, 'Flashpoints in 3D Printing and Trade Mark Law' (2015) 23 *Journal of Law, Information and Science* 30, 46 (noting that 2D fictional characters are often registered as 2D marks).

[2] See, eg, B van Wiele, 'Decentralised, Democratised and Disruptive: How 3D Printing Challenges the Consumer Protection Rationale of Trade Marks' (2019) 41 *European Intellectual Property Review* 313, 319; V Elam, 'The Transfer of Computer-Aided Design Files in the Era of 3D Printing: Trademark Infringement Under the Current European Framework' in *Building a European Digital Space: 12th International Conference on Internet, Law & Politics* (Barcelona, 7–8 July 2016) at cadmus.eui.eu/handle/1814/60440; J Ammar and R Craufurd-Smith, 'When is a Trade Mark use not a Trade Mark Use? A 3D Perspective' (2015) 1 *International Journal of Law and Interdisciplinary Legal Studies* (2015) 4, 4; I Silverman, 'Optimising Protection: IP Rights in 3D Printing' (2016) 38 *European Intellectual Property Review* 5, 6.

[3] J Hornick, '3D Printing and IP Rights: The Elephant in the Room' (2015) 55 *Santa Clara Law Review* 801, 802.

The General Scope of Trade Mark Protection

What exactly does trade mark law protect? Registration may be granted for any sign capable of distinguishing the goods or services of one undertaking from those of another, provided that the sign is capable of being represented in a manner that enables the registrar and the public to determine 'the clear and precise subject matter of the protection afforded to the proprietor'.[4] Registered signs may include letters, numerals, colours, shapes and various other insignia. The famous distinctive shape of the Coca-Cola bottle is one such example.[5] Certain marks are automatically excluded from protection under the absolute grounds for refusal. For instance, this includes signs devoid of a distinctive character and natural shapes necessary to obtain a technical result.[6] Registrability is further limited by the relative grounds for refusal, which typically come into play where an identical or similar mark is already in use.[7] Upon successful registration, the trade mark owner receives a set of exclusive rights, most notably the right to initiate infringement proceedings.[8]

In terms of infringement, liability may arise in several different circumstances, including where a person uses in the course of trade: i) a mark which is identical with a registered mark in relation to goods (or services) which are identical with those for which the proprietor's mark is registered (the so-called 'double identity' provisions); ii) where the marks are identical, the goods are similar, and there is a likelihood of confusion on the part of the public; iii) where the marks are similar, the goods are identical or similar, and there is a likelihood of confusion; and iv) where the marks are identical or similar, the mark has a reputation, and the use of the mark takes unfair advantage of, or is detrimental to, the reputation or distinctive character of the mark (a doctrine known as 'dilution').[9] We will contextually analyse the relevant infringement requirements in more detail below.

[4] Trade Marks Act (TMA) 1994, s 1(1); see also Case C-273/00 *Ralf Sieckmann v Deutsches Patent-und Markenamt*, [2002] ECR I-11737 [50] (the graphical representation had to be clear, precise, self-contained, easily accessible, intelligible, durable, and objective). Although the representation no longer has to be 'graphical', the Sieckmann criteria were incorporated in the Trade Marks Directive 2015; see Directive (EU) 2015/2436 of the European Parliament and of the Council of 16 December 2015 to approximate the laws of the Member States relating to trade marks (recast) OJ L 336, Recital 13 (noting that it is essential that the sign is capable of fulfilling the *Sieckmann* criteria listed above).

[5] UK Registered Trade Mark 2000546.

[6] TMA 1994, ss 3(1)–(2).

[7] TMA 1994, ss 5(1)–(3).

[8] TMA 1994, s 9.

[9] See TMA 1994, s 10(1) (double identity); ss 10(2)(a)–(b) (confusing similarities); s 10(3) (dilution).

Personal 3D Printing and the Boundaries of Trade Mark Infringement

To come within the scope of trade mark infringement, the use of a mark must be 'in the course of trade'.[10] While the precise meaning of this term is not completely clear, in *Arsenal v Reed*, the court defined this as use 'in the context of commercial activity with a view to economic advantage, and not as a private matter'.[11] As further illustrated by AG Colomer in the same case, BMW's trade mark would not be infringed in a scenario where an individual puts it on a key ring for their own personal use.[12] In more recent case law, the court has added that 'the exclusive rights conferred by a trade mark may … be relied on by the proprietor … only as against economic operators and, consequently, only in the context of a trading business'.[13]

Moreover, in the case of *L'Oreal v Ebay*, the court further considered the application of this criterion in the context of sales by individuals in an online marketplace environment. It held that while such activity does not necessarily constitute commercial use by itself (and that not all individual transactions for remuneration will qualify as such), if 'owing to their volume, their frequency or other characteristics, the sales … go beyond the realms of a private activity, the seller will be acting 'in the course of trade''.[14]

Why is this requirement so important in the context of desktop 3D printing? When users manufacture various items at home, this is generally carried out for purposes that are strictly private and non-commercial.[15] In other words, such use is unlikely to amount to 'use in the course of trade' under existing doctrine (and, therefore, infringement action is unlikely to arise). The same principle would apply if the technology is used to make 3D-printed goods for friends and family members, as this would not constitute commercial activity either. Moreover, if the approach in *L'Oreal* is followed, even one-off sales of 3D-printed goods will not necessarily come within the remit of the doctrine – unless, of course, this cumulatively amounts to commercial activity by virtue of the volume and frequency of the sales.

[10] TMA 1994, s 103(1) ('trade' includes 'any business or profession').

[11] Case C-206/01 *Arsenal Football Club plc v Reed* [2002] ECR I-10273 [40]. While it was initially unclear whether 'economic advantage' and 'non-private' are cumulative conditions, it now appears that the latter merely clarifies when usage is in the context of a commercial activity; see *Och Ziff v Och Capital* [2010] EWHC 2599 (Ch), [2011] FSR (11) 289 [55]–[66]; *Unilever v Griffin* [2010] EWHC 899 (Ch), [2010] FSR (33) 814, as cited in Bently and others, *Intellectual Property Law* (Oxford, OUP 2022) 1132.

[12] *Arsenal* (n 11), Opinion of AG Colomer [63]–[64].

[13] Case C-772/18 *A v B*, EU:C:2020:341 [23].

[14] Case C-324/09 *L'Oréal v eBay International* [2011] ECR I–6011 [55]. When assessing this, factors such as the volume, frequency and nature of the goods can override other factors, such as the lack of commercially significant remuneration for the defendant.

[15] See ch 9.

While this issue is not necessarily problematic from a doctrinal perspective, it may nevertheless raise serious concerns among proprietors who may argue that consumers would be less inclined to buy a certain product from the original seller if they can simply 3D print them at home.

Crossing the Non-commercial Line

If we assume that the 'non-commercial' line has been crossed (for instance, where users start selling 3D-printed goods on a sufficiently large scale with a view to economic advantage), trade mark infringement action may arise in several different scenarios, including where the marks and goods in question are identical (under the so-called 'double identity' provisions); where there are 'confusing similarities'; and in the context of dilution. Let's consider a 'classic' double identity scenario under section 10(1) of the Trade Marks Act first.

Assuming that the marks and 3D-printed goods are identical,[16] liability could arise, for example, where a tangible product incorporates a graphical two-dimensional mark on its surface; where users make three-dimensional representations of two-dimensional marks; or where the three-dimensional product itself replicates a three-dimensional shape mark.[17] For example, desktop 3D printing is commonly used to make various toys and products based on fictional characters from popular culture, such as Marvel action figures,[18] and items of this nature are often protected by a registered trade mark. Provided that the relevant trade mark is used in relation to the same category of goods and this is carried out without the owner's consent or authorisation, such activity could, in principle, amount to infringement.[19]

An Overview of the Trade Mark Functions

While liability under the double identity provisions appears absolute at first glance (meaning that as long as the marks and goods are identical, infringement will be found), the Court of Justice has effectively limited the scope of protection afforded by this doctrine through its jurisprudence. In *Arsenal*, it introduced a further element of 'harm' that must be demonstrated in most scenarios involving

[16] For a more detailed analysis of the concept of 'identity' (and similarity) of the goods in the context of 3D printing, see Elam (n 2) 84 (given the 'ease' with which 3D printable files can be converted into tangibles, Elam argues that 'the scope of trademark protection should be broadened, so as to cover both the physical goods, indicated in the application, and their digital representations').

[17] A Daly, *Socio-Legal Aspects of the 3D Printing Revolution* (London, Palgrave Macmillan, 2016) 37.

[18] See www.thingiverse.com/search?q=action+figure.

[19] However, see also Case C-48/05 *Adam Opel AG v Autec* [2007] ETMR 33.

infringement.[20] More specifically, it held that the rights conferred by trade mark law must be 'reserved to cases in which a third party's use of the sign affects or is liable to affect the functions of the trade mark'.[21]

The 'essential' function of a mark (also known as the 'origin' function) enables consumers to distinguish between the goods of competing undertakings. It will generally be adversely affected where a third party sells products in a manner which may lead consumers to believe that they originate from the owner.[22] Furthermore, in *L'Oréal*, the court expanded this principle to include other functions, including 'that of guaranteeing the quality of the goods … and those of communication, investment or advertising'.[23] While the law in this area is controversial and shrouded in mystery,[24] it remains an essential aspect of trade mark infringement.

We will now explore some of the core functions of a trade mark (with a particular emphasis on the essential origin function) in the context of both selling 3D-printed goods and sharing printable files online.

3D Printing and the Origin Function

By separating design from manufacturing, 3D printing further weakens the link between the proprietor and the end product.[25] Any sign that appears on a 3D-printed product may therefore have little to do with the original proprietor, which may, in theory, undermine the ability of trade marks to effectively guarantee the origin of the relevant goods.[26]

However, the mere fact that a mark appears on a 3D-printed good will not necessarily be enough to adversely affect the origin function. In *Adam Opel*, the defendant sold a remote-controlled scale model of an Opel Astra bearing the popular German car manufacturer's lightning logo on its grille.[27] One of the key questions here was whether such use should be regarded as liable to jeopardise the origin function of the mark, especially if we take into account the fact that consumers are generally accustomed to seeing scale models designed with absolute fidelity in mind (so that upon viewing the toy, they would understand that it is merely a scale version). The court held that as long as customers do not assume

[20] See Bently and others (n 11) 1081.

[21] Case C-206/01 *Arsenal Football Club* [2002] ECR I-10273 [51].

[22] Cases C-236/08–238/08 *Google France SARL and Google Inc v Louis Vuitton Malletier SA* [2010] ECR I-2417 [82].

[23] Case C-487/07 *L'Oréal SA v Bellure NV* [2009] ECR I-05185 [58]. For a more detailed overview of the different trade mark functions, see also Bently and others (n 11) 1135.

[24] *L'Oréal v Bellure* [2010] EWCA Civ 535 [30] (describing functions as 'conceptually vague and ill-defined'); Max Planck Institute, *Study on the Overall Functioning of the European Trade Mark System* (2010) [2.184].

[25] L Osborn, *3D Printing and Intellectual Property* (Cambridge, CUP, 2019) 121.

[26] ibid. See also J Grace, 'The End of Post-Sale Confusion: How Consumer 3D Printing Will Diminish the Function of Trademarks' (2014) 28 *Harvard Journal of Law & Technology* 263; Elam (n 2) 86.

[27] Case C-48/05 *Adam Opel AG v Autec* [2007] ETMR 33.

that the toys came from Opel or an economically linked undertaking, the essential function of the mark would not be affected.[28]

This principle would be especially important in the context of 3D printed miniature models and toy cars. Indeed, items of this nature are commonly manufactured by desktop 3D printing users. For example, typing 'Mercedes' or 'Ferrari' in Thingiverse's search bar produces several relevant results.[29]

Beyond the origin of 3D-printed goods, there are some complex issues surrounding the origin of marks associated with 3D printable *files*. Trade marks may appear both within the 3D model itself and on the webpage where the file is uploaded. What source-indicating function do marks perform within this context?

It is important to first emphasise that when users share 3D printable files online, these files are typically accompanied by detailed information about the nature of the digital model as well as other relevant details which enable users to verify what exactly they are about to download and 3D print.[30] What is more, all major file-sharing platforms, including Thingiverse and MyMiniFactory, clearly indicate *who* has made a particular design and whether it is officially authorised or licensed.[31] For instance, consider the following 'real life' example of a user called Black Banshee who has uploaded a file for an 'Apple Watch Stand' with the following short, yet sufficiently informative, description on Thingiverse:

> Yet another Apple watch stand. This one is built from 3 parts. Designed so that the cable is hidden. Also added some holes in the base that are sized to fit a few stacks of American pennies which makes the base quite heavy and stable.[32]

In such scenarios, it would be clear that the file originates from this specific uploader, as opposed to Apple. As put by Bram van Wiele, '[b]y stating that a model is created by a certain entity or person, the platform unmistakably tells the consumer this person is the origin of the model'.[33]

What is more, the text accompanying the file would often be necessary to indicate the particular characteristics of a product and the manner in which it is meant to be used. For example, the name of a certain brand may be mentioned where the item is intended to be used as an accessory or spare part.[34] This could qualify as referential use (in particular, use necessary to indicate the 'intended purpose'

[28] ibid [24].

[29] See www.thingiverse.com/search?q=mercedes and www.thingiverse.com/search?q=ferrari.

[30] van Wiele (n 2) 318; see also Elam (n 2) 85; L Osborn, 'Trademark Boundaries and 3D Printing' (2017) 50 *Akron Law Review* 865, 882–3.

[31] D Mendis and D Secchi, 'A legal and empirical study of 3D printing online platforms and an analysis of user behaviour' (UK Intellectual Property Office 2015/41) 31 at www.gov.uk/government/uploads/system/uploads. See also van Wiele (n 2) 318.

[32] See www.thingiverse.com/thing:806900.

[33] van Wiele (n 2) 318 (arguing that it is unlikely that a reasonable consumer would assume that there is a link between the mark and the origin of the file); Osborn (n 25) 130.

[34] Elam (n 2) 85 ('The use of the trademark «BMW», in order to designate the purpose or intended use of the goods that can be printed, is a purely descriptive one, not capable of being perceived as an indicator of origin'); see also Osborn (n 25) 125.

of the product), which is expressly exempt from infringement under the Trade Marks Act.[35]

Lucas Osborn argues that even where a certain mark is embedded within the 3D model itself, its depiction would not necessarily adversely affect the origin function (illustrating this with an example where a user called 'User123' has uploaded a printable iPhone case bearing Nike's distinctive swoosh mark):

> [What] source-indicating function, if any, does the Nike swoosh logo appearing within the image of the DMF serve? The answer has to be "none." The website context makes plain who the source … is … The trademark appearing on the digital version simply tell users what the object in the DMF is designed to look like, rather than who made the file.[36]

Therefore, the extent to which the essential function is likely to be adversely affected in this context will depend on the manner in which this information is presented and whether the source of the file is clearly and unambiguously indicated.[37] It goes without saying that if this information is misleading or missing, such use could certainly jeopardise the origin function of the mark.[38]

The Quality of 3D Printed Goods

There are several other trade mark functions that are likely to be often adversely affected in this context. For example, the *quality* of the 3D printed product will directly depend on the quality of the printable file itself and the machine used to manufacture it.[39] As put by Elam, '3D printed goods, produced from unauthorized

[35] TMA 1994, s 11(2)(c) (concerning the use of the mark where this is necessary to indicate the intended purposes of the product or services, in particular, as an accessory or a spare part); see also TMA 1994, s 11(2)(b).

[36] Osborn (n 25) 124–5. However, see Elam (n 2) 86 ('[I]f the BMW logo features on the car body panel itself, and, therefore, is incorporated in the CAD file, there can be a question of the trademark used being perceived as a sign indicative of the undertaking of origin. A reasonably well-informed and reasonably observant Internet user might detect with difficulty the origin of the file').

[37] Osborn (n 25) 131.

[38] When it comes to the liability of online platforms hosting infringing content, Regulation 19(a) of the Electronic Commerce Regulations 2002 (SI 2002/2013) provides a 'safe harbour' provision which applies where the website does not have knowledge of unlawful activity or is unaware of the facts from which it would have been apparent (and, upon obtaining information, acts expeditiously to remove it); see also Art 14 of Directive 2000/31; Cases C-236/08–238/08 *Google France v Louis Vuitton* [2010] ECR I–2417 [114]; see also, more generally, D Hong and S Bradshaw, 'Digital Trade Mark Infringement and 3D Printing Implications: What does the Future Hold?' in D Mendis, M Lemley and M Rimmer (eds), *3D Printing and Beyond: Intellectual Property and Regulation* (Cheltenham, Edward Elgar, 2019) 103.

[39] van Wiele (n 2) 317 (noting that the quality of 3D printed goods depends on the quality and integrity of the printable file; the printing settings; and the printing process, including the specific hardware used). For a more detailed analysis of the implications of 3D printing for other functions (beyond origin and quality), see Elam (n 2) 86–87 (arguing that the use of a mark in connection with a printable file to attract more views is not enough to cause detriment to the advertising and investment functions,

CAD files, do not always guarantee quality and safety standards'.[40] There can be significant variations in both hardware capabilities (as most affordable desktop printers are unable to compete with more sophisticated industrial machinery or mass-produced goods when it comes to output quality) and digital design modelling (as some 3D printable files could be based on poor quality designs). Most 'consumer-grade' 3D printers are based on fused filament fabrication technologies which typically leave traces of 'material extrusion', meaning that rough layers and poor finishes can be easily observable with the eye,[41] and there is little doubt that the quality of these products will often be inferior to their mass-produced or 'official' authorised counterpart.[42]

Confusion in the Age of 3D Printing

When it comes to infringement action based on 'confusing similarities', there must also be a likelihood of confusion on the part of consumers.[43] In this context, the similarity between the relevant marks is assessed on the basis of a 'global appreciation' test whereby marks are compared as a whole, paying attention to the dominant and distinctive components of the mark.[44] This assessment (as with other relevant infringement principles) is made through the eyes of the notional average consumer who is well-informed, observant and circumspect.[45] While confusion

given that this does not necessarily prevent the rightsholder from using their mark to effectively inform consumers and gain their loyalty).

[40] Elam (n 2) 86.

[41] van Wiele (n 2) 319.

[42] It is also worth noting that while 3D printing presents new business opportunities and some companies have already released authorised files for a range of printable products (for instance, Nokia has released 3D models allowing users to make their own phone cases), other businesses have been more sceptical. One of the potential explanations for this is the risk of potential reputational damage resulting from the *quality* of these goods. If there is a possibility that users may make a poor quality product bearing a certain mark and subsequently use it in public (which also has relevance for post-sale confusion, a doctrine that we explore further below), it would make little business sense to release such 'DIY' models in the first place. See M Senese, 'Nokia Releases Files for 3-D Printing Your Own Phone Case' (*Wired*, 10 January 2013) at www.wired.com/2013/01/nokia-3d-print-case; see also D Desai and G Magliocca, 'Patents, Meet Napster: 3D Printing and the Digitization of Things (2014) 102 *Georgetown Law Journal* 1713 (arguing that individuals are likely to prefer purchasing a product from a reliable company that guarantees the safety and quality of the files and offers quality customer support, as opposed to printable models issued by an anonymous individual online).

[43] TMA 1994, s 10(2); see also L'Oréal (n 23) [59].

[44] Case C-251/95 *Sabel BV v Puma, Rudolf Dassler Sport* [1997] ECR I-6191, [23–24] (stating that 'the more distinctive the earlier mark, the greater will be the likelihood of confusion'); Case C-39/97 *Canon Kabushiki Kaisha v Metro-Goldwyn-Mayer* [1998] ECR I-5507 [17] (assessing the likelihood of confusion implies some interdependence between the relevant factors, meaning that a lesser degree of similarity between the goods may be offset by a greater degree of similarity between the marks and vice versa).

[45] C-342/97 *Lloyd Schuhfabrik Meyer v Klijsen Handel* [1999] ECR I-3189 [26] (noting that the notional average consumer only rarely has the opportunity to directly compare the different marks and must base this assessment on the imperfect picture of them that they have kept in their mind). The

doctrines have traditionally focused on the origin of goods,[46] these principles have been expanded to include situations where one incorrectly assumes a broader economic connection between the marks.[47]

Confusion is typically assessed at the point of sale. In this regard, 3D printing does not raise any novel or uniquely problematic legal or policy issues. Provided that the other relevant infringement criteria are satisfied, the same general rules and considerations applicable in other circumstances would also apply here. However, courts have extended the scope of the doctrine to also include scenarios where consumers are confused *away* from the point of sale as part of a doctrine known as 'post-sale confusion'.[48] This is precisely where desktop 3D printing has the potential to be especially problematic.

In *Arsenal v Reed*, the defendant sold unofficial Arsenal merchandise with a sign informing customers of the origin of the goods. The Court of Justice recognised that despite the absence of confusion at the point of sale, the mark's essential function may be jeopardised in a post-sale environment given that 'consumers, in particular if they come across the goods after they have been sold … and taken away from the stall where the notice appears, may interpret the sign as designating Arsenal FC as the undertaking of origin'.[49]

To illustrate this further, consider the example of a person who purchases an unauthentic Rolex watch for a fraction of the retail price, with full knowledge of the fact that the item is not genuine. While there is clearly no confusion as to origin at the point of sale, the public may subsequently see it on the wrist of the purchaser and falsely assume that this is a 'real' product sold by Rolex.[50] This could not only harm consumers who have purchased the original (as the perceived value of their products would diminish), but it could also cause economic harm to the proprietor given that this could adversely affect consumers' perception of the mark and thus devalue their brands (especially if the quality of the 'fake' product is visibly inferior).[51]

characteristics of the average consumer vary across sectors. For instance, the purchaser of expensive watches may be more attentive than someone buying bottled water; see, eg, Case C-361/04 *Picasso v OHIM* [2006] ECR I–643, [39]; see also van Wiele (n 2) 322 (discussing who the notional 'average consumer' would be in the context of 3D printing and noting that individuals who are familiar with the technology would be more likely to make different assumptions regarding marks applied to 3D printed objects).

[46] *Comic Enterprises v Twentieth Century Fox Film* [2016] EWCA Civ 41, [2016] FSR (30) 811, [79].

[47] Case C-39/97 *Canon v MGM* [1998] ECR I–55077 [29]–[30].

[48] P O'Byrne and B Allgrove, 'Post-sale Confusion' (2007) 2 *Journal of Intellectual Property Law & Practice* 315; M McKenna, 'A Consumer Decision Making Theory of Trademark Law' (2012) 98 *Virginia Law Rev* 67.

[49] *Arsenal* (n 11) [57] (however, this case concerned a double identity scenario); see also the Opinion of AG Kokott in Case C-412/05 *Alcon v OHIM* [2007] ECR I-3569 [51]; *Picasso* (n 45) [60].

[50] Grace (n 26) 263, 270; A Kozinski, 'Trademarks Unplugged' (1993) 68 *New York University Law Review* 960, 963.

[51] Post-sale confusion can be divided into 'bystander confusion', where a purchaser sees a product in a post-sale environment and makes a negative assessment of it (which may prevent them from purchasing it in the future); and status confusion, where consumers who tend to purchase a product primarily

Why exactly is post-sale confusion problematic in the context of 3D printing? If any individual user with access to a 3D printer is, at least in theory, able to manufacture any item they wish and attach a logo of their choice to it, this may dramatically increase the risk of bystander confusion – that is, confusion among people who see these 3D-printed goods being used in public later. For example, Deven Desai and Gerard Magliocca argue that:

> [In] a world of 3D printers, whatever ground may have supported post-sale confusion is eroded. There will be less, or perhaps no, reason for consumers to think that any popular trade dress observed outside of a store was made by the brand owner. An equally valid conclusion is that products that look similar and are being used by someone else were, in fact, homemade.[52]

Similarly, James Grace argues that given that 3D printing allows users to make their own products bearing a certain mark without any oversight by (or a contractual relationship with) the original rightsholder, this is likely to have a significant impact on how consumers perceive a mark in a post-sale environment.[53] In the long term, the argument goes, if consumers become manufacturers of their own trademarked goods, 'trademarks may cease to function as badges of origin … Consumers may no longer make assumptions about a brand's quality and social status based on casual observations of trademarked products in the post-sale environment'.[54]

The extent to which these risks will actually materialise would, of course, directly depend on the future trajectory of 3D printing and, in particular, the extent to which it becomes more technologically sophisticated and reaches more mainstream adoption.

Printing Famous Marks

The Trade Marks Act offers enhanced protection for marks with a 'reputation'.[55] These doctrines effectively implement a form of dilution, a concept

for its social status may believe that the product is no longer scarce. See Grace (n 26); see also J Sheff, 'Veblen Brands' (2012) 96 *Minnesota Law Review* 769, 773.

[52] Desai and Magliocca (n 42) 1691, 1771 (discussing the issue from the perspective of US law).

[53] Grace (n 26) 265 (arguing that it may gradually become unreasonable for individuals to expect that certain brands maintain any control over the quality of products that display their marks); see also van Wiele (n 2) 318 (arguing that the act of private manufacturing indicates a loss of control over the final product, which can in turn cause reputational damage and loss of customers or revenue).

[54] Grace (n 26) 287. While the doctrine is likely to be critical in the context of printed tangible products, it is likely to have more limited relevance in relation to design files, as these will typically be confined to the user's device; see Osborn (n 25) 133 (arguing that 'a purchaser of a DMF will not use the file in public, and thus third parties cannot be confused by it … If the purchaser chooses to upload the file to a repository, the uploaded file is a separate copy than the purchased copy. Any confusion as to origin of the uploaded copy will be determined by the context of the website, not by the internal contents of the file').

[55] TMA 1994, s 10(3).

originally developed by Frank Shechter that has now been roughly translated into legislation,[56] and operate regardless of whether the essential function of a mark is affected. As explained by Advocate General Jääskinen in the case of *Interflora*:

> [Dilution] relates to the idea that the proper purpose of trade mark law should be to protect the efforts and investments made by the … proprietor and the independent value (good will) of the trade mark. This 'property-based' approach to trade marks differs from the 'deception-based' idea that trade mark law primarily protects the origin function.[57]

For a dilution claim to arise, the relevant mark must be 'known by a significant part of the public'.[58] Among the several conditions that have to be established in these cases, there must be either detriment to the distinctive character or reputation of the earlier mark, or the use in question must take unfair advantage of the said mark.[59] Detriment may include 'blurring' (diminishing the ability of the mark to raise immediate association with the goods) and 'tarnishment' (affecting the mark's power of attraction). Unfair advantage (also known as free-riding), on the other hand, is concerned with exploitation on the coat-tails of the mark.[60] Liability under this doctrine generally arises in scenarios where the image of the mark is likely to transfer to the later mark in a manner that 'unfairly' confers an advantage on it.[61]

The reason why dilution is important when it comes to desktop 3D printing is twofold. First, it is clear that users commonly attach marks belonging to various famous brands to their printed products. Typing 'Gucci' in Thingiverse's search bar instantly generates dozens of different items – including rings, keychains, cups, Xbox controllers and toys – bearing the brand's easily recognisable logo.[62] Given the significant creative freedom that 3D printing technologies enable in terms of product design, it is not difficult to imagine scenarios where proprietors invoke this doctrine on the basis that there has been detriment to the distinctive character of their mark.

Second, while most trade mark infringement scenarios require claimants to demonstrate harm to one of the functions of their mark, the concept of free-riding is primarily concerned with the defendant's benefit instead.[63] Such claims

[56] F Schechter, 'The Rational Basis of Trade Mark Protection' (1927) 40 *Harvard Law Review* 813.

[57] Opinion of AG Jääskinen, Case C-323/09 *Interflora v Marks & Spencer* [2011] ECR I-8625 [50] ('The property-based approach also protects the communication, advertising and investment functions of trade marks with a view of creating a brand with a positive image and independent economic value').

[58] Case *C-375/97 Yplon* [1999] ECR I-5421 [22]–[23].

[59] See *Comic Enterprises* [2016] [107]–[123]; Case C-408/01 *Adidas-Salomon v Fitnessworld* [2003] ECR I-12537; Case C-252/07 *Intel v CPM UK* [2008] *ECR* I-8823.

[60] *L'Oréal* (n 23) [41], [43].

[61] ibid [50] ('[W]here that party seeks by that use to ride on the coat-tails of the mark with a reputation in order to benefit from the power of attraction, the reputation and the prestige of that mark and to exploit, without paying any financial compensation, the marketing effort expended by the proprietor of the mark in order to create and maintain the mark's image').

[62] See www.thingiverse.com/search?q=gucci.

[63] *L'Oréal* (n 23) [41]; see also Bently and others (n 11) 1081.

are therefore likely to be especially valuable to proprietors in cases where they are unable to establish that one of the functions of the mark has been adversely affected. It goes without saying that the lower threshold in this regard could not only dramatically widen liability, but it could also stifle legitimate competition and impinge on free expression in the 3D printing world.[64]

Secondary Liability

In an environment where infringement is highly decentralised (and, therefore, individual acts of infringement are difficult to detect), proprietors could also rely on secondary liability doctrines. There are generally two sources of such liability under UK law.[65] First, there are statutory provisions covering instances where a person (among other things) applies the mark to the packaging, labels or any other means of affixing the mark to the product (or offers for sale such labelling) and there is a risk that these materials could be later applied to goods in an infringing manner.[66] Second, under the principle of joint tortfeasorship, third parties may be held liable where they are actively involved in a 'common design' to infringe.[67] However, this principle requires some active coordination between at least two parties.

Conclusion

Unlike some other IP rights, liability for trade mark infringement would typically only arise where the marks in question are used in the *course of trade* – that is, where there is some commercial benefit involved. Given that 'hobbyists' primarily use the technology for purely private purposes,[68] they are likely to avoid liability

[64] *L'Oreal SA v Bellure NV* [2007] EWCA Civ 968 [27], per Jacob LJ (arguing that free-riding is 'subtly and dangerously emotive: it carries the unwritten message that it ought to be stopped. That is far from being necessarily so. The needs of proper competition and lawful free trade will involve an element at least of 'free riding'); R Burrell and D Gangjee, 'Because You're Worth It: L'Oréal and the Prohibition on Free Riding' (2010) 73 *Modern Law Review* 282; M Senftleben, 'Trade Mark Protection: A Black Hole in the Intellectual Property Galaxy?' (2011) 42 *International Review of Intellectual Property and Competition Law* 383; Osborn (n 25) 138.

[65] See Bently and others (n 11) 1146, citing M Leistner, 'Structural Aspects of Secondary (Provider) Liability in Europe' (2014) 9 *Journal of Intellectual Property Law & Practice* 75; G Dinwoodie (ed), *Secondary Liability of Internet Service Providers* (Cham, Springer, 2017).

[66] For the full text of the provision, see s 10(3B) TMA 1994, transposing Directive (EU) 2015/2436 of the European Parliament and of the Council of 16 December 2015 to approximate the laws of the Member States relating to trade marks (recast) (Text with EEA relevance) OJ L 336, Art 11(a)–(b).

[67] *Unilever plc v Gillette (UK) Ltd* [1989] RPC 583, 589, 596 (joint tortfeasorship could arise either where an individual procures another to infringe by inducement, incitement or persuasion, or where they actively participate in the infringing act: 'joint infringers are two or more persons who act in concert with one another pursuant to a common design in the infringement').

[68] See, eg, the responses in the empirical study in ch 9.

in the vast majority of cases, provided that the use in question is confined to their own personal enjoyment. Once the 'non-commercial' threshold is crossed, proprietors would still generally have to demonstrate that the use in question adversely affects one of the key functions of the mark (for example, liability could arise where the goods and marks are identical and the use in question jeopardises the ability of the mark to guarantee the origin of the goods). As also explored throughout this chapter, since 3D printing is often used to manufacture products bearing the logos of well-known brands, dilution and confusion-based principles are likely to play a key role in this area. Overall, however, there is little evidence to suggest that 3D printing is particularly problematic in the context of trade mark law as far as the application of existing doctrine is concerned.

With regards to the broader policy issues in this area, while some commentators have expressed serious concerns about the impact of decentralised manufacturing on the trade mark system and rightsholders' economic interests more generally, the extent to which these risks are likely to materialise remains to be seen (the reason for this is that, among other things, desktop 3D printing is still a long way from being as technologically sophisticated and widespread as many commentators initially predicted). We will explore this issue in more detail as part of the empirical study in chapter nine.

8

Monopolies, Open Hardware and the Future of Innovation

Introduction

Fritz Machlup, commissioned by the Congress of the United States to evaluate the efficiency of patents in the 1950s, famously concluded that if we did not have a patent system, the evidence would not justify creating one – but since we already had a patent system, the evidence would not justify abolishing it.[1] There was simply not enough evidence at the time to determine whether patents do more harm than good to society (as they confer limited monopolies and thus temporarily restrict competition and public access to innovation).

Fast forward to the twenty-first century, there is now considerably more data on the issue from a range of fields, including economics, business and psychology.[2] However, as Lisa Ouellette puts it, none of these studies confirm 'whether patents have a net positive effect on innovation, much less their net welfare effect'.[3] The relationship between patents and innovation seems to depend greatly on industry, and while patents may be 'worth the cost' in some sectors, such as biomedicine, they would not necessarily survive a cost-benefit assessment in others.[4]

[1] F Machlup, 'An Economic Review of the Patent System' (Study of the Subcommittee on Patents, Committee on Judiciary, US Congress, 85th Congress, 2d sess, Study No 15, 1958), as cited in M Lemley, 'Faith-Based Intellectual Property' (2015) 62 *UCLA Law Review* 1328, 1332 (paraphrased).

[2] Lemley (n 1).

[3] L Ouellette, 'Patent Experimentalism' (2015) 101 *Virginia Law Review* 65; see also Lemley (n 1) 1334, and the sources cited therein.

[4] Lemley (n 1) 1334; J Besen and M Meurer, 'Lessons for Patent Policy From Empirical Research on Patent Litigation' (2005) 9 *Lewis & Clark Law Review* 1. For other critical perspectives on the efficiency of patents more generally, see also M Boldrin and D Levine, 'The Case against Patents' (2013) 27 *Journal of Economic Perspectives* 3, 4 (arguing that there is no empirical evidence that patents increase innovation and that due to political pressures, 'the demand for stronger patent protection comes from old and stagnant industries and firms, not from new and innovative ones'); J Brüggemann and others, 'Intellectual Property Rights Hinder Sequential Innovation: Experimental Evidence' (2016) 45 *Research Policy* 2054, 2054 ('[G]ranting intellectual property rights hinders innovation, especially for sectors characterized by a strong sequentiality in innovation processes'); P Goold, *A Critical Introduction to Intellectual Property Law* (Cambridge, CUP, 2024) 186; see also Thomas Jefferson's famous letter to Isaac McPherson at press-pubs.uchicago.edu/founders/documents/a1_8_8s12.html ('England was, until we copied her, the only country on earth which ever, by a general law, gave a legal right to the exclusive use of an idea … but … other nations have thought that these monopolies produce more embarrassment than advantage to society … [T]he nations which refuse monopolies … are as fruitful').

Why does this matter here? While this book is primarily concerned with the extent to which 3D printing *as a technology* presents a challenge to IP theory and practice (and, indeed, this is what all previous chapters have focused on), the history behind the making of modern 3D printing is itself a fascinating case study that provides valuable insights into the complex relationship between exclusive IP rights, open-source innovation and net social welfare in the digital age. Exploring this issue is also essential to understanding why the existing 3D printing community is based on an exceptionally strong open-source ethos (as further explored in the next chapter).

First, this chapter will outline the foundations of 'open hardware', an innovative licensing model that enables users to disseminate the designs for various tangible items – hardware, devices and machines – in a manner that allows others to easily make, modify and redistribute these models. Second, we will explore the correlation between the expiry of key 3D printing patents and the emergence of an open hardware community which utilised the same technology and made significant advancements in the area, effectively shaping the modern desktop 3D printing sector. Finally, we will situate this discussion within the broader debate on patents and innovation (of course, it goes without saying that I do not aim to provide a general critique of the entire patent system).

The Rise of Open Hardware

Part of the reason why open source came into being is the long reach of IP law.[5] The artificial scarcity introduced through exclusive rights inevitably places restrictions on society's access to large amounts of information.[6] Thus, in the 1980s, a group of software developers – including 'copyleft' pioneers such as Richard Stallman – opposed the idea of proprietary software and founded the free software movement (which later laid the foundations for the broader 'free and open source software' (FOSS) community).[7]

[5] See, eg, H Lipson and M Kurman, *Fabricated: The New World of 3D Printing* (Indianapolis, Wiley, 2013) 235 (argues that open hardware is similar in philosophy to open-source software and that it is 'a response to the limitations of current intellectual property laws').

[6] See L Lessig, *Free Culture* (New York, Penguin Press, 2004) 87–8 ('Today [copyright] includes a large collection of restrictions on the freedom of others: It grants the author the exclusive right to copy, the exclusive right to distribute, the exclusive right to perform, and so on'); see also, more generally, M Lemley, 'IP in a World Without Scarcity' (2015) 90 *New York University Law Review* 460.

[7] The difference between 'free and open-source software' (FOSS) and 'open-source software' is, to a considerable extent, philosophical. FOSS has to comply with four essential freedoms to qualify as 'free' under its original definition: freedom to study, modify, create and distribute the software. See GNU, 'The Free Software Definition' at www.gnu.org/philosophy/free-sw.html; see also L Rosen, *Open Source Licensing: Software Freedom and Intellectual Property Law* (New Jersey, Prentice Hall, 2004) 3; G Coleman, 'Code is Speech: Legal Tinkering, Expertise and Protest Among Free and Open Source Developers' (2009) 24 *Cultural Anthropology* 420, 421; M Maher, 'Open Source Software the Success

In essence, open source is a licensing mechanism that relies on contractual agreements to mitigate the scarcity imposed by IP law and to restore the natural state of abundance of informational content.[8] It makes source code openly available for inspection, modification and redistribution and requires content to be distributed through channels which seek to promote, rather than restrict, access.[9] While critics have called open source 'everything from a virus to socialism',[10] others have praised it for the transparency and collaboration that it facilitates.[11]

Following the success of open-source software, Creative Commons, known for the 'some rights reserved' principle, introduced standardised copyright licences for a wide range of creative works such as text, images, music and videos (and is now also widely used on popular 3D printing file sharing platforms).[12] This is especially important in an age where creativity is increasingly the result of collective effort, despite the fact that areas such as copyright are still largely based on the romantic idea of a sole creative genius.[13]

However, while these licensing mechanisms are already well established, what is less known is that open source principles are increasingly being brought to the

of an Alternative Intellectual Property Incentive Paradigm' (2000) 10 *Fordham Intellectual Property, Media & Entertainment Law Journal* 619.

[8] P de Filippi and P Troxler, 'From Material Scarcity to Artificial Abundance: The Case of FabLabs and 3D Printing Technologies' in B van den Berg, S van der Hof and E Kosta (eds), *3D Printing: Legal, Philosophical and Economic Dimensions* (The Hague, Asser, 2016) 66 (arguing that 'open source practices have managed to 'hack' these [IP] provisions by means of contractual instruments designed to eliminate artificial scarcity so as re-instate the original state of abundance in the information realm'); see also L McDonagh, 'Copyright, Contract and FOSS' in Noam Shemtov and Ian Walden (eds), *Free and Open Source Software* (Oxford, OUP, 2013) 69.

[9] V Vasudeva, 'Open Source Software Paradigm and Intellectual Property Rights' (2012) 17 *Journal of Intellectual Property Rights* 511, 512.

[10] M Boldrin and D Levine, 'Open-Source Software: Who Needs Intellectual Property?' (2007) 57 *The Freeman: Ideas on Liberty* 26, 26.

[11] ibid; see also R Stallman, 'Why Software Should be Free' in A Moore (ed), *Intellectual Property: Moral, Legal, and International Dilemmas* (Lanham, Rowman and Littlefield, 1997); Y Benkler, 'Freedom in the Commons: Towards a Political Economy of Information' (2003) 52 *Duke Law Journal* 1245, 1256 (arguing that open source is the quintessential example of peer production, 'a process by which many individuals, whose actions are coordinated neither by managers nor by price signals in the market, contribute to a joint effort that effectively produces a unit of information'); Y Benkler, 'Coase's Penguin, or, Linux and 'The Nature of the Firm' (2002) 112 *The Yale Law Journal* 369; S Santoso and S Wicker, 'The Future of Three-Dimensional Printing: Intellectual Property or Intellectual Confinement?' (2016) 18 *New Media and Society* 138.

[12] See www.creativecommons.org; M Weinberg, 'What's the Deal with Copyright and 3D Printing?' (*Public Knowledge*, 2013) 20 at www.michaelweinberg.org/docs/WhatstheDealwithCopyright_%20Finalversion2.pdf (arguing that attaching a licence serves both a legal purpose and a cultural one, the latter being 'a signal that the creator wants to include her work in an ever-expanding and evolving network of creativity').

[13] See P de Filippi and P Troxler, 'From Material Scarcity to Artificial Abundance: The Case of FabLabs and 3D Printing Technologies' in B van den Berg, S van der Hof and E Kosta (eds), *3D Printing: Legal, Philosophical and Economic Dimensions* (The Hague, Asser Press, 2016) 71 (argues that while there has been a longstanding emphasis on the idea of a 'sole creator' in the artistic realm (a romantic vision of an author sitting in a secluded studio) and this vision is strongly reflected in how existing laws define and regulate creative output, creative production is increasingly the result of collective effort, as opposed to individual endeavour).

physical world. As defined by the Open-Source Hardware Association (OSHWA), 'Open Source Hardware (OSHW) is a term for tangible artifacts – machines, devices, or other physical things – whose design has been released to the public in such a way that anyone can make, modify, distribute, and use those things'.[14] Like other open-source models, open-source hardware (or open hardware) is based on the collaborative work of many. The model allows users to attach open-source licences to various digital files containing technical drawings, schematics and computer code.[15] By doing so, users can contribute to the design and innovation process and easily share improvements back with the community. Strong advocates of open hardware, such as Alicia Gibb of the Open-Source Hardware Association, have even argued that:

> [Open] hardware is the 21st patent system … The benefit is that you have an entire community contributing to your designs, innovating, and sharing their derivatives to your product. It pushes the original designer to create a better product and continue to improve it rather than lock it in a 20-year stalemate. Open source hardware pushes innovation further and faster …[16]

Open hardware licences have been adopted by major research organisations and companies, including CERN, Arduino and Adafruit.[17] They have already been used to make a remarkably wide range of products, including mechanical components for medical devices, audio equipment and micro-computing devices.[18] However, these licences are not yet as mature as their software counterparts, and the range of available open hardware licences is significantly more limited. Their implementation is also more complex, as this involves hardware, documentation, software and branding, all of which may be covered by different IP rights.[19]

[14] As per the Open-Source Hardware Association's (OSHWA) definition of 'open-source hardware'; see www.oshwa.org/definition.

[15] ibid; see also Lipson and Kurman (n 5) 235 (notes that just like with software licences, open hardware licences grant individuals permission to use and modify another inventor's design).

[16] P Torrone (reporting), 'MAKE's Exclusive Interview with Alicia Gibb – President of the Open Source Hardware Association' (*Makezine*, 23 April 2012) at www.makezine.com/2012/04/23/makes-exclusive-interview-with-alicia-gibb-president-of-the-open-source-hardware-association.

[17] See CERN (European Organization for Nuclear Research), 'Open source for open science' www.home.cern/science/computing/open-source-open-science.

[18] See J Bonvoisin and others, 'What is the 'Source' of Open Source Hardware?' (2017) 1 *Journal of Open Hardware* 1; see also M Weinberg, 'Open hardware for musicians and music lovers' (13 July 2019) at www.michaelweinberg.org/blog/2019/07/13/open-hardware-musicians; S Chiu and others, 'Robotics-assisted Mass Spectrometry Assay Platform Enabled by Open-source Electronics' (2015) 64 *Biosensors and Bioelectronics* 260; C Anderson, *Makers: The New Industrial Revolution* (London, Random House Business, 2012) 107 ('Every day, we see more and more examples of open-hardware business models working brilliantly. The MakerBot 3-D printer is open hardware, as is the RepRap on which it is built. So is Arduino, and the hundreds of products from companies such as Adafruit, Seeed Studio and Sparkfun').

[19] Lipson and Kurman (n 5) 235 (notes that as the movement develops further, the types of available licences is likely to expand accordingly).

Moreover, open hardware may not work for all types of items. It generally works well for relatively complex products (like electronics) where the original creator's expertise is still needed after the source is made available.[20]

Despite these limitations, this model has already played a key role in developing cutting-edge technologies such as modern desktop 3D printing, an issue that we will now focus on.

Patents, Open Source and the Making of Modern 3D Printing

Most modern desktop 3D printers are based on fused filament fabrication,[21] a type of additive manufacturing technology originally developed in the late 1980s and marketed as 'fused deposition modelling' by Stratasys, one of the 'Big Two' in the industry.[22] However, for decades, the technology remained prohibitively expensive and confined to industrial use. While a 3D printer can be purchased for a few hundred US dollars today, it would have cost tens of thousands two decades ago.[23] What took so long to democratise access to 3D printing?

Commentators argue that '[despite] the fact that AM has existed for over 30 years the spread of the technology has been limited due to the initial patents which only more recently have expired'.[24] While correlation does not equate to causation,

[20] ibid 236.

[21] See S Bradshaw and others, 'The Intellectual Property Implications of Low-Cost 3D Printing' (2010) 7(1) *SCRIPT-ed* 1, 8; see also I Gibson, 'The Changing Face of Additive Manufacturing' (2017) 28 *Journal of Manufacturing Technology Management* 10.

[22] A Daly, *Socio-Legal Aspects of the 3D Printing Revolution* (London, Palgrave Macmillan, 2016) 5.

[23] J West and G Kuk, 'The Complementarity of Openness: How MakerBot Leveraged Thingiverse in 3D Printing' (2016) 102 *Technological Forecasting and Social Change* 169, 172 ('The first 20 years were limited to industrial and commercial vendors, who used patented technology to sell … units every year at prices exceeding $100,000').

[24] H Steenhuis and L Pretorius, 'The Additive Manufacturing Innovation: A Range of Implications' (2017) 28(1) *Journal of Manufacturing Technology Management* 122, 137 (AM refers to 'additive manufacturing'); see also S Bechtold, '3D Printing, Intellectual Property and Innovation Policy' (2016) 47 *International Review of Intellectual Property and Competition Law* 517, 532; World Intellectual Property Organization, 'Breakthrough Innovation and Economic Growth' (2015) 105 ('Expiry of these patents may be one of the reasons why the personal 3D printing market took off') at www.wipo.int/edocs/pubdocs/en/wipo_pub_944_2015.pdf; Santoso and Wicker (n 11) 139 ('Critics asserted that 3D printing technology could have reached its current stage more quickly if it had not been for the series of patents filed in the late 1980s and early 1990s, which placed significant limitations on who had access to the technology'); A Scardamaglia, 'Flashpoints in 3D Printing and Trade Mark Law' (2015) 23 *Journal of Law, Information and Science* 34–5 ('[E]specially as the equipment becomes more affordable and the print quality increases, coinciding with the expiry of several early key 3D print patents'), citing US Patent 4,575,330; US Patent 4,863,538; US Patent 5,121,329 and US Patent 5,204,055; T Birtchnell and others, '3D Printing and Intellectual Property Futures' (UK Intellectual Property Office 2018/03) 62 ('The expiry of patents was also widely pointed to as an important event for the dissemination of 3D printing in many countries') at www.assets.publishing.service.gov.uk/government/uploads/system/uploads/attachment_data /file/757767/3D-printing.pdf; Wohlers Associates, 'Wohlers Report 2014: 3D Printing and Additive Manufacturing State of the Industry' (2014) 14 at www.wohlersassociates.

there appears to be a strong link between the expiry of key fused filament fabrication patents and the emergence of an open hardware 3D printing community which utilised the same technology. It built on the existing technology by relying on open source principles and not only made significant improvements in terms of quality, but also dramatically reduced hardware costs. As observed by Stefan Bechtold:

> Open source implementations of fused deposition modeling only appeared after related key patents had expired. Prices for 3D printers based on fused deposition modeling dropped tremendously thereafter … Once the relevant patents had expired, the threat of injunctive relief against open source 3D printers vanished.[25]

Of prime importance here is RepRap, a pioneering open hardware project founded by Adrian Bowyer at Bath University. The project relied on a small number of core contributors and large community support consisting of hardware enthusiasts, hackers and academic researchers.[26] RepRap created a self-replicating 3D printer based on fused filament fabrication with 'an unusual business strategy in mind: its users should never, ever have to buy another RepRap again'.[27] Essentially, the idea was that each 3D printer should be able to fabricate all of its own replacement parts.

RepRap disseminated all of its hardware designs under open-source principles (by primarily relying on the GNU's General Public License), allowing users to modify the designs and improve the existing hardware, as long as they shared the derivatives back with the community.[28] RepRap thus effectively extended its hardware research and development to a virtually infinite pool of participants around the world wishing to contribute. Interestingly, Rod Lipson and Melba Kurman claim that Bowyer intentionally did not seek patents on RepRap's technologies (quoting Bowyer himself):

> Patents do inhibit development – it's unquestionably the case … It's in the nature of patents that they give a monopoly to whoever holds them for 20 years … James Watt patented various vital aspects of the steam engine. Yet, you look at steam engine development and nothing happened for 20 years during the life of Watt's patent. When that patent lapsed, there was a great flaring of steam engine innovation and then the industrial revolution.[29]

com/2014report.htm; E Greenbaum, 'Three-dimensional Printing and Open-source Hardware' (2013) 2 *NYU Journal of IP and Entertainment Law* (2013) 257, 271.

[25] Bechtold (n 24) 532–3 (arguing that although it is difficult to demonstrate that the expiry of key patents caused the emergence of the open-source 3D printing community, anecdotal evidence indicates that there is indeed such a causal link).

[26] Bechtold (n 24) 524; see also www.reprap.org. It should be noted that some of the key relevant patents were still in force when the project started.

[27] Lipson and Kurman (n 5) 232.

[28] Bradshaw and others (n 21) 9.

[29] Lipson and Kurman (n 5) 231–2 (quoting Adrian Bowyer).

Crucially, there appears to be a scholarly consensus that this 'transparent, open-source approach is one of the main reasons why 3D printing has thrived in the last several years',[30] and that RepRap's reliance on open collaboration, community norms and user involvement helped to make 3D printing significantly more sophisticated and accessible. The project effectively helped to lay the foundations of the modern desktop 3D printing sector – in fact, most leading hardware companies in the early 3D printing scene, such as MakerBot, started as RepRap spin-offs.[31] As also observed by Joel West and George Kuk:

> The consumer market was created and grew explosively after 2005 in response to three factors: the "maker" movement of do-it-yourself hobbyists, the formation of the RepRap open hardware community, and the entry of dozens of startup firms selling low-priced printers … after the 2006 expiration of a key industrial patent.[32]

It goes without saying that all of these developments may not have been possible without the early patents and advancements in the industrial sector (as, in theory, the technology may not have even been invented without the lure of exclusive rights).[33] Yet, it does appear that the long reach of IP is at least partially responsible for holding up innovation and keeping the technology outside the reach of individual users for decades.

Can 3D Printing Remain 'Open'?

Despite its success, open-source 3D printing is not without its criticisms. In particular, some commentators have raised concerns that it may be difficult to stay competitive as a business if you rely on an open hardware strategy. For instance, MakerBot – one of the first manufacturers of desktop 3D printers – based its original hardware on RepRap's open-source technology and repeatedly praised this model in its early days. It argued that they have seen substantial participation in research and development by their community, knowing that if users improve a certain aspect of the technology, this will be freely shared and everyone in the community will benefit.[34] It even criticised other companies that took open

[30] Santoso and Wicker (n 11) 151 ('The development of 3D printing technology and the rapid growth of a large, passionate, and dedicated user base has been due to the vast amounts of easily accessible information online about everything from building a 3D printer from scratch, modifying and customizing existing 3D printers to object designs').

[31] See J Moilanen and others, 'Cultures of Sharing in 3D Printing: What Can We Learn from the Licence Choices of Thingiverse Users?' (2015) 6 *Journal of Peer Production* 1.

[32] West and Kuk (n 23) 172 (notes that in 2013 alone, individuals bought more personal 3D printers than were purchased by industrial buyers in the first 25 years and that just like with any other technology that has shifted from industrial to consumer use, this can be linked to making the technology more affordable and easier to use); see also Santoso and Wicker (n 11) 138, 151.

[33] Bechtold (n 24) 534.

[34] A Zaleski, 'The 3D Printing Revolution That Wasn't' (*Wired*, 1 December 2016) at www.wired.com/2016/12/the-3d-printing-revolution-that-wasnt (citing Bre Pettis, co-founder of MakerBot:

designs and subsequently 'closed' their model, arguing that this brought innovation to a dead end and breached ethical norms.[35] As put by Chris Anderson:

> Practically everything about the MakerBot was either developed by a community or given to one to do with as they please. It is a shining example of how abandoning intellectual property protection can actually grant even more protection in the form of community support and goodwill.[36]

However, MakerBot changed business strategies and abandoned its open-source model in 2012, arguing that this was necessary to make the technology more widely accessible.[37] Open-source 3D printers at the time were primarily sold as kits, rather than complete units, aimed at DIY hobbyists who had the passion, time and higher ease of use tolerance to build their own hardware.[38] By designing a proprietary machine that comes fully assembled and ready to use, the company aimed to make the technology more user-friendly.[39]

Crucially, it also expressed concerns about 'cloning' by competitors who offered direct copies of their open-source printers for a fraction of the price. It argued that while claiming patents was not optimal, it was an essential part of 'being a competitive company':[40]

> [We] will not share the way the physical machine is designed or our GUI because we don't think carbon-copy cloning is acceptable and carbon-copy clones undermine our ability to pay people to do development.[41]

Now, more than a decade later, there are several successful open-source 3D printing companies that continue to innovate in this field, including Prusa, Ultimaker and LulzBot. While some of them have raised similar concerns to MakerBot (in particular, about competitors who 'clone' hardware without contributing back to the community; a general lack of attribution and acknowledgment; and

'Because we're open source and the community is so smart, we've seen a lot of participation in the research and development sector … our users know that the code and designs are theirs to hack on. They also know that if they improve their machine, they can share their improvement and everyone in the community benefits').

[35] West and Kuk (n 23) 174, citing Bre Pettis (arguing that where a company makes a derivative of an open-source project and goes to the market without sharing the derivatives back with the community, they are hindering innovation and that this goes against what open-source hardware stands for).

[36] Anderson (n 18) 94.

[37] See also Moilanen and others (n 31) 5 (arguing that MakerBot's newly adopted business strategy does not ideologically align with the licensing model they encourage users to adhere to on Thingiverse, MakerBot's own design sharing platform).

[38] Rough and messy DIY kits are generally not as attractive to *consumers* who may not have the time or knowledge to build their own machines. In contrast, early adopters tend to have a higher ease of use tolerance.

[39] West and Kuk (n 23).

[40] Moilanen and others (n 31) 4, citing Bre Pettis, co-founder of MakerBot (this statement appears to be a reference to TangiBot, a direct copy of MakerBot's hardware manufactured in China and sold for a third of the price of MakerBot's original model).

[41] ibid.

the inadequacy of existing licences in the context of hardware designs)[42] and it remains to be seen whether they will remain 'open' in the long term, it appears that the existing community is based on an exceptionally strong open source ethos – an issue that we will explore further as part of the empirical study in chapter nine.

Conclusion

Although correlation does not equate to causation, anecdotal evidence points to a strong link between the expiry of key patents and the emergence of an open-source hardware community, which – following decades of limited follow-on innovation – utilised the existing 3D printing technology and not only dramatically increased its quality, but also reduced hardware costs by orders of magnitude. It effectively brought a once prohibitively expensive technology that was strictly confined to industrial and business use to the homes of individual users. In this sense, the recent surge of 3D printing was not caused by the invention of a radically new and advanced technology, but rather by *existing* technology being 'freed' from IP law.

While there is little doubt that patents may often hold up valuable follow-on innovation, were they 'worth the cost' here, as far as net social welfare is concerned? I will let the reader decide. What is beyond doubt is that the innovative open hardware model is one of the prime reasons why the desktop 3D printing sector exists. This collaborative model is also likely to play an increasingly important role in advancing future digital innovation.

[42] J Prusa, 'The state of open-source in 3D printing in 2023' (*Prusa Research*, 29 March 2023) at www.blog.prusa3d.com/the-state-of-open-source-in-3d-printing-in-2023_76659. For some of the responses to Prusa's statements, see M Weinberg, 'A(nother) Reply to Josef Průša' (*Michael Weinberg*, 5 April 2023) at https://michaelweinberg.org/blog/2023/04/05/prusa-response.

9

Insights from the 'Real World'

Introduction

In order to further gauge the extent to which 3D printing presents a challenge to the IP framework and to gain a better understanding of the existing 3D printing community – including its values, practices and relationship with the law – I conducted a comprehensive empirical study over a period of several months in 2019. The study consists of two streams of data collection, including interviews (carried out in New York and online) and a large qualitative survey, featuring a total of 171 participants from a diverse range of backgrounds.[1]

The study aimed to shed light on a range of pertinent issues, including the types of products that users most commonly make through 3D printing (which was also essential to understand what IP rights are most likely to be affected in this context); the extent to which IP plays a role in practice (including individual users' concerns, experiences and exposure to infringement or litigation); their views on possible regulatory measures, as well as potential approaches to tackling piracy online; and, finally, the future trajectory of the 'consumer' 3D printing sector (which was essential to assess the urgency and need for law reform).

This chapter will present the findings of the study in a thematically structured manner, drawing attention to commonly recurring patterns, themes and perspectives. I will compare and contrast the results of the two streams of data collection before finally contextually analysing the overall significance of the findings at the end of the chapter. The results will be presented in a primarily descriptive manner, allowing the reader to see as much of the 'raw data' as possible.[2] The most illustrative, compelling and vivid excerpts have been selected as evidence of what participants directly observed.

[1] For more details regarding the methodology, sample, questions and the rationales for carrying out the empirical study, see ch 1 and the Annex. The study included a total of 10 interviews and 161 surveys.

[2] Minor amendments to punctuation and style have been made to aid clarity and readability.

The 3D Printing Scene

Participants were first given the opportunity to explain what they do in their own words and, where applicable, the types of products they typically 3D print.

As *interviewees* came from a diverse range of backgrounds, it was not surprising to see that they used the technology for a remarkably wide range of purposes.[3] When it comes to professionals, for example, one participant (an engineer at a large 3D printing service that manufactures custom products on behalf of customers) stated that their company prints 'literally anything, from toys to car parts and even prosthetics'.[4] Another interviewee (a PR director at a smaller 3D printing service) explained that they make industrial parts and bespoke items on behalf of architects, interior designers and other clients.[5] One professional (the chairperson of a global 3D printing retailer) stated that their company sells hardware and also runs a large 3D printing file-sharing repository, aiming 'to bring the power of 3D printing to everyone'.[6] Some professionals worked within more 'niche' markets. For instance, this included offering a 3D scanning service that captures the likeness of an object or person,[7] and 3D printing bespoke objects using exotic materials such as bamboo and cork.[8]

In contrast with professionals, 'hobbyist' interviewees used the technology to make various aesthetic and functional products at home, typically for purely personal use (or as gifts for others). For example, one user explained that they most commonly print figures for roleplaying games, such as Dungeons and Dragons, and repair parts for fixing broken things at home.[9] Another hobbyist stated that they generally print items from popular culture, such as Marvel action figures, either for themselves or as gifts for friends and family.[10] There is indeed a lucrative market for such products that could potentially be disrupted by 3D printing (and items of this nature are often protected by various IP rights, including trade marks and copyright).

What about the *surveys*? The responses once again demonstrated the versatility of the technology. It was clear that 3D printing is commonly used to produce a remarkably wide range of products at home, including both functional items (such as replacement parts for household appliances, fixtures and tools) and various aesthetic objects (including figurines, models of fictional characters, busts and vases). Specific examples included 'Legos, D&D minis, dice tower',[11] 'tool holders',[12]

[3] Anon interviewee 1 is a legal practitioner; interviewee 2 is a 3D scanning expert; interviewee 3 is a 3D printing engineer; interviewee 4 is the chairperson of a global retailer; interviewee 5 is director of PR at a 3D printing intermediary service; interviewee 6 is a hobbyist *and* professional; interviewee 7 is a hobbyist; interviewee 8 is a hobbyist; interviewee 9 is a professional working at an SME; interviewee 10 is a hobbyist.

[4] Interviewee 3.

[5] Interviewee 5.

[6] Interviewee 4.

[7] Interviewee 2.

[8] Interviewee 9.

[9] Interviewee 7.

[10] Interviewee 10.

[11] Survey respondent 113.

[12] Survey respondent 87.

'hinges for a washing machine, toys, art ... cake molds for a local bakery',[13] 'figures of popular culture characters',[14] 'shower hooks'[15] and 'toys or puzzles but also ... parts to fix things such as a cooler'.[16]

When it comes to professional applications, survey participants commonly used 3D printing as part of various medical and engineering projects at work. Specific examples included 'medical models',[17] a prosthetic foot,[18] and 'whatever my customers want, which can be anything from keychains to prototypes to functional industrial parts'.[19]

Several survey participants reported that they 3D print both at home *and* at work, although this typically involved rather different types of products (which could be explained by the fact that professionals typically have access to more expensive and sophisticated industrial 3D printers). For example, one respondent stated that they print 'components for [their] work as a roboticist' in professional settings, while at home they tend to print items such as toys and 'characters from TV shows'.[20]

Finally, it was also evident that 3D printing is increasingly being used in educational settings, which is consistent with recent trends reported in the academic literature.[21] For example, one survey participant explained that 'as the President of the Makerspace at the University of Wisconsin-Platteville, they help many people in the University and around the community to 3D print, and provide a service to those who are not as well versed in the craft'.[22]

What's So Special About 3D Printing?

Beyond participants' general background, it was also important to gain a more nuanced understanding of their motivation for using the technology – for example, why they choose to create their own products through 3D printing as opposed to purchasing mass-produced goods. This also provided valuable information about the viability of potential business models in this area, an issue that we will explore in more detail later in the study.

Interviewees generally listed a combination of different factors for using the technology, including customisation, precision, costs, efficient prototyping, the

[13] Survey respondent 77.
[14] Survey respondent 22.
[15] Survey respondent 9.
[16] Survey respondent 20.
[17] Survey respondent 134.
[18] Survey respondent 38.
[19] Survey respondent 70 (the respondent was the owner of a small print and design company).
[20] Survey respondent 119.
[21] See, eg, H Steenhuis and L Pretorius, 'The Additive Manufacturing Innovation: A Range of Implications' (2017) 28 *Journal of Manufacturing Technology Management* 122, 131 ('35 percent of engineering jobs now require additive manufacturing skills ... and this is already influencing the educational process. High schools in the USA are increasingly acquiring 3D printers to enhance their curriculum').
[22] Survey respondent 14.

ability to print 'complex geometries' or items that are not on the market, and the 'novelty' of 3D printing itself. Unsurprisingly, the justifications provided by participants typically depended on whether the technology was used professionally or at home. For example, some professionals argued that 3D printing 'improves turnaround time greatly and allows for a huge variety of outputs'.[23] Another professional explained that in their particular field (ceramics), 3D printing 'offers a very different way to make things'.[24] In contrast, hobbyist interviewees more commonly argued that they valued the ability to make their own personalised products and that 3D printing offers them a very cost-efficient method of doing so – for example, one user stated that they had recently printed a Deadpool action figure for a fraction of the retail price.[25] For others, it was personal enjoyment and curiosity. As stated by one hobbyist interviewee, 'It is not even about the part itself but it is mostly a sense of wonder and how this works, which got me into the whole thing'.[26]

When it comes to the *surveys*, participants commonly noted the ability to easily transform a digital model into a tangible item as a key reason for using 3D printing – in the words of one respondent, the technology allows them 'to dump new ideas directly from thought into a real product'.[27] As also put by another user:

> You can model and print anything you can imagine. You can create a one-off that no one else will ever want, but you need. It is a tiny factory in your own home.[28]

It was indeed evident that users especially valued the ability to have a say in the design and production process, without being reliant on a specific manufacturer to make products for them:

> Giving regular people access to precision manufacturing levels the playing field for developing products and solutions.[29]

Several survey respondents explained that 'nobody sells what they print, whether it be odd connectors, specialty items or weird trinkets'.[30] In the words of one participant:

> The ability to make something completely custom is a big draw. For example, I recently made a bracket for a product that has not been manufactured since the late 1980s.[31]

In line with the interviews, cost efficiency often played an important role for many survey participants. In many instances, users reported being able to create an item

[23] Interviewee 2.
[24] Interviewee 5.
[25] Interviewee 10.
[26] Interviewee 7.
[27] Survey respondent 45. Survey respondent 106 similarly stated: '3D printing allows me to take my ideas and make them tangible objects'.
[28] Survey respondent 89.
[29] Survey respondent 13.
[30] Survey respondent 17.
[31] Survey respondent 60.

for a fraction of what it would otherwise cost (if they were to purchase the same mass-produced equivalent):

> One example was a plastic gear for my car's AC unit that was stripped. Reverse engineer and print a $2 gear or buy a $250 new AC motor. Easy choice, in my opinion.[32]

As explained by another participant, 'I like the idea of being able to create something that I can have ready when I need it. Also, some parts are more expensive … A glucose pump holder is $40. I can print one for pennies'.[33]

Other commonly cited factors included 'convenience' and the ability to obtain a certain product quickly: 'Why drive to the store and buy a wall hanger or yarn needle if it takes less time to print one?'[34] As similarly put by another participant:

> I think I print my own things because I can do it quickly. When I'm printing parts for myself, I can quickly change the designs to suit me or to navigate around problems I didn't anticipate.[35]

There was an element of 'personal enjoyment' that several survey respondents linked to the ability to make their own things: 'I love the whole process. Watching something being built from the ground up right in front of you is mesmerising'.[36] As also put by another user:

> It's far … more satisfying for the things I make for myself, and prints make excellent novelty gifts, as they're custom, made at home, and somewhat unique.[37]

Finally, one participant argued that 'there is a sense of satisfaction or accomplishment in having made something without much real effort'.[38] This is reminiscent of the so-called 'IKEA effect', originally coined in the psychology literature, whereby consumers exhibit a cognitive bias and tend to place disproportionately high value on things they have made themselves.[39]

Intellectual Property is not a Marginal Issue

Is IP law a concern among the community? To what extent have users been exposed to issues involving IP enforcement or litigation? While there is already some existing (primarily quantitative) data on these issues, it was also important to

[32] Survey respondent 106.
[33] Survey respondent 76.
[34] Survey respondent 16.
[35] Survey respondent 133.
[36] Survey respondent 29.
[37] Survey respondent 34.
[38] Survey respondent 103.
[39] M Norton, D Mochon and D Airley, 'The IKEA Effect: When Labor Leads to Love' (2011) 22 *Journal of Consumer Psychology* 453; see also R Landers, 'Unfolding the IKEA Effect: Why We Love the Things We Build' (2012) 22 *Journal of Consumer Psychology* 453.

obtain more nuanced qualitative insights into the experiences and views of users and professionals involved in the 3D printing community.[40]

First, intellectual property law was clearly a concern among at least some *interviewees*. For example, one participant argued that 'it is a Wild West once someone with some CAD knowledge sees an STL'.[41] The same interviewee explained that they had recently shared a 3D model of a herb grinder online, following which others tried to claim it as their own and attempted to apply for a patent in relation to it:

> This went a little viral a while ago. I've since had to submit complaints and objections to the US Patents and Trademarks Office (USPTO) … and prevent other people from trying to patent the concept as their own.

They sought advice from patent attorneys and managed to successfully challenge the application on the basis that the grinder was based on old milling plates and the item was not patentable in the first place.

Another hobbyist interviewee stated that, as a 'layman', they find the scope and application of IP rights confusing. For example, they had recently designed a functional 3D model but found it difficult to determine whether this is likely to be protected by any IP rights.[42]

Within the professional space, it was also evident that some participants were particularly mindful of the risk of potential IP infringement. As put by one such interviewee (a 3D scanning expert working at a small business):

> We are aware and really strive to make sure that this trust [between us and our clients] is maintained. Within our industry, this is an easy way for you to hurt yourself. It wouldn't be ethical to recreate someone's exact piece of art and sell it. Anything like that would apply to the digital space as well, so we treat it the same way.[43]

Another professional, working at an intermediary 3D printing service (a business that prints on behalf of customers), explained that although they have not directly dealt with any issues involving IP enforcement or litigation so far, they have previously refused to process orders where it was clear that the model that the client had requested was subject to IP protection, or that it was being used without authorisation.[44]

[40] See D Mendis and D Secchi, 'A Legal and Empirical Study of 3D Printing Online Platforms and an Analysis of User Behaviour' (UK Intellectual Property Office, 2015/41, 2015) 41 ('As 3D printing continues to grow, there is also evidence of intellectual property infringement, albeit on a small scale, on these online platforms. For example, trademarked or copyrighted designs, like an Iron Man helmet or figurines from Games Workshop, Star Wars and the videogame Doom or Disney figures are easy to locate').

[41] Interviewee 9.

[42] Interviewee 8.

[43] Interviewee 2.

[44] Interviewee 5.

Some hobbyist interviewees argued that they do not see IP as a concern, especially as they use 3D printing for purely private purposes (though we should note such use could still, in principle, infringe various IP rights).[45] In the words of one such interviewee:

> If I would print Deadpools and sell them on eBay I would not [be surprised] to get a mail from Marvel.[46]

Moreover, when I asked one of the interviewees – a legal practitioner with substantial experience in this field – whether, based on their observations, rightsholders appear to be concerned about 3D printing at present, they noted that:

> IP owners are much more worried about the platform-based infringement because the goods that come out of those places are much closer to substitutes for existing goods. The stuff that's coming out of desktop 3D printers … They are less concerned about it.[47]

The reason for this is that intermediary services and 3D printing marketplaces typically have access to more sophisticated industrial-grade machinery and are thus able to offer significantly higher output quality. When I pressed for more details and asked the same interviewee about their observations on the adequacy of the existing IP framework more broadly, and whether law reform is likely to be necessary in the future, they stated that:

> The kinds of questions that 3D printing poses at this point don't fundamentally challenge the tenets of IP law. It raises issues that have been dormant and rebalances focus but not in the way that it breaks the entire system … There are many challenges to the IP system right now and 3D printing is one of them, but 3D printing is not uniquely problematic.

What about the *survey respondents*? The response was clearly mixed. Nearly half of the participants stated that they do not see IP law as a concern at all (the remaining participants noted that it is a concern at least to a limited extent).[48] For example, in line with the interviews, several participants argued that they do not regard IP as an issue as they exclusively use 3D printing for purely private purposes:

> No, because everything I do is not for profit and is merely to help people.[49]
>
> So far, everything I have printed is for my personal use at home.[50]

Interestingly, among those who stated that they do not see IP as a concern, one survey respondent simply argued that 'copyright holders do not see 3D printing as a major threat to their IP'.[51] While they did not provide further details,

[45] See, more generally, chs 5 to 7.
[46] Interviewee 10.
[47] Interviewee 1.
[48] Only a small minority described IP law as a major concern.
[49] Survey respondent 76.
[50] Survey respondent 149.
[51] Survey respondent 11.

it could be assumed that this is due to the current technological capabilities of desktop 3D printing and the fact that the technology has not reached more mainstream adoption.

In contrast, some participants argued that they 'take extreme cautions on IP'.[52] One user stated that they 'respect licenses and always ask creators before doing anything commercial'.[53]

Perhaps unsurprisingly, respondents commonly drew a distinction between, on the one hand, the types of products that they 3D print at home for personal use and, on the other, the 3D models that they post online – precisely because of the risk of potential infringement:

> I generally do not share designs to someone else's enforceable IP. I'll make upgrade parts for board games that I don't own IP rights to … If I make a puzzle based on a puzzle I saw in the real world, I wouldn't post it.[54]

Among survey participants who expressed concerns about IP, the risk of appropriation was by far the most commonly cited issue. For example, one respondent argued that they are concerned that 'others may take their designs for profit with no legal recourse to prevent it'.[55]

In fact, some survey participants reported that they had already been directly exposed to issues involving infringement and enforcement, particularly where their 3D models were used without permission or in a manner not permitted by the licence (however, they did not always specify the nature of the items in question, so it was difficult to determine what IP rights were affected or, indeed, whether these items were subject to protection in the first place). As noted by one such participant:

> Commercial use of my models when it is not permitted by license. I simply don't share models that I am not willing to lose.[56]

Similarly, another respondent stated that although they generally share their models under a non-commercial use licence, they 'have seen them resold in other countries'.[57] In such instances, it was evident that users often relied on takedown requests or similar measures to request the removal of infringing copies:

> People will sell my designs, especially the Google Home Hub hanger, on Pinterest or eBay without attributing me. In one case, I had to start a DMCA takedown request.[58]

[52] Survey respondent 76.
[53] Survey respondent 70.
[54] Survey respondent 89.
[55] Survey respondent 123.
[56] Survey respondent 64.
[57] Survey respondent 93.
[58] Survey respondent 45. Survey respondent 82 similarly stated: 'I have had people claim my designs as their own. Instagram was quick to act on these matters … But I do feel IP enforcement will become an issue on file sharing websites as I feel these are not adequately regulated.' The Digital Millennium Copyright Act (DMCA) is a US copyright statute which allows rightsholders to request the removal of infringing content from websites.

Interestingly, some users chose not to take action where others used their models without permission, or without respecting the licence (though they did not explain why):

> I have had (and currently have) some of my non-commercial models sold. Never done anything about it though.[59]

In some cases, users were aware that their own actions (for instance, uploading a file online) may infringe certain IP rights, but proceeded to do so anyway:

> I share some 3D models of video games, the design is not mine, but I share it under my name and using a Creative Commons license. Blizzard could just delete my uploads if they wanted to because they are the original model owners.[60]

Several survey participants stated that while they have not dealt with any IP issues firsthand, they have seen others' models being used without authorisation, or content being removed from websites due to alleged IP violations. As put by one respondent, 'I have lost access to content I had used previously due to IP enforcement of others.'[61] Others stated that they have observed instances of 'litigious threats and deletions on various sites',[62] 'people who have received cease-and-desist letters for selling IP protected items',[63] and users seeking legal advice online.[64]

Finally, some participants raised concerns about companies 'shutting down' files without offering an authorised 3D model that they could use to make their own prints:

> It's only a concern because of a desire to print items from popular culture. Many companies shut down IP files but don't even offer a commercial alternative.[65]

This can be illustrated with Lego's recent takedown orders, where the company reportedly asked several websites to remove files that allegedly contained unauthorised versions of their models.[66] While Lego described the use of 3D printing to make Lego-like products as 'exciting and innovative', it dismissed the possibility of integrating the technology within their production methods for the time being, given that – in their own words – it cannot yet match their 'extraordinarily rigorous safety and quality requirements'.[67]

[59] Survey respondent 49.
[60] Survey respondent 137.
[61] Survey respondent 26.
[62] Survey respondent 44.
[63] Survey respondent 136.
[64] Survey respondent 118.
[65] Survey respondent 71.
[66] A Lalani, 'Lego Targeting Maker Community's 3D Models with Infringement Notices' (*All3DP*, 2 October 2019) www.all3dp.com/4/lego-targeting-maker-communitys-3d-models-with-infringement-notices; see also M Weinberg, 'Lego's IP Grab Bag' (19 October 2019) at www.michaelweinberg.org/blog/2019/10/10/lego-ip-grab-bag (the letter reportedly stated: 'LEGO … hold[s] exclusive worldwide rights to the LEGO® intellectual property, including but not limited to the famous LEGO word mark, the famous red-square LEGO logo and the Minifigure figurine').
[67] Lalani (n 66) ('3D printing is not a viable alternative to the injection molding we currently use to make the Lego bricks you find in stores').

'You Wouldn't Download a Car. Yes, I Would!'

As a particularly contentious issue identified by commentators in the academic literature – and an aspect that is critical in the context of *desktop* 3D printing – participants were also asked about their views on the non-commercial use exemption in patent law (present in several major jurisdictions, including the UK).[68] The application of the provision was illustrated with the act of 3D printing a patented invention at home (for instance, Lego bricks were formerly patented, and items of this nature are commonly shared on 3D printing platforms).[69]

Most *interviewees* were firmly in favour of maintaining the exception, regardless of whether they were hobbyists or professionals. For example, one participant pointed out that even if there was no such exception in place, the decentralised nature of 3D printing would make it exceptionally difficult to effectively monitor and take action against such private reproductions.[70] When it comes to the question of potential reform in this area, one of the interviewees – a legal practitioner – warned against hasty legislative action and argued that policymakers must first understand all nuances before any such measures are considered:

> I think it's certainly something to keep an eye on … It is an issue, but it's more dormant than not. As the desktop technology gets better, if it gets better, and you see it easier as an end user to print something that infringes a high-value patent, then obviously it significantly elevates the issue.[71]

The general sentiment was no different among the *survey respondents*. Virtually all participants in the survey expressed support for having such an exemption in place (it is also worth noting that the majority were based in the US, where no such legal provision exists).[72] In terms of justifications, it was commonly argued that private reproductions would have little, if any, impact on rightsholders' economic interests. For example, one participant argued that 'one reproduction for personal or non-commercial use does not automatically equal one lost sale'.[73] Another respondent similarly contended that 'there is no harm to a company other than not having a customer buy their part'.[74]

[68] See, eg, Patents Act (UK) 1977, s 60(5)(a) ('An act which … would constitute an infringement … shall not do so if … it is done privately and for purposes which are not commercial'); see also, more generally, ch 6.

[69] See, eg, US Patent 3005282A.

[70] Interviewee 2.

[71] Interviewee 1.

[72] See L Osborn, *3D Printing and Intellectual Property* (Cambridge, CUP, 2019) 85; see also D Doherty, 'Downloading Infringement: Patent Law as a Roadblock to the 3D Printing Revolution' (2012) 26 *Harvard Journal of Law & Technology* 353, 368–9; D Desai and G Magliocca, 'Patents, Meet Napster: 3D Printing and the Digitization of Things (2014) 102 *Georgetown Law Journal* 1691, 1716 ('Congress did not exempt personal production from patent infringement, because few could make patented devices at home. Now that this physical limit is disappearing, maintaining a liability standard created for another age does not make sense').

[73] Survey respondent 150.

[74] Survey respondent 100.

Consistent with the interview data, several participants argued that the exemption is unlikely to be a significant concern to rightsholders at present, given the general state of the technology:

> As of right now, the 3D printed versions are fan-made and generally of inferior quality, so I don't think it's such a big deal. If 3D printing can match real products in price and quality, this becomes a much bigger issue.[75]
>
> Current print times and quality make a widespread sale of counterfeit items unlikely.[76]

Moreover, in line with the arguments made by commentators in the academic literature (and consistent with the interview data), several survey respondents argued that taking enforcement action against private reproductions would be particularly difficult in practice (given that this would typically take place at individuals' own homes):[77]

> Yes, among other reasons, because it can't be enforced effectively.[78]

Others took the view that whatever takes place in private should not be within the reach of IP:

> Personally, I have no regard for any IP if it is in the confines of my own residence.[79]

Interestingly, some participants answered the question with reference to an (infamous) anti-piracy campaign advertisement that aimed to address illegal file sharing in the early 2000s:[80]

> Private use should absolutely be permitted. 'You wouldn't download a car'. Yes, I would![81]

When it comes to the question of reform, some survey respondents argued that even though the issue of private use may not be a major concern for rightsholders at present, the exemption may have to be monitored and potentially revisited in the future, especially 'should home production become the norm rather than the niche'.[82] As also stated by another participant:

> As the market grows and 3D printing becomes more accessible, then I think that is a question that would need to be revisited.[83]

[75] Survey respondent 49.
[76] Survey respondent 72 (though it should be noted that in the specific scenario outlined by the respondent, the exemption is unlikely to apply).
[77] See, eg, Desai and Magliocca (n 72).
[78] Survey respondent 111.
[79] Survey respondent 109.
[80] 'Getting inside a downloader's head' (*BBC News*, 18 June 2009) at www.news.bbc.co.uk/1/hi/magazine/8106805.stm. For a recent parody version of the advertisement that features 3D printing, see Fairbairn Films, 'You Wouldn't Download a Car' (*YouTube*, 11 September 2021) at www.youtube.com/watch?v=Fb7N-JtQWGI.
[81] Survey respondent 129.
[82] Survey respondent 43.
[83] Survey respondent 87.

Overall, while the private and non-commercial use exemption enjoyed significant support within the community, it is important to avoid overstating the significance of the results, given that many participants were hobbyists who primarily print at home – and, therefore, it could be assumed that they would directly benefit from the exception.

'Patent Protected by a Monopolist Company'

When it comes to the impact of IP law on 3D printing more generally, and in line with the observations made in the academic literature,[84] there was a widely held view within the community that patents have negatively affected 3D printing's technological development and accessibility.[85] This was generally a reference to fused filament fabrication patents, a type of 3D printing technology commonly used in the desktop sector today. As put by one *interviewee*:

> The follow-on innovation that you saw from the patent-holding companies doesn't appear to be particularly innovative … When the first patents expired, a bunch of people who were … starting from scratch … were able to completely upend that industry. This suggests that the additional innovation that happened over the 20 years … was not so compelling.[86]

The same interviewee explained that this is not a blanket statement on patents and that the issue should be approached in a more nuanced manner:

> Patents obviously prevent follow-on creators from doing things, this is what they do. The question is not, 'did they prevent other people from doing these things'? Because the answer would always be 'yes'. The question is – did they serve as enough of an incentive for the first thing to be developed that is worth the cost of preventing people from doing things afterwards?

Similar concerns were raised by a large number of *survey participants*. As put by one such respondent:

> Only mildly impacted by IP concerns on a day-to-day basis. Stratasys copyrighted (sic) enclosed fused filament fabrication printers, setting back some fundamental additive manufacturing research by a decade.[87]

Another user similarly stated that 'the expiry of patents in the last decade or so is one of the main reasons $300 (instead of $100,000) printers exist'.[88]

[84] For more details, see ch 8.

[85] These comments were typically made when participants were asked whether they had any views or concerns about IP and about their thoughts on the effect of IP law on 3D printing.

[86] Interviewee 1.

[87] Survey respondent 83.

[88] Survey respondent 44.

Moreover, one survey participant expressed concerns about 'large manufacturers patenting community developed concepts',[89] which appeared to be a reference to recent allegations that some desktop 3D printing manufacturers have appropriated community-developed concepts and claimed them as their own.[90]

Overall, these observations are consistent with Stephanie Santoso and Stephen Wicker's earlier empirical study which similarly concluded that users tend to be 'primarily concerned about ownership of key patents limiting the development of 3D printing technology'.[91]

An Exceptionally Strong Open Source Ethos

Several participants linked the emergence of modern desktop 3D printing not only to the expiry of key patents but also to the role that open-source projects have played in this regard. For example, in the words of one *interviewee*:[92]

> Consumer 3D printing is a massive open-hardware success story. The reason we have consumer 3D printing is because the initial patents expired and then the community acted together and said, "These machines cost tens of thousands of dollars today, we think we can co-op to re-engineer them down to hundreds of dollars". You saw an explosion of companies take that core technology that's been collectively designed and bring it to the market in hundreds of different ways.[93]

Several *survey respondents* expressed similar views:

> Fused filament fabrication tech was available since the early 1980s, but being patent protected by a monopolist company, it wasn't publicly available until recently. Once the patents were out of the picture the … technology jumped forward, mainly thanks to the open-source society that then could reiterate a lot faster than any one company.[94]

> 3D printing … has only really taken off in the last decade or so since the patents for FDM printing expired. Prior to this, Stratasys were one of the only manufacturers of FDM 3D printers with little to no progress made. The inception of the RepRap project which had open-source at the core of its values led to the boom in 3D printing we see today.[95]

[89] Survey respondent 150.

[90] See J Biggs, 'MakerBot Responds To Critics Who Claim It Is Stealing Community IP' (*TechCrunch*, 28 May 2014) at www.techcrunch.com/2014/05/28/makerbot-responds-to-critics-who-claim-it-is-stealing-community-ip; see also B Benchoff, 'MakerBot Files Patents, Internet Goes Crazy' (*Hackaday*, 24 May 2014) at www.hackaday.com/2014/05/24/makerbot-files-patents-internet-goes-crazy.

[91] S Santoso and S Wicker, 'The Future of Three-Dimensional Printing: Intellectual Property or Intellectual Confinement?' (2016) 18 *New Media & Society* 138, 142.

[92] These comments were typically made when participants were asked whether open-source 3D printing projects are important for the future of the technology.

[93] Interviewee 1.

[94] Survey respondent 96.

[95] Survey respondent 118.

Another survey respondent further argued that 'a HUGE part of the reason 3D printers are as advanced and accessible as they are now is due to these open-source designs'.[96] Indeed, it was clear that the existing 3D printing community is based on an exceptionally strong open-source ethos, and virtually all participants expressed support for this model.

Yet, given that some of the leading open-source 3D printer manufacturers have expressed concerns about 'cloning' and free-riding (whereby competitors sell 'copied' versions of open-hardware 3D printers for a fraction of the price and generally do not contribute back to the community),[97] participants were also asked whether open-hardware businesses can stay competitive while relying on such a model as a follow-up question.

When it comes to the *interviewees*, several participants pointed out that if a product is successful, copying 'would happen anyway, regardless of whether [the model] is proprietary or not'.[98] As explained by another interviewee:

> The problem with cheaper and imitation components is they will always exist. If you have a good product or idea, the world will try and take it from you and claim it as their own, bypassing R&D, as you say.[99]

In terms of the specific measures that open hardware companies can adopt to stay competitive in light of these concerns, several interviewees argued that the best way to do so is to focus on providing quality components and reliable support and that reputation plays a key role in this regard:

> Quality … because a lot of those copied machines are fire hazards. If you pay a little bit more but your house doesn't burn down, that is a strong argument to consider … If you can get your name out there and build a strong reputation, you can charge a bit more.[100]

Another interviewee argued that 'a company is only as good as the products they make' and that open source can be viable 'as long as you are at the top of your game'.[101]

[96] Survey respondent 88.

[97] See, eg, See R Brown, 'Pulling back from open source hardware, MakerBot angers some adherents' (*CNET*, 27 September 2012) at www.cnet.com/tech/tech-industry/pulling-back-from-open-source-hardware-makerbot-angers-some-adherents ('With these new products, MakerBot has veered away from open source. In a recent blog post, Pettis says, "For the Replicator 2, we will not share the way the physical machine is designed or our GUI because we don't think carbon-copy cloning is acceptable and carbon-copy clones undermine our ability to pay people to do development"'); see also J West and G Kuk, 'Proprietary Benefits from Open Communities: How MakerBot Leveraged Thingiverse in 3D Printing' (2014) at www.ssrn.com/abstract=2544970 ('Open source hardware has many of the same implications for firms as open source software, but questions remain as the former is both a less common phenomenon and less often studied. These questions include both the viability of open hardware business models, and also the ability of firms (or communities) to tightly regulate IP access to support those business models'); J Prusa, 'The state of open-source in 3D printing in 2023' (*Prusa Blog*, 29 March 2023) blog.prusa3d.com/the-state-of-open-source-in-3d-printing-in-2023_76659.

[98] Interviewee 2.

[99] Interviewee 9.

[100] Interviewee 7.

[101] Interviewee 9.

Similarly, *survey respondents* commonly argued that open hardware companies can stay competitive provided that they find a way to 'add value' and establish a reputation as a manufacturer of quality products. As put by one participant:

> There are hundreds of cheaper … copies of [Prusa's] machines, but they still come out on top because they use quality parts, have reliable quality control, great customer service team, and keep innovating and providing new features and upgrades to their machines.[102]

Others pointed out that while 'clones' may function similarly, there is no guarantee that they will be as reliable or of equal quality.[103] In the words of one such survey participant:

> When you buy a printer from a [reputable] company … You are paying for the guarantee of a working … printer from a reputable source, you are paying for future advancements … and the long-term support of the company. Competitors can copy the tech all they want, but they can't copy the company.[104]
>
> Yes, clones will always exist. However, reputation carries loads of weight.[105]

Some survey respondents pointed out that while there are plenty of copies of popular open hardware printers, many people 'are much more inclined to buy the real deal, so to speak'.[106]

Consistent with the interviews, several survey participants also argued that if a company or product is successful, it will be copied either way – for example, one respondent argued that they see 'copies of non-open-sourced hardware just as often'.[107]

Interestingly, it was also evident that community norms play an important role in this respect. There was a general sense that manufacturers of open-hardware 'clones' are not held in high regard, unless they contribute back to the community in a meaningful way:

> Yes. The critics are correct that it can be easily copied and sold at a much lower price. However, there is significant pushback against the copycats unless they actually make improvements to the model.[108]

Yet, despite the above responses, some survey participants nevertheless argued that if a company's primary goal is to make a profit, it might be challenging to stay competitive when relying on an open-source model.[109]

[102] Survey respondent 55.
[103] Survey respondent 75 ('Yes, just because a competitor can make the same parts cheaper doesn't promise that those parts will be good quality').
[104] Survey respondent 152.
[105] Survey respondent 27.
[106] Survey respondent 14.
[107] Survey respondent 3.
[108] Survey respondent 73.
[109] Survey respondent 131 ('I think it depends on the end-goal. If a business is entirely motivated by profit, then it is obviously not a good model. However, I think that companies can still be profitable in an open-source arena by providing high quality products and more importantly, user support').

Tackling Piracy Through New Business Models

As a potential measure that stakeholders and industry could utilise to protect their IP rights (and to potentially stem piracy online by offering consumers more choice), participants were asked about their views on the adoption of a 'streaming' model whereby users can purchase one-off access to an authorised digital model and print it without receiving a permanent copy of the file, as proposed in a recent UK Intellectual Property Office report:

> This model removes the need for a CAD file to be sent to the consumer; instead the build instructions are sent directly to the printer, which, in turn, prints out the number of objects that have been purchased. It is an effective business model for manufacturers and designers who wish to protect their intellectual property whilst giving the consumers the option of printing toys and other smaller products at home.[110]

This is clearly reminiscent of the business models adopted by the content industry in recent years – where users are given the option to conveniently and legally access content – and this approach is now widely used by popular audio and video streaming services such as Spotify and Netflix. However, is there demand for such a model within the 3D printing community?

While some *interviewees* expressed support for the model (arguing that it could make the 3D printing process more seamless and user-friendly),[111] many expressed doubts as to its viability on the basis of concerns about reliability and consistency. As put by one such interviewee:

> I do not know how this could be manageable, as 3D printing is so unstable at the moment. Printing something one-time does not mean that you receive a finished print. Sometimes it takes lots of tries and adjustment to get a good print.[112]

One professional stated that this *used to be* their company's business model, as their idea was to offer 'an iTunes store for 3D models'.[113] However, there were often instances where customers' hardware failed to properly print the item (in which case they had to restart the entire process). Given that they were unable to offer

[110] D Mendis and D Secchi, 'A Legal and Empirical Study of 3D Printing Online Platforms and an Analysis of User Behaviour' (Intellectual Property Office, Report 2015/41) 44–45 assets.publishing.service.gov.uk/government/uploads/system/uploads/attachment_data/file/549045/Study-I.pdf (the report makes several other recommendations for industry, government and intermediaries); see also S Bechtold, '3D Printing, Intellectual Property and Innovation Policy (2016) 47 *International Review of Intellectual Property and Competition Law* 517, 531 ('Some 3D design file marketplaces … offer the possibility to securely stream files directly to the consumer's 3D printer. In such an environment, the consumer does not receive the 3D design file, thereby reducing the risk of unauthorized 3D design file-sharing').

[111] Interviewees 6 and 9.

[112] Interviewee 10.

[113] Interviewee 5.

clients a guarantee that they will consistently receive the final product as intended, they eventually decided to abandon the model:

> We just cannot control it and it does not make sense to sell things that you cannot control.

Another interviewee highlighted the potential risk of circumvention, where customers could 'print an object, 3D scan it, and then create their own file', which would make it difficult to effectively run such a model in practice.[114]

Among *survey respondents*, there was no clear consensus on the issue. Consistent with the interview data, one of the most commonly cited concerns was the issue of reliability and effective implementation from a technical standpoint. For example, some participants argued that this would be 'nearly technically impossible to do'[115] or that 'it would be a nightmare to implement'.[116] The possibility of print failure, in particular, was once again a key concern:

> Absolutely not. The likelihood of a print failing and you being out of luck is huge. This model would not work unless there was some guarantee of success, which would not happen without a physical space run by the business.[117]

Others raised concern about the risk of circumvention, stating that 'unless the service controls the whole chain, once you have the file, you can crack it'.[118] As put by another respondent:

> While it would be possible for such a service to exist, it is key to remember the backgrounds of most people that can keep a 3D printer running … The average user would be able to fairly easily circumvent a streaming service, because there is no good way to encrypt GCODE on a printer's end to prevent from writing down the commands and duplicating them.[119]

Survey participants also raised questions about the issue of payments – what happens if the print fails due to connectivity problems? One respondent argued that there should be a mechanism to take this risk into account and ensure that customers do 'not have to pay for the file five times'.[120] However, some pointed out that even if there was such a system in place, it could easily be abused:

> No, if you buy a one-time-print file, and the print fails, you would be wasting money. People would abuse [this] if there was a refund system by buying the file, printing the file, claiming it failed, then refunding the money.[121]

[114] Interviewee 2.
[115] Survey respondent 70.
[116] Survey respondent 37.
[117] Survey respondent 105.
[118] Survey respondent 97.
[119] Survey respondent 17.
[120] Survey respondent 16 ('Partially. There should be some way to account for … failed prints. You should not have to pay for the file five times if only one print ends up working the way you want it to').
[121] Survey respondent 75.

What is more, some survey respondents were opposed to the concept of paying for a one-off print out of principle: 'Paying and not owning a model is bad. If I pay for a model, I want to print it as many times as I want.'[122] As similarly put by another participant:

> Doubtful. I would not have bought files that I knew I could only use once. What if the print did not turn out correctly for some reason? I would not purchase music to only be able to listen to it once or a book only to be able to read it once.[123]

Indeed, many users argued that they would prefer purchasing a *permanent* digital copy of a certain 3D printable model instead – for example, if it was offered at a lower price compared to its ready-made physical counterpart (though, in this case, there is a higher risk that the file could then be shared without authorisation, unless there is some additional protection in place).[124]

Finally, a sizeable number of survey participants nevertheless expressed approval for the proposed streaming model. For example, one respondent argued that 'this would be the next logical evolution of the Shapeways plus Netflix business model, if 3D printing becomes commonplace'.[125] However, those who expressed approval typically set some important conditions. For instance, one respondent argued that providers relying on this model would be expected 'to have a rich library with high quality content that people could not just get elsewhere for free'.[126] As similarly put by another user:

> I think so. Honestly, I thought a lot of tabletop games like Warhammer would run some sort of business. I would certainly buy on a one-off basis but would expect the machines to create the models perfectly.[127]

The Future of 'Consumer' 3D Printing – And Why this Matters for IP

While commentators have often theorised that 3D printers will become ubiquitous,[128] it is becoming increasingly uncertain whether this will actually ever

[122] Survey respondent 137.

[123] Survey respondent 149.

[124] For example, survey respondent 113 stated: 'I would consider paying less for a digital CAD file over buying the actual product if I thought I could make it myself' (this suggestion was made when discussing the private use exemption in patent law). See also, more generally, M Senese, 'Nokia Releases Files for 3-D Printing Your Own Phone Case' (*Wired*, 10 January 2013) at www.wired.com/2013/01/nokia-3d-print-case.

[125] Survey respondent 135.

[126] Survey respondent 77.

[127] Survey respondent 76.

[128] See, for instance, M Ratto and R Ree, 'Materializing Information: 3D Printing and Social Change' (2012) 17 *First Monday* 1 ('Another thread that was quite evident … was that of 'futurism' – and more specifically, what the impending ubiquity of desktop 3D printing will mean for consumer culture'); H Lipson and M Kurman, *Fabricated: The New World of 3D Printing* (Indianapolis, Wiley,

materialise. This is especially important in the context of IP law. As explored in previous chapters, the extent to which the technology presents a significant challenge to the law and to the economic interests of rightsholders is likely to directly depend on how widespread and sophisticated the technology is and how easily individual users can interfere with various IP rights. I therefore asked participants – including 3D printing professionals, engineers and users with substantial knowledge of the latest technological developments in the field – whether they expected 3D printing to eventually become sufficiently accessible so as to reach 'average consumers' (or, in other words, whether it is likely to achieve mainstream adoption).[129]

There was no clear consensus on the issue among the *interviewees*. Some participants argued that this would happen eventually at some undefined point in the future, but typically argued that several important limitations would have to be addressed first (we will separately explore these in more detail in the next section):

> In short, yes. However, these [3D printers] will not be printing the plastics the industry is used to. All … filament options on the market are not environmentally viable for such widespread use.[130]

Others were clearly more sceptical. Several interviewees argued that despite the initial 'hype' around 3D printing and the expectation that everyone would want to have a printer in their home, there has been a notable decline in that enthusiasm in recent years:

> We are at this moment … where the first rush of "everyone in three years is going to have this magic box that prints them out breakfast and then another phone" has passed. People are now in a much more nuanced understanding of the technology and … have a realistic roadmap.[131]

Another professional – who could provide especially valuable insights on the issue in light of their position as the chairperson of a global 3D printing retailer – argued that:

> At this stage, I wouldn't call it a huge interest yet. The interest is real, it exists. But it [falls] into a sub-category, which is the geek oriented, futuristic thinking, you name it. We call them Makers. And these people are a limited fraction of the population.[132]

When pressed for more details, the same interviewee stated that we are currently 'nowhere near' mainstream adoption and that most people are not 'even thinking of having one – what would I do with it?'.

2013) 103 ('Once 3D printing becomes ubiquitous … everyone can become a manufacturer'); see also The Standard, '3D printers: every home should have one' (*The Standard*, 10 April 2012) at www.standard.co.uk/news/tech/3d-printers-every-home-should-have-one-7308091.html.

[129] The term 'average consumer' was given its ordinary meaning and referred to individuals who do not qualify as electronics hobbyists, early adopters, or experts with specialist knowledge in the field.

[130] Interviewee 9.

[131] Interviewee 1.

[132] Interviewee 4.

Another interviewee argued that, in their view, the future market is likely to focus on providing 'access to the industrial side of things' (essentially, intermediary services that print on behalf of customers), as opposed to desktop 3D printing.[133]

Compared with the interviews, a greater proportion of *survey participants* (constituting a clear majority) argued that they expect 3D printing to reach average consumers *eventually*:

> Absolutely, from printing presses to inkjets, so will go the 3D printer.[134]

Several survey participants argued that this is merely a matter of time and, consistent with the academic literature, often drew comparisons to earlier digital technologies:

> Yes, similar to how computers were mainly used as scientific equipment until the mid-1970s, then mainly hobbyist or developer equipment until the late 1980s.[135]

However, there was often an important caveat attached to these statements. As explained by one participant, 'there are a lot of hurdles to overcome':

> The whole industry, for home use, needs to be simplified, reduced in price, reliable … It also needs to be safe. So, do I believe they will become household appliances? Yes, I absolutely do, but I think it's going to be many, many years before that's a reality.[136]

Perhaps surprisingly, a few survey respondents argued that the technology has *already* reached 'average consumers'. Some even identified as such – one participant claimed that they are 'a consumer who has purchased a complicated device', as opposed to an electronics hobbyist.[137] As similarly put by two other participants:

> I think they are already at that point … The technology is now cheap enough that 3D printing is accessible to the layman. I think now it is just the mental barrier where people don't feel like they have the knowledge or expertise to do their own 3D printing.[138]

> 100%. In a way I think they already are. Apart from building and setting up, it is super simple to just upload a 3D model, have the software to check it … and just press print.[139]

However, not everyone agreed that 3D printing will enter the mainstream, at least not in the immediate future. As bluntly put by one sceptical survey respondent:

> It isn't going to be a push-button toaster kind of device any time soon.[140]

[133] Interviewee 3.
[134] Survey respondent 62.
[135] Survey respondent 130. See also J West and G Kuk, 'Proprietary Benefits from Open Communities: How MakerBot Leveraged Thingiverse in 3D Printing' (2014) 1, 15 at www.ssrn.com/abstract=2544970 15 ('[T]he use cases for the first generation of consumer 3D printers are in as many ways as fanciful for first generation PCs, with printing desktop trinkets in the 2010s the equivalent of storing recipes in the 1970s. As with personal computers, professionals (such as designers or engineers) who want a home device have a reason to buy hardware but the average consumer does not').
[136] Survey respondent 6.
[137] Survey respondent 78.
[138] Survey respondent 14.
[139] Survey respondent 69.
[140] Survey respondent 44.

Among those who expressed doubts, several participants argued that there may simply be a lack of consumer *demand* for 3D printers. For example, one participant stated that 'there is no need or want for consumers to bring manufacturing into the home; quality is poorer, it costs more, it's slower and less capable than … industrial processes'.[141] Another user argued that:

> I really don't think there will be one in every home. Not everyone needs one. I do expect them to be more widely used in small to medium businesses. I feel the hobby market will become somewhat saturated in the next few years.[142]

In line with the interviews, others argued that 3D printing is likely to remain a 'niche' market targeted at hobbyists and technology enthusiasts, as opposed to 'consumers':

> No. Printers fill a niche that just isn't super important to most people. Even if a printer worked 100% perfectly every time, you'd still have to wonder what a person would want to print with it … The original premise that the printer will be completely reliable will probably not happen. They are complicated pieces of machinery with a lot of stuff going on.[143]

Finally, one participant argued that unless future 3D printers are capable of functioning like 'Star Trek Replicators', widescale adoption is unlikely:

> 3D printers are too slow and too meticulous to achieve mainstream success … Consumers demand instantaneous results. Multiday print times to make a large model are not going to win over a quick drive to the store for the average consumer. The way that current 3D printers are designed to function inherently limits their appeal to average consumers.[144]

The Uncertain Road to Mainstream Adoption

While it appears that 3D printing is still a long way from mainstream adoption, what specific issues and technological limitations have to be addressed to facilitate this process?

Interviewees most commonly argued that 'ease of use' has to be substantially improved. For example, one participant explained that while 3D printing is becoming increasingly accessible, users still need considerable experience and skills to consistently achieve quality output.[145] Another participant argued that the printing process currently takes too long and requires substantial technical

[141] Survey respondent 64.
[142] Survey respondent 70.
[143] Survey respondent 2.
[144] Survey respondent 121.
[145] Interviewee 2.

knowledge – including maintenance and troubleshooting – which is likely to put off most consumers:

> My friends … have zero interest in anything but receiving the finished product. They only laugh when they hear it takes eleven hours to print a small figure … Only a 3D printer as simple as a modern inkjet printer would make it to the mass market.[146]

Indeed, this comparison to inkjet printers (as far as ease of use is concerned) was a commonly recurring theme throughout the study:

> We still have a long way to go because current printers are not plug-and-play. Just like with 2D printers, they need to be plug-and-play or no one will use them.[147]

One interviewee argued that when most people hear the term '3D printing', there is a common misconception that you can just push a button and have an object instantly generated in front of you.[148] However, they argued that there is, in fact, substantial effort and skill involved in creating a quality 3D model and ensuring that the item is accurately manufactured. As similarly put by another participant:

> You cannot just … describe something and get a print … You need to internalize a lot of information, so it's not only being able to use CAD in the sense of being able to navigate the virtual environment. You have to know how to print it, which is itself hard.[149]

The ability to use modelling software, in particular, was cited as an especially challenging task for many.[150] Interestingly, OpenAI – the company responsible for ChatGPT – has recently developed a diffusion-based AI model that allows users to generate 3D point clouds by using simple textual prompts (for example, 'a 3D printable gear … 3 inches in diameter and half inch thick').[151] As explained by the authors of the study:

> [T]his model has the ability to support the creation of point clouds that can then be used to fabricate products in the real world, for example through 3D printing.[152]

Such AI tools have the potential to dramatically increase ease of use in the future, especially as far as the 3D modelling process is concerned.

Other commonly cited limitations (or areas that need to be addressed to facilitate wider adoption) included reliability and health and safety. For example, one interviewee argued that further research is needed on 'how hazardous those

[146] Interviewee 10.
[147] Interviewee 7.
[148] Interviewee 2.
[149] Interviewee 1.
[150] Interviewee 8.
[151] A Nichol and others, 'Point E: A System for Generating 3D Point Clouds from Complex Prompts' (*arXiv*, 2022) at arxiv.org/pdf/2212.08751.
[152] ibid. See also OpenAI, 'Point-E: A system for generating 3D point clouds from complex prompts' (*OpenAI*, 16 December 2022) at www.openai.com/index/point-e.

materials are because as soon as there is a wider market for these kinds of printers, there will be more issues that arise'.[153] Some interviewees also raised concerns about environmental issues, including the use of non-biodegradable materials and single-use prints, which could be especially concerning if the technology becomes more widespread.[154]

Among the *survey respondents*, ease of use was once again the most commonly identified barrier to mainstream adoption:

> 3D printers have not been developed with ease of use or reliability or even safety in mind to a sufficient degree that they would be acceptable as a ubiquitous household appliance. Calibration or maintenance … are still very much hobbyist tasks, as opposed to something like an inkjet printer which handles most of its processes automatically. Most printers still look more natural in a workshop or a garage than a desk.[155]

As put by another participant, there is a need for a more streamlined and consumer-friendly 'one-button' user experience:

> Ease of use is going to be the most important aspect to getting a 3D printer into every home. A system … where you click 'print' and have the printer do absolutely everything else is going to be close to what an average person would need.[156]

Indeed, like many interviewees, several survey respondents contrasted 3D printers with more conventional consumer electronics devices that typically require little or no maintenance and handle most of the relevant processes automatically, or at least without the need for significant user involvement and specialist knowledge:

> Printers need to be 'plug-and-play' to an extent that it shouldn't be harder to maintain and troubleshoot than a 'regular' office 2D printer … CAD modelling needs to be intuitive enough for an average computer user to be comfortable with.[157]

There was a general feeling that the learning curve is still too steep for most consumers:

> The majority of the people who own 3D printers have had to learn lots about the subject in order to fully utilise their machines. I would struggle to envision regular … consumers putting in that time commitment in order to understand and utilise what they have.[158]

[153] Interviewee 7.
[154] Interviewee 9 ('The 3D printing industry needs to change. The use of petrol chemical plastics and non-biodegradable plastics … seriously needs addressing. The industry is riddled with misconceptions as to the eco nature of PLA and this is rather distressing … I often find the entire industry a contradiction in itself').
[155] Survey respondent 38 (also noting that 'it's possible that the average consumer would not be comfortable with a machine that looks the way most 3D printers do').
[156] Survey respondent 138.
[157] Survey respondent 96.
[158] Survey respondent 85.

Consistent with the interview data, survey participants once again commonly referred to 3D modelling as a particularly challenging task for many:

> Current printing technologies will never reach this state … The true usefulness of a 3D printer is when a user is able to create their own designs to suit their needs, but even if the printers were to become sufficiently simple to use, the 3D design process will most likely not.[159]

Beyond ease of use, factors such as print quality and attractive use cases for consumers were some of the most commonly cited other factors:

> I don't think the results for many printers are really as good as what could be purchased otherwise. So, the real question might be whether or not the more widescale consumer would ultimately have need of such a device … Being able to fabricate simple objects out of plastic only is of very limited use to average consumers, especially if they are limited to designs that other people have created.[160]

To a lesser extent, other commonly cited factors in this regard included speed,[161] environmental issues involving waste and recycling,[162] and health and safety. As put by one survey participant, 'The safety issue of a completely unskilled consumer interacting with the high temperatures found in 3D printing would have to be addressed in some way.'[163]

Interestingly, costs no longer appeared to be a significant issue due to the availability of affordable desktop 3D printers. However, a higher price tag was often associated with better output quality and reliability.

Analysis and Concluding Remarks

There is a vibrant desktop 3D printing scene. It is evident that the technology is already widely used to make a remarkably diverse range of things at home, from Marvel action figures and models for tabletop games to more 'mundane' items such as repair parts for AC units and shower curtain hooks. As one participant stated, 'You can model and print anything you can imagine … It is a tiny factory in your home.'[164] However, as explored in previous chapters, it is also precisely this aspect of 3D printing that has led to significant concerns among IP scholars and policymakers.

[159] Survey respondent 38.

[160] Survey respondent 143 ('This could change if a radically different or more advanced print process were to become available').

[161] Survey respondent 67 ('Prints take so long to print and that alone might put some people off').

[162] Survey respondent 26 ('Many models require a support structure … and often that means that they have a lot of waste that needs to be thrown out … This issue will need to be addressed for wider adoption to take place').

[163] Survey respondent 160.

[164] Survey respondent 89.

While IP was not necessarily a concern for many participants – at least as far as their everyday usage of 3D printing is concerned – it was clear that it is not a completely marginal issue either. Users most commonly expressed concerns about unauthorised use of their 3D models or violations of their licensing terms. Indeed, several participants took action to protect their work. Yet, there was little evidence to suggest that infringement is rampant, or that it is taking place in any way comparable to the peer-to-peer file sharing issues experienced in the recent past – observations that are consistent with recent reports in the area.[165] It also did not appear that the core of the existing IP framework and the remedial tools available to rightsholders are inadequate in this context. As put by one interviewee (a legal practitioner with substantial experience in the field) – 'there are many challenges to the IP system right now and 3D printing is one of them, but 3D printing is not uniquely problematic'.[166] In fact, some participants argued that IP rightsholders do not appear to be especially concerned about products coming out of *desktop* 3D printers at present, given that they are still unable to compete with mass-produced goods in terms of output quality.

At a more general level, several participants expressed concerns about the effect that patents have had on the development of 3D printing, which is consistent with the observations made in the academic literature.[167] Users commonly linked the expiry of key fused filament fabrication patents to the emergence of an open-source hardware community that utilised the same technology and helped to dramatically increase the accessibility of 3D printing. It was therefore not surprising that there was exceptionally strong support for open-source principles within the community.

When it comes to the adoption of new 'streaming' models as a way to protect IP rights online (as proposed in a recent UK government report),[168] while there was some support within the community, many participants expressed concerns that this may not work in practice due to the risk of print failure and circumvention. Instead, some participants stated that they would consider paying more for a permanent copy of a 3D printable model if it was offered at a lower price compared to its ready-made physical counterpart (so that they can make it themselves).

Finally, as explored throughout this book, the extent to which 3D printing poses a significant challenge to the IP framework and proprietors' economic

[165] See, eg, D Mendis, D Secchi and P Reeves, 'A Legal and Empirical Study into the Intellectual Property Implications of 3D Printing: Executive Summary' (Intellectual Property Office, Report 2015/41) 5 ('Whilst there is little to indicate infringement at a noticeable level in the current landscape, interest and activity is growing exponentially every year') at assets.publishing.service.gov.uk/government/uploads/system/uploads/attachment_data/file/549044/Legal-Empirical-_Executive-Summary.pdf.

[166] Interviewee 1.

[167] Bechtold (n 110) 517.

[168] D Mendis and D Secchi, 'A Legal and Empirical Study of 3D Printing Online Platforms and an Analysis of User Behaviour (UK Intellectual Property Office, Report 2015/41) 44–45 at assets.publishing.service.gov.uk/media/5a7f5d6ced915d74e33f5fb4/Study-I.pdf.

interests is likely to primarily depend on future technological developments and whether the technology achieves more mainstream success.[169] However, the empirical data in this study suggest that 3D printing is still a long way from widescale consumer adoption, and it is, in fact, becoming increasingly unclear whether it will ever enter the mainstream.[170]

[169] See J Hornick, '3D Printing and IP Rights: The Elephant in the Room' (2015) 55 *Santa Clara Law Review* 801, 802 ('3D printing has the potential to democratize manufacturing, meaning that almost anyone may be able to make almost anything').

[170] This is consistent with recent reports and studies in the area; see T Birtchnell and others, '3D Printing and Intellectual Property Futures' (Intellectual Property Office, Report 2018/03) 12–13 ('"citizen empowerment" through household 3D printing is constrained by the current technical aspects and competencies'); see also, A Daly, *Socio-Legal Aspects of the 3D Printing Revolution* (London, Palgrave Macmillan, 2016).

10

Conclusion

3D printing brings both opportunities and challenges. By equipping individual users with access to design and manufacturing tools, it also allows them to make various creative decisions – and, therefore, to play an active (as opposed to merely passive) role in production. As one participant in the empirical study explained, 'it is a tiny factory in your home'. Indeed, there is already a remarkably diverse and vibrant universe of 3D printable products that users make at home on a regular basis – from artworks and action figures from popular culture to various functional items such as hardware components. It is also precisely this aspect of the technology – and the fact that users can reproduce various tangible products on a highly decentralised basis – that has attracted significant attention and led to serious concerns among rightsholders, policymakers and IP scholars.[1]

However, we now have a much more nuanced understanding of the technology, its capabilities, and the risks it poses than we did a decade ago. In practice, there has been significantly less consumer uptake than expected. Part of the reason for this is that existing 3D printers are neither able to offer a 'plug-and-play' experience comparable to conventional consumer electronics, nor sufficiently attractive use cases for most consumers. Therefore, the technology's potential to truly 'democratise' manufacturing may be more modest than previously anticipated – at least for the time being. Moreover, the output quality of desktop 3D printers is generally inferior to that of many mass-produced goods, which means that products made at home would not necessarily be able to act as a substitute for the original and, therefore, to seriously undermine the economic interests of proprietors (as many commentators had initially predicted).[2] This is also why several participants

[1] J Hornick, '3D Printing and IP Rights: The Elephant in the Room' (2015) 55 *Santa Clara Law Review* 801, 806 ('When anyone can 3D print things with virtually any functionality, the risk of IP infringement away from control will become increasingly high'); see also World Intellectual Property Organization, 'World Intellectual Property Report: Breakthrough Innovation and Economic Growth' (2015) 106–7 ('Any person with access to a 3D printer can print any object as long as they have digital representations of that object … Thus, personal 3D printing potentially raises issues of large-scale infringement of existing IP rights by 3D printing users') at www.wipo.int/edocs/pubdocs/en/wipo_pub_944_2015.pdf; H Lipson and M Kurman, *Fabricated: The New World of 3D Printing* (Indianapolis, Wiley, 2013) 7.

[2] See, eg, V Elam, 'The Transfer of Computer-Aided Design Files in the Era of 3D Printing: Trademark Infringement Under the Current European Framework' in *Building a European Digital Space: 12th International Conference on Internet, Law & Politics* (7–8 July 2016) 79 at dialnet.unirioja.es/servlet/libro?codigo=963258.

in the empirical study argued that IP rightsholders do not even see 3D printing as a threat at present (though it was also evident that several major companies have already initiated enforcement action targeting 3D printable versions of their products).[3]

What about the IP framework itself? Is it fit for purpose, as far as existing doctrines and substantive provisions are concerned? There are certainly areas that require attention and should continue to be closely monitored. For example, the private and non-commercial use exemption in patent law is a vulnerable area that may require reform in the future, especially *if* the technology becomes significantly more widespread and sophisticated and there is empirical evidence to support such action. The case for reform in this area would be even more compelling if desktop 3D printing eventually allows individual users to interfere with high-value patents on a decentralised basis and the end products are of sufficiently high quality.

Moreover, given that much of the existing patent system was designed in the analogue age (and not necessarily with digitisation in mind), there are several areas that would benefit from further guidance. For instance, it is not completely clear whether existing indirect patent infringement principles cover the dissemination of *intangible* 3D printable versions of patented inventions (where a physical product is claimed) within their remit. At the same time, this doctrine would be a critical remedial tool for patentees, given that no underlying act of direct infringement has to be demonstrated for contributory liability to arise under UK patent law.

In other fields, such as copyright law, there have been extensive debates on issues such as whether 3D scans (should) qualify for protection under the existing framework. While there is no scholarly consensus on the issue, I have argued that 3D scans will almost invariably fail to qualify for protection on the basis that the technology is predominantly used to make faithful reproductions of the original through a technical process that leaves little room for creative choices (of course, where the object being scanned is subject to copyright, the act of reproduction itself may amount to infringement). From a policy perspective, denying fresh protection in such cases is also important to ensure that copyright is not abused to exercise monopoly control over otherwise unprotectable works (for example, public domain works such as the Bust of Nefertiti).

Yet, despite these issues, it does not appear that the IP system as a whole is deficient or inherently incompatible with the technology as far as existing doctrine is concerned. As one interviewee put it, it is becoming increasingly clear that 3D printing is 'not uniquely problematic' so as to require a major overhaul of existing norms and principles.

As further observed in the empirical study, while IP law is clearly not a marginal issue within the 3D printing community and there have already been some early

[3] See, eg, M Weinberg, 'Lego's IP Grab Bag' (19 October 2019) at www.michaelweinberg.org/blog/2019/10/10/lego-ip-grab-bag.

legal skirmishes between proprietors and users, there is nothing to suggest that piracy is rampant, let alone that infringement is taking place on a scale that is in any way comparable to the peer-to-peer file sharing issues experienced during the Napster era.[4] Although many participants expressed concerns about appropriation of their 3D models or violations of their licensing terms, they were generally able to successfully enforce their rights by relying on the existing remedial tools without any significant difficulties.

How should the law, therefore, respond? As I have argued throughout this book, the extent to which 3D printing presents a significant challenge to the IP framework is likely to primarily depend on future technological developments and whether the technology achieves more mainstream success. In a world where, as hypothesised in the early academic literature, 'anyone may be able to make almost anything',[5] desktop 3D printing certainly has the potential to disrupt some of the core tenets of the IP system. However, we still appear to be a long way from such a scenario, and certainly significantly farther than many had initially predicted. While it would be futile to attempt to predict what the future holds, the normative case for major reform action – including introducing entirely new principles or dramatically strengthening existing IP protection – remains weak at present, with the exception of addressing the specific legal and policy issues identified above. Until we are certain that this is strictly necessary and there is compelling empirical and economic evidence to support such action, it would be best to avoid introducing major changes to the law.

In terms of practical recommendations for rightsholders and industry, and as potential solutions to address concerns about piracy online, it would be sensible to explore the adoption of new business models and approaches that offer users a more convenient way to legally access authorised content online.[6] While some commentators may recommend the adoption of digital rights management systems to enhance the protection available to rightsholders, their deployment should be treated with great caution as there is a risk of stifling the legitimate use of the technology and harming honest consumers.

It goes without saying that when considering potential regulatory responses in the future, it is essential that policymakers and rightsholders are attentive to the concerns, values and practices of the community and that they avoid relying on any indiscriminate or excessive measures that could deprive the technology of its immense potential and social value.

[4] While the empirical study is primarily qualitative and does not aim to provide a definite statement on the issue, the views expressed by participants are broadly consistent with recent quantitative studies in the area. See, eg, D Mendis and D Secchi, 'A Legal and Empirical Study of 3D Printing Online Platforms and an Analysis of User Behaviour' (UK Intellectual Property Office, 2015/41, 2015) 41.

[5] Hornick (n 1) 802 (arguing that as 3D printing has the potential to democratise manufacturing, 'almost anyone may be able to make almost anything').

[6] See, eg, Mendis and Secchi (n 4) 41; however, see also the discussion in ch 9.

ANNEX – INTERVIEW AND SURVEY QUESTIONS

In designing the interviews and surveys, I aimed to ensure that all questions are presented in a sufficiently accessible manner so that they could easily be understood by a non-lawyer. Given that the interviews were semi-structured, I relied on follow-up questions to clarify certain points or to request additional information where relevant – for example, some participants were able to provide more detailed information regarding a particular issue, in light of their individual expertise and experiences. Therefore, while the interviews and surveys followed the same basic structure, the questions and their precise formulation (including the order in which some questions were presented) varied slightly. Data for this monograph were primarily extracted from the following general categories of questions.[1]

Part A – General Involvement with 3D Printing

Participants were first given the opportunity to explain what they do in their own words, including their motivation for using 3D printing. These questions had direct relevance for several pertinent issues discussed throughout the book, such as the relationship between the technology and IP law (including what rights are most likely to be affected in this context).

Q1. Please briefly describe your involvement with 3D printing in your own words.

Q2. If applicable, please explain what type of products you typically model or print.

Q3. Why is 3D printing important to you? Why do you print your own items, as opposed to purchasing similar readily available products?

Part B – Intellectual Property Law

Participants were asked a range of questions about their views and exposure to IP, which was essential to understand the extent to which the law is a concern among

[1] While the original interviews and surveys included some additional questions on issues that are not covered in this monograph, in light of this book's general scope and limitations, the data used for its purposes were primarily extracted from the questions outlined here.

the community as well as the degree to which the technology poses a challenge to the existing legal framework. This also helped to identify new issues and themes that were not previously discussed in the academic literature.

Q4. Is IP law a concern for you in your everyday usage of the technology?[2]

Q5. As a 3D printing user, have you encountered any specific issues involving IP law (for example, litigation or enforcement action involving IP rights)?

Q6. In some jurisdictions, the IP system has been described as being very favourable in relation to home 3D printing. Part of the reason for this is the availability of private use exemptions in areas such as patent law, which means that 3D printing a patented invention (for example, items such as Lego bricks may be patented) for personal and non-commercial use will not infringe the owner's rights under UK patent law. Do you think that such private use should be permitted?

Q7. In your view, what effect does IP law have on 3D printing?[3]

Part C – Tackling Piracy and New Business Models

As a measure that industry could adopt to protect their IP rights and to potentially help address concerns about piracy online, participants were asked about their views on the adoption of a 'streaming' model whereby users can purchase one-off access to an authorised digital model and 3D print it themselves, without receiving a permanent copy of the file (this model was proposed in a recent UK Intellectual Property Office report).

Q8. In your view, are 'pay-per-print' business models viable in this context (a service which allows users to 'stream' and 3D print an item on a one-off basis without receiving a permanent copy of the file)?[4]

Part D – Open-source 3D Printing

Given the important role that open-source hardware has played in the context of desktop 3D printing, participants were asked about their views on open-source 3D printing.

[2] Survey participants had the option to reply with the following pre-set answers: 'Major concern'; 'It is a concern to a limited extent'; 'No, I generally don't think about IP at all', or 'Other' (which allowed them to provide further details).

[3] Survey participants had the option to reply with the following pre-set answers: 'Positive'; 'Negative'; 'It has little or no effect', or 'Other' (which allowed them to provide further details).

[4] Survey participants had the option to reply with the following pre-set answers: 'Yes'; 'No'; 'I don't know'; or 'Other' (which allowed them to provide further details).

Q9. Do you think that open-source 3D printing projects such as RepRap and Prusa are important for the future of the technology?[5]

Q10. In your opinion, can companies relying on an open-source hardware model be successful and competitive? Critics argue that open hardware designs may easily be copied and sold at a much lower price by a competitor.

Part E – The Future of 'Consumer' 3D Printing

As explored throughout this book, the extent to which desktop 3D printing poses a significant challenge to IP theory and practice is likely to depend on whether the technology achieves more mainstream adoption in the future (and allows users to print high-quality output). Participants were therefore also asked whether they expected the technology to become sufficiently accessible and reach 'average consumers' and what specific issues would have to be addressed to facilitate this process.

Q11. Do you expect desktop 3D printers to eventually become sufficiently accessible so that average consumers may have a 3D printer at home (as opposed to primarily hobbyists)?

Q12. What issues have to be addressed to facilitate the wider adoption of desktop 3D printing (for example, costs, ease of use)?

End of the Interview or Survey

At the end of the interviews and surveys, participants were given the opportunity to make additional comments or to raise any issues that were not previously discussed in the study.

[5] Survey participants had the option to reply with the following pre-set answers: 'Yes'; 'No'; or 'Other' (which allowed them to provide further details).

BIBLIOGRAPHY

Secondary Sources

Journal Articles

Ahn, G, Kim, H and Lee, S, 'Fabrication Direction Optimization to Minimize Post-machining in Layered Manufacturing' (2007) 47 *International Journal of Machine Tools and Manufacture* 593

Arnold, R, 'The Need for a New Copyright Act: A Case Study in Law Reform' (2015) 5 *Queen Mary Journal of Intellectual Property* 110

Austin, G, 'Copyright's Modest Ontology: Theory and Pragmatism in *Eldred v. Ashcroft*' (2003) 16 *The Canadian Journal of Law & Jurisprudence* 163

Ballardini, R and Norrgård, M, 'Digitising Patent Law: Challenges from 3D Printing Technologies' (2016) 38 *European Intellectual Property Review* 519

Ballardini, R, Norrgård, M and Minssen, T, 'Enforcing Patents in the Era of 3D Printing' (2015) 10 *Journal of Intellectual Property Law & Practice* 850

Bechtold, S, '3D Printing, Intellectual Property and Innovation Policy' (2016) 47 *International Review of Intellectual Property and Competition Law* 517

Beebe, B, 'Semiotic Analysis of Trademark Law' (2004) *51 UCLA Law Review* 621

Benkler, Y, 'Coase's Penguin, or, Linux and "The Nature of the Firm"' (2002) 112 *The Yale Law Journal* 369

Benkler, Y, 'Freedom in the Commons: Towards a Political Economy of Information' (2003) 52 *Duke Law Journal* 1245

Bently, L, 'The Return of Industrial Copyright?' (2012) 34 *European Intellectual Property Review* 654

Besen, S and Raskind, L, 'An Introduction to the Law and Economics of Intellectual Property' (1991) 5 *The Journal of Economic Perspectives* 3

Besen, J and Meurer, M 'Lessons for Patent Policy From Empirical Research on Patent Litigation' (2005) 9 *Lewis & Clark Law Review* 1

Boldrin, M and Levine, D 'Open-Source Software: Who Needs Intellectual Property?' (2007) 57 *The Freeman: Ideas on Liberty* 26

Boldrin, M and Levine, D 'The Case against Patents' (2013) 27 *Journal of Economic Perspectives* 3

Bonvoisin, J and others 'What is the "Source" of Open Source Hardware?' (2017) 1 *Journal of Open Hardware* 1

Bradshaw, S, Bowyer, A and Haufe, P, 'The Intellectual Property Implications of Low-Cost 3D Printing' (2010) 7 *ScriptEd* 5

Brean, D, 'Patenting Physibles: A Fresh Perspective for Claiming 3D-Printable Products' (2015) 55 *Santa Clara Law Review* 837

Brüggemann, J and others 'Intellectual Property Rights Hinder Sequential Innovation: Experimental Evidence' (2016) 45 *Research Policy* 2054

Burrell, R and Gangjee, D 'Because You're Worth It: L'Oréal and the Prohibition on Free Riding' (2010) 73 *Modern Law Review* 282

Calandrillo, S, 'An Economic Analysis of Intellectual Property Rights: Justifications and Problems of Exclusive Rights, Incentives to Generate Information, and the Alternative of a Government-Run Reward System' (1998) 9 *Fordham Intellectual Property, Media, & Entertainment Law Journal* 301

Calignano, F and others, 'Overview on Additive Manufacturing Technologies' (2017) 105 *Proceedings of the IEEE* 593
Campbell, R, Bourell, D and Gibson, I, 'Additive Manufacturing: Rapid Prototyping Comes of Age' (2012) 18 *Rapid Prototyping Journal* 255
Carolo, L and Cooper, R, 'A Review on the Influence of Process Variables on the Surface Roughness of Ti-6Al-4V by Electron Beam Powder Bed Fusion' (2022) 59 *Additive Manufacturing* 103103
Chiu, S and Urban, P, 'Robotics-Assisted Mass Spectrometry Assay Platform Enabled by Open-Source Electronics' (2015) 64 *Biosensors and Bioelectronics* 260
Coleman, G, 'Code is Speech: Legal Tinkering, Expertise and Protest Among Free and Open Source Developers' (2009) 24 *Cultural Anthropology* 420
Conrad, S, 'The Making of a Global Icon: Nefertiti's Twentieth-Century Career' [2024] *Global Intellectual History* 1
Cozmei, C and Caloian, F, 'Additive Manufacturing Flickering at the Beginning of Existence' (2012) 3 *Procedia Economics and Finance Volume* 457
Dagne, T and Dubeau, C, '3D Printing and the Law: Are CAD Files Copyright-Protected?' (2015) 28 *Intellectual Property Journal* 101
Dagne, T, 'The Left Shark, Thrones, Sculptures and Unprintable Triangle: 3D Printing and its Intersections with IP' (2015) 25 *Albany Law Journal of Science & Technology* 573
Depoorter, B, 'Intellectual Property Infringements & 3D Printing: Decentralized Piracy' (2014) 65 *Hastings Law Journal* 1483
Desai, D and Magliocca, G, 'Patents, Meet Napster: 3D Printing and the Digitization of Things' (2014) 102 *Georgetown Law Journal* 1691
Diamond, S, 'The Historical Development of Trademarks' (1975) *65 TM Rep* 265
Dickson, K and Coles, A, 'Textile Design Protection: Copyright, CAD and Competition' (2000) 20 *Technovation* 47
Dinev, P, 'Machine Inventorship' (2025) *141 Law Quarterly Review* 43
Dogan, S and Lemley, M, 'Trademarks and Consumer Search Costs on the Internet' (2004) 41 *Houston Law Review* 777
Doherty, D, 'Downloading Infringement: Patent Law as a Roadblock to the 3D Printing Revolution' (2012) 26 *Harvard Journal of Law & Technology* 353
Drescher, T, 'The Transformation and Evolution of Trademarks: From Signals to Symbols to Myth' (1992) *82 TM Rep* 301
Dumitrescu, G and Tanase, I, '3D Printing – A New Industrial Revolution' (2016) 8 *Knowledge Horizons – Economics* 32
Ebrahim, T, '3D Printing: Digital Infringement & Digital Regulation' (2016) 14 *Northwestern Journal of Technology and Intellectual Property* 37
Eisenberg, R, 'Patents and the Progress of Science: Exclusive Rights and Experimental Use' (1989) 56 *University of Chicago Law Review* 1017
Elam, V, 'CAD Files and European Design Law' (2016) 7 *Journal of Intellectual Property, Information Technology and Electronic Commerce Law* 146
Ford S, Mortara, L and Minshall, T, 'The Emergence of Additive Manufacturing: Introduction to the Special Issue' (2016) 102 *Technological Forecasting & Social Change* 156
Frischmann, B, 'An Economic Theory of Infrastructure and Commons Management' (2005) 89 *Minnesota Law Review* 917
Gershenfeld, N, 'How to Make Almost Anything: The Digital Fabrication Revolution' (2012) 91 *Foreign Affairs* 43
Ghosh, S, 'Decoding and Recoding Natural Monopoly, Deregulation, and Intellectual Property' [2008] *University of Illinois Law Review* 1125
Giblin, R, 'The P2P Wars: How Code Beat Law' (2012) *IEEE Internet Computing*, May/June, 92
Gibson I, 'The Changing Face of Additive Manufacturing' (2017) 28 *Journal of Manufacturing Technology Management* 10

Gordon, W, 'A Property Right in Self-Expression: Equality and Individualism in the Natural Law of Intellectual Property' (1993) *102 Yale Law Journal* 1533

Gordon, W, 'Fair Use as Market Failure: A Structural and Economic Analysis of the "Betamax" Case and Its Predecessors' (1982) 82 *Columbia Law Review* 1600

Grace, J, 'The End of Post-Sale Confusion: How Consumer 3D Printing Will Diminish the Function of Trademarks' (2014) 28 *Harvard Journal of Law & Technology* 263

Greenbaum, E, 'Three-Dimensional Printing and Open-Source Hardware' (2013) 2 *NYU Journal of IP and Entertainment Law* 257

Grimmelmann, J, 'Indistinguishable from Magic: A Wizard's Guide to Copyright and 3D Printing' (2014) 71 *Washington and Lee Law Review* 683

Hamilakis, Y, 'Stories from Exile: Fragments from the Cultural Biography of the Parthenon (or "Elgin") Marbles' (1999) 31 *World Archaeology* 303

Handig, C, 'Infopaq International A/S v Danske Dagblades Forening (C-5/08): Is the Term 'Work' of the CDPA 1988 in Line with the European Directives?' (2010) 32 *European Intellectual Property Review* 53

Hettinger, E, 'Justifying Intellectual Property' (1989) 18 *Philosophy and Public Affairs* 31

Holbrook, T and Osborn, L, 'Digital Patent Infringement in an Era of 3D Printing' (2015) 48 *UC Davis Law Review* 1319

Holzmann, P and others, 'User Entrepreneur Business Models in 3D Printing' (2017) 28 *Journal of Manufacturing Technology Management* 75

Hornick, J, '3D Printing and IP Rights: The Elephant in the Room' (2015) 55 *Santa Clara Law Review* 801

Huang, S and others, 'Additive Manufacturing and its Societal Impact: A Literature Review' (2013) 67 *International Journal of Advanced Manufacturing Technology* 1191

Hughes, J, 'The Philosophy of Intellectual Property' (1998) *77 Georgetown Law Journal* 287

Hughes, J, 'The Photographer's Copyright – Photograph as Art, Photograph as Database' (2012) 25 *Harvard Journal of Law and Technology* 339

Hutchinson, T, 'The Doctrinal Method: Incorporating Interdisciplinary Methods in Reforming the Law' (2015) 8 *Erasmus Law Review* 130

Johnson, P, 'Mr Skemp's Preposterous Provision: The Drafting of the Patents Act 1977 and Harmonization in the 1970s' (2015) 5 *Queen Mary Journal of Intellectual Property* 367

Johnson, P, 'Contributing to the Wrong: Indirect Infringement of Patents' (2010) 5 *Journal of Intellectual Property Law & Practice* 514

Karp, J, 'Experimental Use as Patent Infringement: The Impropriety of a Broad Exception' (1991) 100 *Yale Law Journal* 219

Kietzmann, J, Pitt, L and Berthon, P, 'Disruptions, Decisions, and Destinations: Enter the Age of 3-D Printing and Additive Manufacturing' (2015) 58 *Business Horizons* 209

Kozinski, A, 'Trademarks Unplugged' (1993) 68 *New York University Law Review* 960

Kurtz, P, 'The Industrial-technological Revolution' (2007) *27 Free Inquiry* 4

Landes, W and Posner, R, 'An Economic Analysis of Copyright Law' (1989) 18 *The Journal of Legal Studies* 325

Leistner, M, 'Structural Aspects of Secondary (Provider) Liability in Europe' (2014) 9 *Journal of Intellectual Property Law & Practice* 75

Lemley, M, 'Faith-Based Intellectual Property' (2015) 62 *UCLA Law Review* 1328

Lemley, M, 'IP in a World Without Scarcity' (2015) 90 *New York University Law Review* 460

Lemley, M and Reese, R, 'Reducing Digital Copyright Infringement Without Restricting Innovation' (2004) 56 *Stanford Law Review* 1345

Lemley, M, 'The Economics of Improvement in Intellectual Property Law' (1997) 75 *Texas Law Review* 989

Li, P and others, 'Intellectual Property and 3D Printing: A Case Study on 3D Chocolate Printing' (2014) 9 *Journal of Intellectual Property Law and Practice* 322

Mahamood, R, Akinlabi, E and Pityana, S, 'Revolutionary Additive Manufacturing: An Overview' (2014) *Lasers in Engineering* 161

Maher, M, 'Open Source Software: The Success of an Alternative Intellectual Property Incentive Paradigm' (2000) 10 *Fordham Intellectual Property, Media & Entertainment Law Journal* 619

Malaquias, P, 'Consumer 3D Printing: Is the UK Copyright and Design Law Framework Fit for Purpose' (2016) 6 *Queen Mary Journal of Intellectual Property* 321

Mansfield, E, 'Patents and Innovation: An Empirical Study' (1986) *32 Management Science* 173

Marquis, D, 'The Anatomy of Successful Innovations' (1969) 1 *Innovation* 28

Mazzone, J, 'Copyfraud' (2006) 81 *New York University Law Review* 1026

McCutcheon, J, 'Levola Hengelo BV v. Smilde Foods BV: The Hard Work of Defining a Copyright Work' (2019) 82 *Modern Law Review* 936

McDonagh, L, 'From Brand Performance to Consumer Performativity: Assessing European Trade Mark Law after the Rise of Anthropological Marketing' (2015) 42 *Journal of Law and Society* 611

McKenna, M, 'A Consumer Decision Making Theory of Trademark Law' (2012) 98 *Virginia Law Review* 67

Mellor S, Hao, L and Zhang, D, 'Additive Manufacturing: A Framework for Implementation' (2014) *149 International Journal of Production Economics* 194

Mendis, D, 'Clone Wars Episode II – The Next Generation: The Copyright Implications Relating to 3D Printing and Computer-Aided Design (CAD) Files' (2014) 6 *Law, Innovation and Technology* 265

Mendis, D, 'Clone Wars: Episode I – The Rise of 3D Printing and Its Implications for Intellectual Property Law: Learning Lessons from the Past?' (2013) 35 *European Intellectual Property* 155

Mendis, D, 'In Pursuit of Clarity: The Conundrum of CAD Software and Copyright – Seeking Direction Through Case Law' (2018) 40 *European Intellectual Property Review* 694

Merryman, J, 'Thinking about the Elgin Marbles' (1985) 83 *Michigan Law Review* 1881

Mimler, M, '3D Printing, the Internet and Patent Law – A History Repeating?' (2013) 62 *La Rivista di Diritto Industriale* 352

Moilanen, J and others, 'Cultures of Sharing in 3D Printing: What Can We Learn from the Licence Choices of Thingiverse Users?' (2015) 6 *Journal of Peer Production* 1

Moore, A, 'Intellectual Property: Theory, Privilege, and Pragmatism' (2003) 16 *Canadian Journal of Law & Jurisprudence* 191

Murphy, S and Atala, A, '3D Bioprinting of Tissues and Organs' (2014) 32 *Nature Biotechnology* 773

Navangul, G, Paul, R and Anand, S, 'Error Minimization in Layered Manufacturing Parts by Stereolithography File Modification Using a Vertex Translation Algorithm' (2013) 135 *Journal of Manufacturing Science and Engineering* 031006

Nielsen, J and Liddicoat, J, 'The Multiple Dimensions of Intellectual Property Infringement in the 3D Printing Era' (2017) 27 *Australian Intellectual Property Journal* (2017) 184

Norton, M, Mochon, D and Ariely, D, 'The IKEA Effect: When Labor Leads to Love' (2011) 22 *Journal of Consumer Psychology* 453

O'Byrne, P and Allgrove, B 'Post-Sale Confusion' (2007) 2 *Journal of Intellectual Property Law & Practice* 315

Oppenheim, S, 'A New Approach to Evaluation of the American Patent System' (1951) 33 *Journal of the Patent and Trademark Office Society* 555

Oropallo, W and Piegl, L, 'Ten Challenges in 3D Printing' (2016) 32 *Engineers with Computers* 135

Oruç, P, '3D Digitisation of Cultural Heritage: Copyright Implications of the Methods, Purposes and Collaboration' (2020) 11 *Journal of Intellectual Property, Information Technology and E-Commerce Law* 149

Oruç, P, 'Rethinking Who "Keeps" Heritage: 3D Technology, Repatriation and Copyright' (2022) 71 *GRUR International* 1138

Osborn, L 'Trademark Boundaries and 3D Printing' (2017) 50 *Akron Law Review* 865

Osborn, L and Holbrook, T, 'Digital Patent Infringement in an Era of 3D Printing' (2015) 48 *UC Davis Law Review* 1319

Osborn, L, 'Doctrinal Quandaries with 3D Printing and Intellectual Property' (2016) 27 *Intellectual Property Litigation* 18

Osborn, L, 'Of PhDs, Pirates and the Public: Three-Dimensional Printing Technology and the Arts' (2014) 1 *Texas A&M Law Review* 811

Osborn, L, 'Regulating Three-Dimensional Printing: The Converging Worlds of Bits and Atoms' (2014) 51 *San Diego Law Review* 553

Ouellette, L 'Patent Experimentalism' (2015) 101 *Virginia Law Review* 65

Patterson, L and Joyce, C, 'Copyright in 1791: An Essay Concerning the Founders' View of Copyright Power Granted to Congress in Article 1, Section 8, Clause 8 of the US Constitution' (2003) 52 *Emory Law Journal* 1

Pattishall, B, 'Trade Marks and the Monopoly Phobia' (1952) 42 *TM Rep* 588

Petrick, I and Simpson, T, '3D Printing Disrupts Manufacturing: How Economies of One Create New Rules of Competition' (2013) 56 *Research-Technology Management* 12

Petrovic, V and others, 'Additive Layered Manufacturing: Sectors of Industrial Application Shown Through Case Studies' (2011) 49 *International Journal of Production Research* 1061

Phatak, A and Pande, S 'Optimum Part Orientation in Rapid Prototyping Using Genetic Algorithm' (2012) 31 *Journal of Manufacturing Systems* 395

Posner, R, 'Intellectual Property: The Law and Economics Approach' (2005) 19 *The Journal of Economic Perspectives* 57

Ratto, M and Ree, R, 'Materializing Information: 3D Printing and Social Change' (2012) 17 *First Monday* 1

Rayna, T and Striukova, L, 'From Rapid Prototyping to Home Fabrication: How 3D Printing is Changing Business Model Innovation' (2016) 102 *Technological Forecasting and Social Change* 214

Reichman, J, 'Charting the Collapse of the Patent-Copyright Dichotomy: Premises for a Restructured International Intellectual Property System' (1995) 13 *Cardozo Arts and Entertainment Law Journal* 475

Rimmer, M, '3D printing Jurassic Park: Copyright Law, Cultural Institutions, and Makerspaces' [2016] *Pandora's Box* 1

Rimmer, M, 'Metal 3D Printing: Patent Law, Trade Secrets, and Additive Manufacturing' (2022) 7 *Frontiers in Research Metrics and Analytics* 1

Rimmer, M, 'The Maker Movement: Copyright Law, Remix Culture and 3D Printing' (2017) 41 *The University of Western Australia Law Review* 51

Rosati, E, 'CJEU Rules That Copyright Protection for Designs Only Requires Sufficient Originality' (2019) 14 *Journal of Intellectual Property Law and Practice* 931

Rosati, E, 'Originality in a Work, or a Work of Originality: The Effects of the Infopaq Decision' (2011) 58 *Journal of the Copyright Society of the USA* 795

Russell, A, 'Telecommunications Standards in the Second and Third Industrial Revolutions' (2006) 5 *The Journal of the Communications Network* 100

Samuelson, P and Wheatland, T, 'Statutory Damages in Copyright Law: A Remedy in Need of Reform' (2009) 51 *William & Mary Law Review* 439

Santoso, S and Wicker, S 'The Future of Three-Dimensional Printing: Intellectual Property or Intellectual Confinement?' (2016) 18 *New Media and Society* 138

Scardamaglia, A 'Flashpoints in 3D Printing and Trade Mark Law' (2015) 23 *Journal of Law, Information and Science* 30

Schechter, F, 'The Rational Basis of Trade Mark Protection' (1927) 40 *Harvard Law Review* 813

Schiff, D, 'Socio-Legal Theory: Social Structure and Law' (1976) 39 *The Modern Law Review* 287

Senftleben, M 'Trade Mark Protection: A Black Hole in the Intellectual Property Galaxy?' (2011) 42 *International Review of Intellectual Property and Competition Law* 383

Shapiro, I, 'Resources, Capacities, and Ownership: The Workmanship Ideal and Distributive Justice' (1991) 19 *Political Theory* 47

Shavell, S and van Ypersele, T, 'Rewards versus Intellectual Property Rights' (2001) 44 *The Journal of Law & Economics* 525
Sheff, J, 'Veblen Brands' (2012) 96 *Minnesota Law Review* 769
Silverman, I, 'Optimising Protection: IP Rights in 3D Printing' (2016) 38 *European Intellectual Property Review* 5
Stallman, R, 'Did You Say 'Intellectual Property'? It's a Seductive Mirage' (2006) 4 *Policy Futures in Education* 334
Steenhuis, H and Pretorius, L, 'The Additive Manufacturing Innovation: A Range of Implications' (2017) 28 *Journal of Manufacturing Technology Management* 122
Stigler, G, 'The Economies of Scale' (1958) 1 *The Journal of Law & Economics* 54
Teece, D, 'Business Models, Business Strategy and Innovation' (2010) 43 *Long Range Planning* 172
Twomey, P, 'A New Dimension to Intellectual Property Infringement: An Evaluation of the Intellectual Property Issues Associated with 3D Printing' (2014) 17 *Trinity College Law Review* 14
van Overwalle, G and Leys, R, '3D Printing and Patent Law: A Disruptive Technology Disrupting Patent Law?' (2017) 48 *International Review of Intellectual Property and Competition Law* 504
van Wiele, B, 'Decentralised, Democratised and Disruptive: How 3D Printing Challenges the Consumer Protection Rationale of Trade Marks' (2019) 41 *European Intellectual Property Review* 313
Vasudeva, V 'Open Source Software Paradigm and Intellectual Property Rights' (2012) 17 *Journal of Intellectual Property Rights* 511
Vogel, B, 'Intellectual Property and Additive Manufacturing / 3D Printing: Strategies and Challenges of Applying Traditional IP Laws to a Transformative Technology' (2016) 17 *Minnesota Journal of Law, Science & Technology* 881
von Tunzelmann, G, 'Innovation and Industrialisation: A Long-term Comparison' (1997) 56 *Technological Forecasting & Social Change* 1
Wallace, A, and Euler, E, 'Revisiting Access to Cultural Heritage in the Public Domain: EU and International Developments' (2020) 51 *IIC – International Review of Intellectual Property and Competition Law* 823
Weller, C, Kleer, R and Piller, F, 'Economic Implications of 3D Printing: Market Structure Models in Light of Additive Manufacturing Revisited' (2015) 164 *International Journal of Production Economics* 43
West, J and Kuk, G, 'The Complementarity of Openness: How MakerBot Leveraged Thingiverse in 3D Printing' (2016) 102 *Technological Forecasting and Social Change* 169
Yen, A, 'Restoring the Natural Law: Copyright as Labour and Possession' (1990) *51 Ohio State Law Journal* 517

Books

Anderson, C, *Makers: The New Industrial Revolution* (London, Random House Business, 2006)
Barnatt, C, *3D Printing: Third Edition* (CreateSpace, 2016)
Bently, L and others, *Intellectual Property Law* (Oxford, OUP, 2022)
Bently, L, Suthersanen, U and Torremans, P, *Global Copyright: Three Hundred Years since the Statute of Anne, from 1709 to Cyberspace, Proceedings of the ALAI Congress London 2009* (Cheltenham, Edward Elgar, 2009)
Bernstein, W, *The Birth of Plenty, How the Prosperity of the Modern World Was Created* (New York, McGraw-Hill, 2004)
Boyle, J, *Shamans, Software, and Spleens: Law and the Construction of the Information Society* (Cambridge, MA, Harvard University Press, 1997)
Budmen, I and Rotolo, A, *The Book On 3D Printing* (CreateSpace, 2013)

Chan, H, Choo, H, Osuji, O and Griffin, J, *Intellectual Property Rights and Emerging Technology: 3D Printing in China* (Abingdon, Routledge, 2020)
Daly, A, *Socio-Legal Aspects of the 3D Printing Revolution* (London, Palgrave Macmillan, 2016)
Darling, K and Perzanowski, A, *Creativity without Law: Challenging the Assumptions of Intellectual Property* (New York, NYU Press, 2017)
Doctorow, C, *Makers* (New York, Tor Books, 2010)
Gebhardt, A and Hötter, J, *Additive Manufacturing: 3D Printing for Prototyping and Manufacturing* (Munich, Hanser, 2016)
Gibson, I, Rosen, D and Stucker, B, *Additive Manufacturing Technologies Rapid Prototyping to Direct Digital Manufacturing* (Cham, Springer, 2010)
Goold, P, *A Critical Introduction to Intellectual Property Law* (Cambridge, CUP, 2024)
Griffin, J, *The State of Creativity: The Future of 3D Printing, 4D Printing and Augmented Reality* (Cheltenham, Edward Elgar, 2019)
Hatch, M, *The Maker Movement Manifesto: Rules for Innovation in the New World of Crafters, Hackers, and Tinkerers* (New York, McGraw-Hill, 2013)
Hornick, J, *3D Printing Will Rock the World* (CreateSpace, 2015)
Kalpakjian, S and Schmid, S, *Manufacturing Engineering & Technology* (London, Pearson, 2013)
Karapapa, S and McDonagh, L, *Intellectual Property Law* (Oxford, OUP, 2019)
Kirk, J and Miller, M, *Reliability and Validity in Qualitative Research* (Beverly Hills, Sage, 1986)
Landes, W and Posner, R, *The Economic Structure of Intellectual Property Law* (Cambridge, MA, Harvard University Press, 2003)
Lessig, L *Free Culture* (New York, Penguin Press, 2004)
Lessig, L, *Code: And Other Laws of Cyberspace, Version 2.0*, 2nd edn (New York, Basic Books, 2006)
Lessig, L, *Remix: Making Art and Commerce Thrive in the Hybrid Economy* (New York, Penguin Press, 2008)
Lessig, L, *The Future of Ideas* (New York, Random House, 2002)
Lipson, H and Kurman, M, *Fabricated: The New World of 3D Printing* (Indianapolis, Wiley, 2013)
Loewenheim, U and Schricker, G, *Urheberrecht. Kommentar* (Munich, C H Beck, 2010)
Machlup, F, *Production and Distribution of Knowledge in the United States* (New Jersey, Princeton University Press, 1962)
Malecki, E, *Technology and Economic Development: The Dynamics of Local, Regional and National Competitiveness* (Essex, Longman, 1997)
Mazzone, J, *Copyfraud and Other Abuses of Intellectual Property Law* (Stanford, Stanford Law Books, 2011)
McDonagh, L, *European Patent Litigation in the Shadow of the Unified Patent Court* (Cheltenham, Edward Elgar, 2016)
Menell, P and others, *Intellectual Property in the New Technological Age 2023 Vol. I: Perspectives, Trade Secrets and Patents* (Berkeley, Clause 8 Publishing, 2023)
Mowery, D and Rosenberg N, *Technology and the Pursuit of Economic Growth* (Cambridge, CUP, 1995)
Osborn, L, *3D Printing and Intellectual Property* (Cambridge, CUP, 2019)
Patton, M, *Qualitative Research and Evaluation Methods* (Thousand Oaks, Sage, 2002)
Rosati, E, *Copyright in the Digital Single Market* (Oxford, OUP, 2021)
Rosen, L, *Open Source Licensing: Software Freedom and Intellectual Property Law* (New Jersey, Prentice Hall, 2004)
Scherer, F and Ross, D, *Industrial Market Structure and Economic Performance* (Boston, Houghton Mifflin, 1980)
Simmons, A, *The Lockean Theory of Rights* (New Jersey, Princeton University Press, 1992)
Stearns, P, *The Industrial Revolution in World History* (Boulder, Westview Press, 2013)
Torremans, P, *Intellectual Property Law* (Oxford, OUP, 2019)
Watt, R, *Copyright and Economic Theory: Friends or Foes?* (Cheltenham, Edward Elgar, 2000)

Edited Collections

Ballardini, R, Norrgård, M and Partanen, J (eds), *3D Printing, Intellectual Property and Innovation* (Alphen aan den Rijn, Kluwer Law International, 2017)

Dinwoodie, G (ed), *Secondary Liability of Internet Service Providers* (Cham, Springer, 2017)

Dosi, G and Galambos, L (eds), *The Third Industrial Revolution in Global Business* (Cambridge, CUP, 2013)

Mendis, D, Lemley, M and Rimmer, M (eds), *3D Printing and Beyond: Intellectual Property and Regulation* (Cheltenham, Edward Elgar, 2019)

van der Berg, B, van der Hof, S and Kosta, E (eds), *3D Printing: Legal, Philosophical and Economic Dimensions* (The Hague, Asser Press, 2016)

Chapters in Books

Antikainen, M and Jongsma, D, 'The Art of CAD: Copyrightability of Digital Design Files' in R Ballardini, M Norrgård and J Partanen (eds), *3D Printing, Intellectual Property and Innovation* (Alphen aan den Rijn, Kluwer Law International, 2017)

Ballardini, R and Lee, N, 'The Private and Non-commercial Use Defence Revisited: The Case of 3D Printing Technologies' in R Ballardini, M Norrgård and J Partanen (eds), *3D Printing, Intellectual Property and Innovation: Insights from Law and Technology* (Alphen aan den Rijn, Kluwer Law International, 2017)

Chynoweth, P, 'Legal Research' in L Ruddock and A Knight (eds), *Advanced Research Methods in the Built Environment* (Chichester, Wiley, 2003)

Daly, A, 'Don't Believe the Hype? Recent 3D Printing Developments for Law and Society' in D Mendis, M Lemley and M Rimmer (eds), *3D Printing and Beyond* (Cheltenham, Edward Elgar, 2019)

de Filippi, P and Troxler, P, 'From Material Scarcity to Artificial Abundance: The Case of FabLabs and 3D Printing Technologies' in B van den Berg, S van der Hof and E Kosta (eds), *3D Printing: Legal, Philosophical and Economic Dimensions* (The Hauge, Asser, 2016)

Fisher, W, 'Theories of Intellectual Property' in S Munzer (ed), *New Essays in the Legal and Political Theory of Property* (Cambridge, CUP, 2001)

Gangjee, D, 'Property in Brands: The Commodification of Conversation' in H Howe and J Griffiths (eds), *Property Concepts in Intellectual Property Law* (Cambridge, CUP, 2013)

Hong, D and Bradshaw, S 'Digital Trade Mark Infringement and 3D Printing Implications: What Does the Future Hold?' in D Mendis, M Lemley and M Rimmer (eds), *3D Printing and Beyond: Intellectual Property and Regulation* (Cheltenham, Edward Elgar, 2019)

Keymolen, E, 'The Focal Practice of 3D Printing' in B van den Berg, S van der Hof and E Kosta (eds), *3D Printing: Legal, Philosophical and Economic Dimensions* (The Hague, Asser Press, 2016)

Margoni, T, 'Design Rights and 3D Printing in the UK: Balancing Innovation and Creativity in a (dis) harmonised and Fragmented Legal Framework' in D Mendis and others (eds), *3D Printing and Beyond: Intellectual Property and Regulation* (Cheltenham, Edward Elgar, 2019)

McDonagh, L 'Copyright, Contract and FOSS' in N Shemtov and I Walden (eds), *Free and Open Source Software* (Oxford, OUP, 2013)

Mendis, D, 'Back to the Future': From Engravings to 3D Printing – Implications for UK Copyright Law' in D Mendis, M Lemley and M Rimmer (eds), *3D Printing and Beyond: Intellectual Property and Regulation* (Cheltenham, Edward Elgar, 2019)

Mendis, D, 'Fit for Purpose? 3D Printing and the Implications for Design Law: Opportunities and Challenges' in T Aplin (ed), *Research Handbook on Intellectual Property and Digital Technologies* (Cheltenham, Edward Elgar, 2019)

Osborn, L, '3D Printing and Intellectual Property' in F Olleros Xavier and M Zhegu (eds), *Research Handbook on Digital Transformations* (Cheltenham, Edward Elgar, 2016)

Rahmatian, A, 'Copyright Protection for the Restoration, Reconstruction and Digitisation of Public Domain Works' in E Derclaye (ed), *Copyright and Cultural Heritage: Preservation and Access to Works in a Digital World* (Cheltenham, Edward Elgar, 2010)

Rayna, T and Striukova, L, 'A Taxonomy of Online 3D Printing Platforms' in B van den Berg, S van der Hof and E Kosta (eds), *3D Printing: Legal, Philosophical and Economic Dimensions* (The Hague, Asser Press, 2016)

Rayna, T and Striukova, L, 'Adaptivity and Rapid Prototyping: How 3D Printing Is Changing Business Model Innovation' in B van den Berg, S van der Hof and E Kosta (eds), *3D Printing: Legal, Philosophical and Economic Dimensions* (The Hague, Asser Press, 2016)

Stallman, R, 'Why Software Should Be Free' in A Moore (ed), *Intellectual Property: Moral, Legal, and International Dilemmas* (Lanham, Rowman and Littlefield, 1997)

Troxler, P and van Woensel, C, 'How Will Society Adopt 3D Printing?' in B van den Berg, S van der Hof and E Kosta (eds), *3D Printing: Legal, Philosophical and Economic Dimensions* (The Hague, Asser Press, 2016)

Webley, L, 'Qualitative Approaches to Empirical Legal Research' in P Cane and H Kritzer (eds), *Oxford Handbook of Empirical Legal Research* (Oxford, OUP, 2010)

Weinberg, M, 'Copyright Implications of 3D Scanning' in R Ballardini, M Norrgård and J Partanen (eds), *3D Printing, Intellectual Property and Innovation: Insights from Law and Technology* (Alphen aan den Rijn, Kluwer Law International, 2017)

Weinberg, M, 'When 3D Printing and the Law Get Together, Will Crazy Things Happen?' in B van den Berg, S van der Hof and E Kosta (eds), *3D Printing: Legal, Philosophical and Economic Dimensions* (The Hague, Asser, 2016)

Other Sources

Ammar, J and Craufurd, R, 'When is a Trade Mark use not a Trade Mark Use? A 3D Perspective' (2015) 1 at papers.ssrn.com/sol3/papers.cfm?abstract_id=2760947

Barron, L, 'Back on record – the reasons behind vinyl's unlikely comeback' (The Conversation, 17 April 2015) at theconversation.com/back-on-record-the-reasons-behind-vinyls-unlikely-comeback-39964

BBC News, 'Getting Inside a Downloader's Head' (*BBC News*, 18 June 2009) at www.news.bbc.co.uk/1/hi/magazine/8106805.stm

BBC News, 'L'Oreal to start 3D-printing skin' (*BBC News*, 19 May 2015) at www.bbc.co.uk/news/technology-32795169

BBC News, 'Man Who Used 3D Printer to Build Gun Jailed' (*BBC News*, 25 November 2024) at www.bbc.com/news/articles/crmz9dn941eo

Bechtold, S, '3D Printing and the Intellectual Property System' (*Economic Research Working Paper No 28*, World Intellectual Property Organization 2015) at www.wipo.int/edocs/pubdocs/en/wipo_pub_econstat_wp_28.pdf

Benchoff, B, 'MakerBot Files Patents, Internet Goes Crazy' at www.hackaday.com/2014/05/24/makerbot-files-patents-internet-goes-crazy (*Hackaday*, 24 May 2014)

Biggs, J, 'MakerBot Responds To Critics Who Claim It Is Stealing Community IP' (*TechCrunch*, 28 May 2014) at www.techcrunch.com/2014/05/28/makerbot-responds-to-critics-who-claim-it-is-stealing-community-ip

Birtchnell, T and others '3D Printing and Intellectual Property Futures' (UK Intellectual Property Office 2018/03) at assets.publishing.service.gov.uk/government/uploads/system/uploads/attachment_data/file/757767/3D-printing.pdf

Bogle, A, 'Good News: Replicas of 16th-Century Sculptures Are Not Off-Limits for 3-D Printers' (*Slate*, 26 January 2015) at www.slate.com/technology/2015/01/3-d-printing-and-copyright-replicas-of-16th-century-sculptures-are-not-off-limits.html

Bower, J and Christensen, C, 'Disrupting technologies: catching the wave' (1995) *January-February Issue, Harvard Business Review* 43 at hbr.org/1995/01/disruptive-technologies-catching-the-wave

Brown, F, 'Firm 'refuses to give blueprint' for coronavirus equipment that could save lives' (*Metro News*, 16 March 2020) at www.metro.co.uk/2020/03/16/firm-refuses-give-blueprint-coronavirus-equipment-save-lives-12403815

Brown, R, 'Pulling back from open source hardware, MakerBot angers some adherents' (*CNET*, 27 September 2012) at www.cnet.com/tech/tech-industry/pulling-back-from-open-source-hardware-makerbot-angers-some-adherents

Bursey, L, 'The Parthenon Marbles Dispute – Is the End in Sight?' (*The New York Times*, 26 September 2024) at blogs.lse.ac.uk/europpblog/2024/09/26/the-parthenon-marbles-dispute-is-the-end-in-sight/

Butts, J, '3D Printer Maker Bambu Lab Faces Patent Infringement Lawsuits That Could Threaten Hobbyist 3D Printing in General' (*Tom's Hardware*, 11 August 2024) at tomshardware.com/3d-printing/3d-printer-maker-bambu-lab-faces-patent-infringement-lawsuits-that-could-threaten-hobbyist-3d-printing-in-general

CERN (European Organization for Nuclear Research) 'Open Source for Open Science' at www.home.cern/science/computing/open-source-open-science

Christensen, C, Raynor, M and McDonald, R, 'What Is Disruptive Innovation?' (*Harvard Business Review*, December 2015) at hbr.org/2015/12/what-is-disruptive-innovation

Curry, A, 'Here Are the Ancient Sites ISIS Has Damaged and Destroyed' (*National Geographic*, 1 September 2015) at www.nationalgeographic.com/history/article/150901-isis-destruction-looting-ancient-sites-iraq-syria-archaeology

D'Aveni, R, 'The 3-D Printing Revolution' (2015) May Issue, Harvard Business Review at hbr.org/2015/05/the-3-d-printing-revolution

Flaherty, J, '3-D Printed Prosthetics That Look Fit for a Sci-Fi Warrior' (*Wired*, 7 January 2015) at www.wired.com/2015/01/3-d-printed-prosthetics-look-fit-sci-fi-warrior

Elam, V, 'The challenge of three-dimensional printing: questioning established concepts in intellectual property law' (Doctoral thesis, EUI 2019) at www.cadmus.eui.eu/handle/1814/60404

Elam, V, 'The Transfer of Computer-Aided Design Files in the Era of 3D Printing: Trademark Infringement Under the Current European Framework' in *Building a European Digital Space: 12th International Conference on Internet, Law & Politics* (7–8 July 2016) at dialnet.unirioja.es/servlet/libro?codigo=963258

Engineering.com, 'SpaceX Launches 3D Printed Parts to Space' (5 August 2014) at www.engineering.com/spacex-launches-3d-printed-parts-to-space

European Commission, 'Digital Single Market: EU Negotiators Reach a Breakthrough to Modernise Copyright Rules' (13 February 2019) at www.ec.europa.eu/commission/presscorner/detail/en/ip_19_528

European Commission, 'Reflection Paper on Harnessing Globalisation' (Communication) COM (2017) 240 final at commission.europa.eu/publications/reflection-paper-harnessing-globalisation_en

European Copyright Society, 'Comment of the European Copyright Society on the Implementation of Art.14 of the Directive (EU) 2019/790 on Copyright in the Digital Single Market' (26 April 2020) at https://europeancopyrightsociety.org/wp-content/uploads/2020/04/ecs_cdsm_implementation_article_14_final.pdf

European Parliament resolution of 3 July 2018 on three-dimensional printing, a challenge in the fields of intellectual property rights and civil liability (2017/2007(INI)) [2020] OJ C118/10 at eur-lex.europa.eu/legal-content/EN/TXT/?uri=CELEX%3A52018IP0274

European Patent Office, 'Guidelines for Examination' (3.6.1) at www.epo.org/en/legal/guidelines-epc/2024/g_ii_3_6_1.html

European Patent Office, 'Guidelines for Examination' (3.6) at www.epo.org/law-practice/legal-texts/html/guidelines/e/g_ii_3_6.htm

Fairbairn Films, 'You Wouldn't Download a Car' (YouTube, 11 September 2021) at www.youtube.com/watch?v=Fb7N-JtQWGI

Freeman, D, 'Israeli Scientists Create World's First 3D-Printed Heart Using Human Cells' (*NBC*, 19 April 2019) at nbcnews.com/mach/science/israeli-scientists-create-world-s-first-3d-printed-heart-using-ncna996031

GNU, 'The Free Software Definition' at www.gnu.org/philosophy/free-sw.html

Greenberg, A, '3D-Printed Gun's Blueprints Downloaded 100,000 Times In Two Days (With Some Help From Kim Dotcom)' (*Forbes*, 8 May 2013) at www.forbes.com/sites/andygreenberg/2013/05/08/3d-printed-guns-blueprints-downloaded-100000-times-in-two-days-with-some-help-from-kim-dotcom

Greene, A, 'The 50 Worst Decisions in Music History' (*Rolling Stone*, 29 November 2022) at au.rollingstone.com/music/music-lists/the-50-worst-decisions-in-music-history-44119

Hargreaves, I, 'Digital Opportunity: A Review of Intellectual Property and Growth' (2011) 5 at www.gov.uk/government/publications/digital-opportunity-review-of-intellectual-property-and-growth

Haria, R, 'Keeping 3D Printing Open, Petition Against 'Restrictive' US Copyright Office' (3D Printing Industry, 22 December 2017) at www.3dprintingindustry.com/news/keeping-3d-printing-open-petition-restrictive-us-copyright-office-exemptions-126572

Harris, J, 'Vinyl Is Back for Good and That's Exciting. Don't Let the Greed of Big Labels Ruin It' (*The Guardian*, 31 December 2023) at www.theguardian.com/commentisfree/2023/dec/31/vinyl-labels-mainstream-music-price

Helmore, E, 'Suspect in UnitedHealthcare CEO shooting charged with murder by New York prosecutors' (*The Guardian*, 10 December 2024) at www.theguardian.com/us-news/2024/dec/09/brian-thompson-shooting-suspect-mayor

Hitch, G and Fennell, M, 'Parthenon Marbles Recreated from 3D Scans to Sway British Museum to Return Them to Greece' at www.abc.net.au/news/2024-06-17/parthenon-elgin-marbles-greece-british-museum/103969352

Hong, D, 'An Analysis of UK Copyright and Design Laws on 3D Printing and Product Design' (Doctoral thesis, Bournemouth 2020) at www.eprints.bournemouth.ac.uk/35915

Hurst, N, 'HBO Blocks 3-D Printed Game of Thrones iPhone Dock' (*Wired*, 13 February 2013) at www.wired.com/2013/02/got-hbo-cease-and-desist

Intellectual Property Office, 'Manual of Patent Practice' (19 February 2016, updated 2 January 2025) at www.gov.uk/guidance/manual-of-patent-practice-mopp/section-1-patentability

Jones, D, 'Ariadne' (1974) 64 *New Scientist* 80

Koten, J, 'A Revolution in the Making' (The Wall Street Journal, 10 June 2013) at www.wsj.com/articles/SB10001424127887324063304578522812684722382

Lalani, A, 'Lego Targeting Maker Community's 3D Models with Infringement Notices' (*All3DP*, 2 October 2019) at www.all3dp.com/4/lego-targeting-maker-communitys-3d-models-with-infringement-notices

Lamont, T, 'Napster: The Day the Music Was Set Free' (*The Guardian*, 24 February 2013) at www.theguardian.com/music/2013/feb/24/napster-music-free-file-sharing

Lancaster, C, 'Man Jailed for 3D-Printed Gun and Terror Offences' (*BBC News*, 14 October 2024) at www.bbc.com/news/articles/c20myxlrrn1o

Machemer, T, '3-D Scans of the Bust of Nefertiti Are Now Available Online' (*Smithsonian Magazine*, 22 November 2019) at www.smithsonianmag.com/smart-news/3-d-scans-bust-nefertiti-are-now-available-online-180973628

Machlup, F, 'An Economic Review of the Patent System' (Study of the Subcommittee on Patents, Committee on Judiciary, US Congress, 85th Congress, 2d sess, Study No 15, 1958) at cdn.mises.org/An%20Economic%20Review%20of%20the%20Patent%20System_Vol_3_3.pdf

Marshall, A, 'After 220 Years, the Fate of the Parthenon Marbles Rests in Secret Talks' (*The New York Times*, 17 January 2023) at www.nytimes.com/2023/01/17/arts/design/parthenon-sculptures-elgin-marbles-negotiations.html

Max Planck Institute, *Study on the Overall Functioning of the European Trade Mark System* (2010) at op.europa.eu/en/publication-detail/-/publication/5f878564-9b8d-4624-ba68-72531215967e

McDonagh, L, 'UK Patent Law and Copyright Law after Brexit: Potential Consequences' (Centre for International Governance Innovation Paper No 3, 2017) at www.cigionline.org/sites/default/files/documents/Brexit%20Series%20Paper%20no3.pdf

Mendis, D and others, 'The Intellectual Property Implications of the Development of Industrial 3D Printing' (European Commission Final Report, 12 February 2020) at op.europa.eu/en/publication-detail/-/publication/e193a586-7f8c-11ea-aea8-01aa75ed71a1

Mendis, D and Secchi, D, 'A Legal and Empirical Study of 3D Printing Online Platforms and an Analysis of User Behaviour' (Intellectual Property Office, Report 2015/41) at assets.publishing.service.gov.uk/government/uploads/system/uploads/attachment_data/file/549045/Study-I.pdf

Mendis, D, Secchi, D and Reeves, P, 'A Legal and Empirical Study into the Intellectual Property Implications of 3D Printing' (UK Intellectual Property Office Report 2015/41) at assets.publishing.service.gov.uk/government/uploads/system/uploads/attachment_data/file/549044/Legal-Empirical-_Executive-Summary.pdf

Menell, P, 'Intellectual Property: General Theories' (1999) at www.sfu.ca/~allen/intellectual.pdf

Moore, A and Himma, K, 'Intellectual Property' in Zalta E and Nodelman U (eds), *The Stanford Encyclopedia of Philosophy* (2022) at plato.stanford.edu/archives/fall2022

Nichol, A and others, 'Point E: A System for Generating 3D Point Clouds from Complex Prompts' (*arXiv*, 2022) at arxiv.org/pdf/2212.08751

O'Neal, B, 'Sioux Falls Maker Accused of Infringing on Copyright Laws with 3D Models of Michelangelo's Statues' (*3DPrint*, 21 January 2015) at www.3dprint.com/38631/michelangelo-copyright-models

OpenAI, 'Point-E: A System for Generating 3D Point Clouds from Complex Prompts' (OpenAI, 16 December 2022) at www.openai.com/index/point-e

O'Rourke, M, 'A 3D Printed Future' (2013) 60 *Risk Management* 1 at www.rmmagazine.com/articles/article/2013/05/02/-A-3D-Printed-Future-

Peels, J, 'Shapeways interviews Bre Pettis of MakerBot Industries' (*Shapeways Blog*, January 2010) at www.shapeways.com/blog/shapeways-interviews-bre-pettis-of-makerbot-industries

Petch, M, 'LEGO 3D Printing Takedowns: A Lawyer Responds and LEGO Replies' (9 October 2019) at www.3dprintingindustry.com/news/lego-3d-printing-takedowns-a-lawyer-responds-and-lego-replies-163104

Prusa, J, 'From Design to Mass 3D printing of Medical Shields in Three Days' (*Prusa Blog*, 18 March 2020) at blog.prusa3d.com/from-design-to-mass-3d-printing-of-medical-shields-in-three-days_32578

Prusa, J, 'The state of open-source in 3D printing in 2023' (*Prusa Blog*, 29 March 2023) blog.prusa3d.com/the-state-of-open-source-in-3d-printing-in-2023_76659

Pyne, C, '3D Printing Brings New Dimension to Australian Manufacturing' (19 November 2015) at www.pyneonline.com.au/media-centre/media-releases/3d-printing-brings-new-dimension-to-australian-manufacturing

Razzall, K, 'Parthenon Sculptures: Pressure Growing on British Museum' (*BBC News*, 21 July 2023) at www.bbc.co.uk/news/entertainment-arts-66239150

Schwaar, C, 'A 3D Printer On Every Desk? Why Companies Are Buying More 3D Printers' (*Forbes*, 2 May 2024) at www.forbes.com/sites/carolynschwaar/2024/05/02/a-3d-printer-on-every-desk-why-companies-are-buying-more-3d-printers

Shaheen, K, 'Isis Destroys Tetrapylon Monument in Palmyra' (*The Guardian*, 20 January 2017) at www.theguardian.com/world/2017/jan/20/isis-destroys-tetrapylon-monument-palmyra-syria

Shaheen, K, 'Isis Fighters Destroy Ancient Artefacts at Mosul Museum' (*The Guardian*, 26 February 2015) at www.theguardian.com/world/2015/feb/26/isis-fighters-destroy-ancient-artefacts-mosul-museum-iraq

Shapeways, '2017 Transparency Report' (2017) at www.shapeways.com/legal/transparency/2017

Shapeways, '2018 Transparency Report' (2018) at www.shapeways.com/legal/transparency/2018

Senese, M, 'Nokia Releases Files for 3-D Printing Your Own Phone Case' (*Wired*, 10 January 2013) at www.wired.com/2013/01/nokia-3d-print-case

The Economist, 'The Third Industrial Revolution' (*The Economist*, 21 April 2012) at www.economist.com/node/21552901
The Standard, '3D Printers: Every Home Should Have One' (*The Standard*, 10 April 2012) at www.standard.co.uk/news/tech/3d-printers-every-home-should-have-one-7308091.html
The White House, 'President Barack Obama's State of the Union Address – As Prepared for Delivery' (12 February 2013) at obamawhitehouse.archives.gov/the-press-office/2013/02/12/president-barack-obamas-state-union-address-prepared-delivery
Torrone, P 'MAKE's Exclusive Interview with Alicia Gibb – President of the Open Source Hardware Association' (Makezine, 23 April 2012) at www.makezine.com/2012/04/23/makes-exclusive-interview-with-alicia-gibb-president-of-the-open-source-hardware-association
Varotsis, A, '3D Printing vs. CNC machining' (Undated) at www.3dhubs.com/knowledge-base/3d-printing-vs-cnc-machining
Vincent, J, 'Japanese man jailed for two years for creating 3D printed guns' (*The Independent*, 21 October 2014) at www.independent.co.uk/life-style/gadgets-and-tech/japanese-man-jailed-for-two-years-for-creating-3d-printed-guns-9807765.html
Weinberg, M, 'Open Hardware for Musicians and Music Lovers' (13 July 2019) at www.michaelweinberg.org/blog/2019/07/13/open-hardware-musicians
Weinberg, M, 'What's the Deal with Copyright and 3D Printing?' (*Public Knowledge*, 2013) at michaelweinberg.org/docs/WhatstheDealwithCopyright_%20Finalversion2.pdf
Weinberg, M, '3D Scanning: A World Without Copyright' (2016) at www.michaelweinberg.org/docs/white-paper-3d-scanning-world-without-copyright.pdf
Weinberg, M, 'Cultural Institutions Behaving Badly: Stupid Reactions to 3D Scanning' (Public Knowledge, 22 January 2015) at www.publicknowledge.org/cultural-institutions-behaving-badly-stupid-reactions-to-3d-scanning
Weinberg, M, 'It Will Be Awesome If They Don't Screw It Up: 3D Printing, Intellectual Property, and the Fight over the Next Great Disruptive Technology' (*Public Knowledge* 2010) at publicknowledge.org/it-will-be-awesome-if-they-dont-screw-it-up-3d-printing/
Weinberg, M, 'Keep 3D Printers Unlocked (the win! 2023)' (1 November 2024) at michaelweinberg.org/blog/2024/11/01/1201-win
Weinberg, M, 'Keep 3D Printers Unlocked' (13 July 2023) at www.michaelweinberg.org/blog/2023/07/13/1201-kickoff
Weinberg, M, 'Lego's IP Grab Bag' (2019) at michaelweinberg.org/blog/2019/10/10/lego-ip-grab-bag
Weinberg, M, 'The Bust of Nefertiti is Free (With One Strange Caveat)' (13 November 2019) at www.michaelweinberg.org/blog/2019/11/13/nefertiti-scan-nc-license
Weinberg, M, 'The Nefertiti Bust Meets the 21st Century: When a German Museum Lost Its Fight Over 3D-Printing Files of the 3,000-Year-Old Artwork, It Made a Strange Decision' (*Slate*, 15 November 2019) at www.slate.com/technology/2019/11/nefertiti-bust-neues-museum-3d-printing.html
Weinberg, M, 'A(nother) Reply to Josef Průša' (5 April 2023) at michaelweinberg.org/blog/2023/04/05/prusa-response
Wenman, C, 'Secret 3D Scans in the French Supreme Court' (29 September 2024) at cosmowenman.substack.com/p/secret-3d-scans-in-the-french-supreme
Wilder, C, 'Nefertiti 3-D Scanning Project in Germany Raises Doubts' (*New York Times*, 10 March 2016) at www.nytimes.com/2016/03/11/arts/design/nefertiti-3-d-scanning-project-in-germany-raises-doubts.html
Wilder, C, 'Swiping a Priceless Antiquity … With a Scanner and a 3-D Printer' The New York Times (*New York Times*, 1 March 2016) at www.nytimes.com/2016/03/02/arts/design/other-nefertiti-3d-printer.html
Wohlers Associates, 'Wohlers Report 2014: 3D Printing and Additive Manufacturing State of the Industry' (2014) at www.wohlersassociates.com/2014report.htm
Wohlers Associates, 'Wohlers Report 2016' (2016) at www.wohlersassociates.com/wp-content/uploads/2016/05/2016-ExSum.pdf